James Ensor

JAMES ENSOR

THE CREATIVE YEARS

by Diane Lesko

PRINCETON UNIVERSITY PRESS | PRINCETON NEW JERSEY

Copyright © 1985 by Princeton University Press
Published by Princeton University Press, 41 William Street, Princeton, New Jersey 08540
In the United Kingdom: Princeton University Press, Guildford, Surrey

All Rights Reserved
Library of Congress Cataloging in Publication Data will be found on the last printed
page of this book
ISBN 0-691-04030-3

This book has been composed in Linotron Trump type

The ornament used on the title page and chapter openings is adapted from
James Ensor's coat of arms

Clothbound editions of Princeton University Press books are printed on acid-free paper, and
binding materials are chosen for strength and durability. Paperbacks, although satisfactory
for personal collections, are not usually suitable for library rebinding

Printed in the United States of America by Princeton University Press
Princeton, New Jersey

In Memory of My Mother and Father

TABLE OF CONTENTS

List of Illustrations   ix

Acknowledgments   xv

Introduction: "Cabin on the Beach"   3

I. Ensor's Early Life in Ostend and His Isolation   6

II. "Peculiar Insects": Brussels; Another World Revealed   29

III. Of Sirens and Fallen Angels: The Lure of Wiertz and Rops   59

IV. Literature as Inspiration for Ensor's Art   83

V. Tribulations, Temptations and Transformations: Ensor's Debt
to Religion and History   115

VI. Ensor's Last Years of Creativity and the Decline of His Art   146

Bibliography   159

Photographic Credits   167

Index   169

LIST OF ILLUSTRATIONS

COLOR PLATES

1. Ensor. *Cabin on the Beach*, 1877. Oil on cardboard, 7½ inches × 9½ inches. Koninklijk Museum voor Schone Kunsten, Antwerp. *facing 32*

2. Ensor. *Woman Eating Oysters*, 1882. Oil on canvas, 81½ inches × 59¹/₁₆ inches. Koninklijk Museum voor Schone Kunsten, Antwerp. *facing 33*

3. Ensor. *Scandalized Masks*, 1883. Oil on canvas, 53 inches × 44¾ inches. Musées Royaux des Beaux-Arts de Belgique, Brussels. *facing 48*

4. Ensor. *Children Dressing*, 1886. Oil on canvas, 53 inches by 43¼ inches. Private Collection. *facing 49*

5. Ensor. *Self-Portrait in a Flowered Hat*, 1883. Oil on canvas, 29⅝ inches × 24¼ inches. Stedelijk Museum voor Schone Kunsten, Ostend. *facing 80*

6. Ensor. *Skeletons Trying to Warm Themselves*, 1889. Oil on canvas, 25⅕ inches × 18 inches. Kimbell Art Museum, Fort Worth, Texas. *facing 81*

7. Ensor. *The Tribulations of St. Anthony*, 1887. Oil on canvas, 46⅜ inches × 66 inches. Museum of Modern Art, New York. *facing 96*

8. Ensor. *The Ray*, 1892. Oil on canvas, 31½ inches × 39¼ inches. Musées Royaux des Beaux-Arts de Belgique, Brussels. *facing 97*

BLACK-AND-WHITE FIGURES

1. Ensor. *Dunes of Ostend*, c. 1876. Oil on cardboard. 7½ inches × 9⅜ inches. Private collection. 7

2. Ensor. *Classic Academy Model*, 1878. Charcoal on paper, 31½ inches × 23⅝ inches. Stedelijk Museum voor Schone Kunsten, Ostend, inventory number 657. 7

3. Ensor. *Pears*, 1881. Oil on canvas, 15¾ inches × 19⅝ inches. Private collection, Brussels. 8

4. Ensor. *The Ray*, 1882. Oil on canvas, 31½ inches × 39¼ inches. Koninklijk Museum voor Schone Kunsten, Antwerp. 10

ix

5. Ensor. *The Rower*, 1883. Oil on canvas, 31 inches × 38⅞ inches. Koninklijk Museum voor Schone Kunsten, Antwerp.　　12

6. Ensor. *Baths at Ostend*, 1899. Etching, 8¾ inches × 10 inches, II/II. Private collection.　　13

7. Ensor. *Sleeping Woman*, c. 1882. Pencil on paper, 8⅞ inches × 6½ inches. G. van Geluwe, Brussels.　　13

8. Ensor. *Portrait of the Artist's Aunt*, c. 1883. Pencil on paper, 8¼ inches × 6¼ inches. J. Boogaerts, Brussels.　　14

9. Ensor. *Portrait of the Artist's Sister*, 1881. Charcoal on paper, 29⅛ inches × 22⅞ inches. The Art Institute of Chicago, The Margaret Day Blake Collection.　　14

10. Ensor. *The Convalescent*, 1880. Oil on canvas, 32¼ inches × 19⅝ inches. Private collection.　　15

11. Ensor. *Portrait of Mitche*, 1883. Oil on canvas, dimensions unknown. Location unknown. Archives, Stedelijk Museum voor Schone Kunsten, Ostend.　　15

12. Ensor. *Pair in an Open Landau*, 1883. Pen and ink. Koninklijk Museum voor Schone Kunsten, Antwerp. Inventory number 2712/57.　　16

13. Ensor. *Intrigue*, 1890. Oil on canvas, 35⅜ inches × 58⅞ inches. Koninklijk Museum voor Schone Kunsten, Antwerp.　　16

14. Ensor. *Mitche with Child*, n.d. Drawing. Private Collection.　　17

15. Ensor. *The Artist's Mother in Death*, 1915. Oil on canvas, 19½ inches × 23⅝ inches. Stedelijk Museum voor Schone Kunsten, Ostend.　　18

16. Ensor. *Portrait of the Artist's Father*, 1881. Oil on canvas, 39⅜ inches × 31½ inches. Musées Royaux des Beaux-Arts de Belgique, Brussels.　　18

17. Ensor. *The Artist's Father in Death*, 1887. Conte crayon on paper. 6¾ inches × 8⅞ inches. Koninklijk Museum voor Schone Kunsten, Antwerp.　　19

18. *Photograph of Ensor in Death*, November 1949. Archives, Stedelijk Museum voor Schone Kunsten, Ostend.　　19

19. Ensor. *The Drunkards*, 1883. Oil on canvas, 45³⁄₁₆ inches × 64¾ inches. G. DeGraeve, Brussels.　　20

20. Odilon Redon. *Interior with Skeletons*, c. 1882. Charcoal and black pencil on paper, 17¼ inches × 14⅛ inches. Rijksmuseum Kröller-Müller, Otterlo, The Netherlands.　　21

21. Postcard of Ensor drawing *Le Buveur*, c. 1882. Archives, Stedelijk Museum voor Schone Kunsten, Ostend.　　22

22. Ensor. *Portrait of Ensor's Mother*, 1882. Oil on canvas, 39⁵⁄₁₆ inches × 31½ inches. Musées Royaux des Beaux-Arts de Belgique, Brussels.　　26

23. Ensor. *Portrait of the Artist's Mother*, 1887. Conte and colored crayon on paper, 7 inches × 8¾ inches. B. Goldschmidt, Brussels.　　27

24. Ensor. *A Fisherman*, 1880. Charcoal on paper, 28⅞ inches × 21¼ inches. Stedelijk Museum, Leuven.　　28

25. *Photograph of Ensor in a Crowd*, 1888. R. Hespel, Ghent.　　29

26. Ensor. *Two Waders*, n.d. Pen and ink on paper. Private collection, Ghent.　　30

27. Ensor. *Ernest Rousseau*, 1887. Etching, 9⅜ inches × 7 inches, IV/IV. Private collection.　　31

28. Ensor. *Peculiar Insects*, 1888. Drypoint, 4⅝ inches × 6⅛ inches, V/V. Private collection.　　33

29. Ensor. *The Garden of Love*, 1888. Oil on canvas, 37¾ inches × 44 inches. Private collection.　　34

30. Ensor. *Ensor and General Leman Discussing Painting*, 1890. Oil on panel, 4¾ inches × 6¼ inches. M. Mabille, Brussels.　　35

31. Ensor. *Death and a Doctor By a Gravestone*, n.d. Pen and ink on paper, 7¾ inches × 5 inches. Koninklijke

Museum voor Schone Kunsten, Antwerp. Inventory number 2712/18. 37

32. Louis Boulenger. *Dead at Age Fifteen, Beautiful, Happy, and Adored*, 1829. Lithograph by C. Motte. Bibliothèque Nationale, Paris. 38

33. Honoré Daumier. *Peace, an Idyl*, 1871. Lithograph, 9¼ inches × 7¼ inches. The Metropolitan Museum of Art, New York, Rogers Fund, 1922. (22.61.275) 39

34. Ensor. *Death Pursuing the People*, 1896. Etching, 9¼ inches × 6¾ inches. III/IV. Private collection. 40

35. Karl Gottfried Merkel. *The Pest-Death*. Engraving from *Pictures of Death*, Leipzig, 1850. 40

36. Ensor. *The Sad and Broken: Satan and his Fantastic Legions Tormenting the Crucified Christ*, 1886. Charcoal and conte crayon on paper, 23⅜ inches × 29⅛ inches. Musées Royaux des Beaux-Arts de Belgique, Brussels. 41

37. Ensor. *Ensor and Death*, December 25, 1887. Pen and ink drawing on a letter, 4⅛ inches × 4⅞ inches. Archives of Contemporary Art in Belgium, Musées Royaux des Beaux-Arts de Belgique, Brussels. 42

38. Ensor. *My Portrait in 1960*, 1888. Etching, 2¾ inches × 4¾ inches, II/II. Private collection. 44

39. Ensor. *My Portrait Skeletonized*, 1889. Etching, 4¾ inches × 3⅛ inches, III/III. Private collection. 45

40. Photograph of Ensor, 20 rue Vautier, Brussels, 1889. Archives of Contemporary Art in Belgium, Musées Royaux des Beaux-Arts de Belgique Brussels, Inventory number 2571. 45

41. Ensor. *Skeleton Painter in His Studio*, c. 1896. Oil on canvas, 14⅝ inches × 17¾ inches. Koninklijk Museum voor Schone Kunsten, Antwerp. 46

42. Titian. *Death in Armor*, n.d. Engraving after drawing (engraver unknown), location unknown. 47

43. Léon Frédéric. *Studio Interior*, 1882. Oil on canvas, remounted on panel. 62¼ inches × 46 inches. Musée d'Ixelles, Brussels. 48

44. Ensor. *Skeletons Fighting for the Body of a Hanged Man*, 1891. Oil on canvas, 23¼ inches × 29⅛ inches. Koninklijk Museum voor Schone Kunsten, Antwerp. 49

45. Ensor. *Skeleton Studying Chinoiseries*, 1885. Oil on canvas, 39¼ inches × 25⅜ inches. Private collection, New York. 51

46. Ensor. *Woman on the Breakwater*, 1880. Oil on canvas, 12⅝ inches × 9½ inches. Private collection. 52

47. Ensor. *Demons Taunting Me*, 1888. Pencil and black chalk on paper, 8⅝ inches × 11¾ inches. The Art Institute of Chicago, Ada Turnbull Hertle Fund. 54

48. J. J. Grandville. *Petites Misères de la vie humaine*, 1843. Engraving for *Petites Misères de la vie humaine* (Paris: Fournier, 1843). 55

49. Félicien Rops. *Hamlet*, n.d. Pen and ink. Dimension unknown, location unknown. 60

50. Antoine Wiertz. *The Triumph of Christ*, n.d. Oil study, 6⅝ inches × 11¼ inches. Musée Antoine Wiertz, Brussels. 61

51. Antoine Wiertz. *The Revolt of Hell Against Heaven*, n.d. Oil study, 6⅞ inches × 4¼ inches. Musée Antoine Wiertz, Brussels. 61

52. Ensor. *The Fall of the Rebel Angels*, 1889. Oil on canvas, 42½ inches × 51⅞ inches. Koninklijk Museum voor Schone Kunsten, Antwerp. 62

53. Antoine Wiertz. *The Apotheosis of the Queen*, 1856. Oil on paper, 36 inches × 24 inches. Musée Antoine Wiertz, Brussels. 64

54. Ensor. *Capture of a Strange City*, 1888. Etching, 7 inches × 9⅜ inches, IV/IV. Private collection. 64

55. Félicien Rops. *Printemps*, 1858. Lithograph, 16 inches × 22¾ inches. *Uylenspiegel*, no. 14 (May 9, 1858). 65

56. Félicien Rops. *Garde Civique*, 1858. Lithograph, 15⅜ inches × 22½ inches. *Uylenspiegel*, no. 20 (June 20, 1858).   65

57. Ensor. *The Entry of Christ into Brussels*, 1888. Oil on canvas, 101⅜ inches × 149¼ inches. Private collection, on loan to Koninklijk Museum voor Schone Kunsten, Antwerp.   67

58. Ensor. *The Call of the Siren*, 1893. Oil on panel, 38 inches × 47 inches. Comte Baudouin de Grunne, Wezembeek-Oppem.   68

59. Félicien Rops. *Essuie-Mains Réactifs Belges*, n.d. Etching, second state, 9¼ inches × 6¼ inches.   69

60. Félicien Rops. *Déballage*, 1856. Lithograph, 9 inches × 7⅝ inches. *Uylenspiegel*, no. 28 (August 10, 1856).   69

61. Ensor. *The Consoling Virgin*, 1892. Oil on panel. 19 inches × 15 inches. Private collection.   70

62. Ensor. *Flaying a Convict*, 1888. Drypoint and etching, 5¼ inches × 3⅝ inches, I/II. Private collection.   71

63. Ensor. *The Flagellation*, 1886. Etching, 3¾ inches × 2½ inches, only state. Private collection.   72

64. Ensor. *Satyr*, n.d. Drawing, 6 inches × 3¾ inches. Koninklijk Museum voor Schone Kunsten, Antwerp, Inventory number 2712/61.   73

65. Ensor. *Four Nudes*, n.d. Drawing, 5⅜ inches × 9 inches. Koninklijk Museum voor Schone Kunsten, Antwerp. Inventory number 2712/64.   73

66. Ensor. *Nymph Embracing a Herm*, c. 1920. Colored pencil on paper, 6 inches × 3½ inches. Bibliothèque Royale Albert Ier, Cabinet des Estampes, Brussels.   74

67. Félicien Rops. *Hommage à Pan*, 1900. Engraving, 13 inches × 9¼ inches.   74

68. Félicien Rops. *La Médaille de Waterloo*, 1858. Lithograph, 23 inches × 17⅛ inches.   75

69. Ensor. *Skeletons Playing Billiards*, 1903. Pencil and colored crayon on paper. 5 inches × 6⅞ inches. Stedelijk Museum voor Schone Kunsten, Ostend.   75

70. Photograph of an Ensor letter, 1885. Ensor-Museum, Ostend.   76

71. Félicien Rops. *L'Eventail*, n.d. Etching, 9⅛ inches × 6⅜ inches.   77

72. Ensor. *Self-Portrait Surrounded by Masks*, 1899. Oil on canvas, 47 inches × 31½ inches. Private collection.   79

73. Félicien Rops. *Diaboli virtus in lumbis*. 8½ inches × 5⅜ inches. Frontispiece for Joséphin Péladan, *La Décadence latine* (Paris: G. Edinger, 1887).   80

74. Antoine Wiertz. *La Jeune Sorcière*, 1857. Oil on canvas, 86⅝ inches × 53⅛ inches. Musée Antoine Wiertz, Brussels.   82

75. Félicien Rops. *Petite Sorcière*, 1895. Etching and aquatint, 4¾ inches × 2½ inches. Reproduced in *L'Epreuve*, Ire année, no. 1, 1895, under the title *Départ pour le Sabbat*.   82

76. Ensor. *The Cathedral*, 1886. Etching, 9¾ inches × 7½ inches. I/V. Private collection.   87

77. Ensor. *The Cathedral*, 1896. Etching, 9⅜ inches × 7 inches, only state. Private collection.   88

78. Ensor. *Detail of The Cathedral*, 1896.   89

79. Photograph of The Cathedral of Sts. Peter and Paul, Ostend, 1978.   89

80. Ensor. *Skeletons Trying to Warm Themselves*, 1895. Etching, 5½ inches × 4 inches, II/II. Private collection.   92

81. Ensor. *The Domain of Arnheim*, 1890. Oil on canvas, 31½ inches × 39¼ inches. Private collection.   94

82. Ensor. *Plague Here, Plague There, Plague Everywhere*, 1904. Etching, 7¾ inches × 11¾ inches, only state. Private collection.   97

83. Ensor. *Auto-Da-Fé*, 1893. Etching, 3⅜ inches × 4¾ inches, only state. Private collection. 98

84. Ensor. *The Infernal Cortège*, 1887. Etching, 8¼ inches × 10⅛ inches, II/II. Private collection. 99

85. Ensor. *The Pisser*, 1887. Etching, 5¾ inches × 4⅛ inches, only state. Private collection. 100

86. Ensor. *Haunted Furniture*, 1885. Oil on canvas, 35 inches × 40½ inches. Formerly Stedelijk Museum voor Schone Kunsten (destroyed during World War II). 103

87. Ensor. *Astonishment of the Mask Wouse*, 1889. Oil on canvas, 42¾ inches × 51½ inches. Koninklijk Museum voor Schone Kunsten, Antwerp. 104

88. Ensor. *My Sad and Splendid Portrait*, 1886. Black chalk on paper, 8¾ inches × 6¼ inches. Private collection. 106

89. Ensor. *The Haunted Mantelpiece*, 1888. Colored pencil on wood, 24 inches × 16 inches. Private collection. 106

90. Ensor. *The Devil's Mirror*, 1888. Pencil and charcoal. 8⅞ inches × 6¾ inches. Private collection. 107

91. Ensor. *Haunted Furniture*, 1888. Etching, 5⅜ inches × 3½ inches. III/III. Private collection. 108

92. Hieronymous Bosch. *Pride*, detail from *The Seven Deadly Sins*, date unknown. Oil on wood, 47¼ inches × 59 inches. Prado Museum, Madrid. 109

93. Jacques Callot. *The Temptation of St. Anthony*, 1635. Etching, 12⅜ inches × 18⅛ inches, Lieure 1416, III/V. Museum of Art, Rhode Island School of Design. 116

94. Gustave Doré. *Baron Munchausen aboard the Dutch ship in a sea of wine about to be swallowed by a monster*, 1865. Engraving from *The Adventures of Baron Munchausen* (London: Cassell, Petter and Galpin, 1865). 117

95. Charles Meryon. *Le Pont-au-change*, 1854. Engraving, 5½ inches × 12¹³⁄₁₆ inches. D-W 34, V/XII. The Art Institute of Chicago, Gift of Howard Mansfield. 119

96. Ensor. *The Temptation of St. Anthony*, 1927. Oil on canvas, 23¾ inches × 27¾ inches. Private collection. 121

97. Pieter Huys. *The Temptation of St. Anthony*, 1547. Oil on panel, 28 inches × 13 inches. Louvre, Paris, inventory number R.F. 3936. 122

98. Félicien Rops. *La Lyre*, 1887. Etching, 10 inches × 4⅜ inches. 123

99. Ensor. *The Temptation of St. Anthony*, 1887. Conte crayon on paper, 66⅞ inches × 59 inches. Frédéric Speth, Kapellen. 127

100. Ensor. *The Fight of the Demons*, 1888. Etching, 10¼ inches × 11⅞ inches, only state. Private collection. 129

101. Martin Schongauer. *The Temptation of St. Anthony*, c. 1470-1475. Engraving, 12¼ inches × 9 inches. British Museum, London. 130

102. Ensor. *Stars at the Cemetery*, 1888. Etching, 5¼ inches × 6¾ inches, II/II. Private collection. 131

103. Ensor. *Hail Jesus, King of the Jews (The Alive and Radiant: The Entry of Christ into Jerusalem)*, 1885. Charcoal and pencil on paper. 76⅝ inches × 55 inches. Museum voor Schone Kunsten, Ghent. 133

104. Detail of Christ in *The Entry of Christ into Brussels*, 1888. 137

105. George Cruikshank and Henry Mayhew. *London in 1851*. Illustration, *From 1851, or, The Adventures of Mr and Mrs Sandboys and Family, Who Came up to London to 'Enjoy Themselves,' and to See the Great Exhibition*. Published by David Bogue, London, 1851. 139

106. Detail of lower left in *The Entry of Christ into Brussels*, 1888. 141

107. Hieronymous Bosch. Detail of *The Hay-Wain*, 1485-1490. Oil on wood, 53⅛ inches × 33⅝ inches. Prado Museum, Madrid. 142

108. Ensor. *The Gendarmes*, 1892. Oil on panel, 7½ inches × 21¾ inches. Stedelijk Museum voor Schone Kunsten, Ostend. 143

109. Detail of lower right in *The Entry of Christ into Brussels*, 1888. 144

110. Ensor. *Double Portrait*, 1905. Oil on panel, 15½ inches × 13 inches. Claes-Boogaerts Collection, Brussels. 147

111. Ensor. *The Ray*. Copy of the 1892 painting (date unknown), 31 inches × 39 inches. Private collection. 148

112. Ensor. *Droll Smokers*, 1920. Oil on canvas, 29½ inches × 25¼ inches. Private collection. 149

113. Photograph of Ensor in his studio, c. 1893. Archives of Contemporary Art in Belgium, Musees Royaux des Beaux-Arts de Belgique, Brussels. 153

114. Ensor. *The Miraculous Draught of the Fishes*, n.d. Pencil, pen and ink on paper, 9¼ inches × 12⅜ inches. Private collection. 155

115. Ensor. *Poster for the Carnival at Ostend*, 1931. Colored lithograph, 18½ inches × 12¾ inches, only state. Private collection. 157

ACKNOWLEDGMENTS

This book began with a challenge from Max Kozloff, who was editor of *Artforum* in 1976 and 1977 when the Art Institute of Chicago and the Guggenheim Museum presented an Ensor exhibition. His suggestion that I use the exhibition as the basis for an article on Ensor resulted in "Ensor in His Milieu" (*Artforum*, May, 1977)—the first step toward a doctoral dissertation and subsequently this book. It is Max Kozloff, then, who deserves the first acknowledgment and my sincere appreciation for his inspired directive.

It is with profound admiration and continuing gratitude that I thank Kenneth C. Lindsay, Professor Emeritus of Art History at the State University of New York at Binghamton. A few sentences cannot adequately express this debt. Professor Lindsay is a remarkable role model who is continually giving of himself; for ten years as teacher, advisor, and friend, he has offered encouragement and direction, sparked by his genuine enthusiasm and intellectual commitment to art history. This Ensor study and much of my other work reflect the influence of his care and attention.

A number of readers have reviewed this manuscript and the preceding dissertation and have offered excellent advice.

Early on, Penelope Mayo, Marilyn Gaddis Rose, and Eunice Lipton helped as members of the dissertation committee. Reinhold Heller and Sharon Hirsh read the completed dissertation with great care. Their expertise has resulted in a number of clarifications, expansions, and deletions that have made a significant difference in the final manuscript. Peg Weiss not only offered similar help, but also actively participated in finding a publisher. During this period James Elesh, who published his study of Ensor prints (*James Ensor, The Complete Graphic Work*) in 1982, volunteered photographs and assistance, and I have benefited from his thorough knowledge of Ensor graphics, as well as his advice on other aspects of this manuscript.

During two visits to Belgium in 1977 and 1979, and in subsequent correspondence, I received invaluable assistance from Belgian scholars. Francine-Claire Legrand and Gisèle Ollinger-Zinque of the Musées Royaux des Beaux-Arts de Belgique patiently answered countless questions, as did Frank Patrick Edebau, then director of the Stedelijk Museum voor Schone Kunsten in Ostend. Mr. Edebau and his staff introduced me to the Ensor archive and the museum's large collection of Ensor publications. Recently, the museum's new curator, Norbert Hostyn, has been most generous with information and photographs. Lydia Schoonbaert of the Koninklijk Museum voor Schone Kunsten, Antwerp, and Nicole Walch of the Cabinet des Estampes in the Bibliothèque Royale Albert Ier, Brussels, have continued to offer their service, as has H. Coenen, Attaché at the Institut Royal du Patrimoine Artistique.

A number of other scholars have helped with information relevant to Ensor and Belgian art. Besides those already mentioned I owe thanks to John David Farmer, Gert Schiff, Julius Held, and James Marrow.

Belgian collectors have been most generous in allowing me to see their collections and to reproduce their works by Ensor. Although they remain anonymous, to them I extend sincere appreciation for their willingness to share Ensor's oeuvre through this book.

Assistance with translations, data gathering, photographs, typing, and all the time-consuming work peripheral, but critical, to the completion of a manuscript was undertaken by a number of colleagues and friends. Christine Lindsay, of Binghamton, New York, made numerous improvements by checking the French and the text during the book's early stages. Although responsibility for all translations remains mine, Marilyn Gaddis Rose, Professor of Comparative Literature and Director of the Translation Research and Instruction Program at the State University of New York at Binghamton, was extremely helpful in scrutinizing the translations for accuracy. Hugo Uyttenhove, then a doctoral candidate at the State University of New York at Binghamton and now back home in Europe, translated the Dutch;

Robert Maples, Associate Professor of Foreign Languages at Lycoming College, Williamsport, Pennsylvania, assisted with passages quoted from Symbolist literature. Thanks also go to my colleagues Paul MacKenzie and Richard Barker of the Foreign Language Department for their answers to various questions concerning titles and to Emily Jensen, Department of English, a perfectionist with prose, who came to my aid on a number of occasions. Special photographic assignments were undertaken by Michael Roskin and Rome Hanks, and the staff of the Lycoming College library was often ingenious in their methods of information retrieval; Susan Beidler and Martin Jamison deserve special mention. Glen McCreary performed a number of key tasks that helped to bring this manuscript to completion, and Esther Henninger proved to me the worth of a word processor, as well as of her own talents as a typist.

At Princeton University Press Christine Ivusik, Fine Arts Editor, has been consistently enthusiastic and helpful. Copyeditor Margaret Riccardi did an admirable job; in addition to editing for style and clarity, she caught inconsistencies, and I am indebted to her for making this text a better book. Sue Bishop's attentive care and expertise resulted in the fine design of this book.

Professional Development Grants from Lycoming College served to ease the financial burden a book of this type presents. There are other burdens as well, and so I offer a second dedication of this book—to Jennifer, Greg, and Charles Lesko—for their enduring care and support.

Williamsport, Pennsylvania
July 1984

xvi

JAMES ENSOR

Frissonnant, solitaire, et le coeur plein de fiel
Tu souris dans ta nuit, et ta gaîté macabre
Se moque en sanglotant de la douceur du ciel.

Georges Rency. September 2, 1898. *La Plume*

INTRODUCTION: "CABIN ON THE BEACH"

As a youth in Ostend, a Belgian coastal resort seventy-seven miles west of Brussels, James Ensor painted a small seascape on cardboard of a wooden bathing cabin standing alone on the sand (Pl. 1). He was just seventeen at the time, but the brushstroke is sure, the color evocative of a hazy blue, cloudy afternoon, and the composition compelling in its simplicity.

The painting still looks fresh; it has a lightness of touch and a general sense of grace that seem remarkable for such a young artist. And there is something else as well: a mood of quiet mystery that imbues the painting with the suggestion of autobiographical content. Ensor's cabin, with its solitary, narrow window and its closed door, is like a shell hiding a silent inhabitant who fears to reveal its self to the dangers of nature. It is a compact fortress at rest, its singular shadow casting the only mark on the empty beach as it waits to be wheeled back to the boundary of the sand's end to be counted among the other numbered cabins amassed there.

Throughout his youth and early maturity, Ensor was like his cabin: solitary, fearful of outside contact and fortified against it. In the ensuing years he produced an art that was radical and hallucinatory, containing individual images of extreme alienation, and crowd scenes of fear and panic. At the same time his was an art capable of bold beauty, poetic nuance, and of a vividly accurate reflection of reality.

Although Ensor's art spanned more than seven decades, and he continued to paint almost until his death in 1949, his brilliant creativity was confined for the most part to the years between 1877 and 1899—intensely fertile years in Europe, when artists like Cézanne, Van Gogh, Gauguin, and Munch were creating their own remarkable visions. Ensor's art both epitomized the era and remained unique, idiosyncratic, and highly personal.

It has often been suggested that the deeply introspective nature of much of Ensor's art defies explanation. Thus, despite extensive inquiry,[1] questions still abound regarding the meaning of his art, the short span of his creativity, and the

---

[1] For a bibliography that was published over twenty years ago, yet contains more than 1,000 titles, consult Hubert de France, *James Ensor, essai de bibliographie commentée—James Ensor: proeve van gencommentariëerde* *bibliografie.* Bibliographia Belgica, Vol. 53 (Brussels: Bibliographia Belgica 1960). A recently published monograph and two catalogs that were not available to the author at the time of writing are: Robert Delevoy, *Ensor*

subsequent dissolution of his artistic powers. Ensor has been characterized as a loner, a recluse who shunned travel and who hid within the city of Ostend and the walls of his studio. His consuming loves were his art, his birthplace, and the sea. These preoccupations, it has been claimed, kept him isolated from the mainstream of European society, a society he vilified and condemned in his art. But this view is somewhat misleading. Ensor's indifference to travel related to a conscious effort to preserve the authenticity of his personal world. Like Huysmans's Des Esseintes in the novel *À Rebours*, Ensor was an armchair traveler. His knowledge of art and his familiarity with the literary, philosophical, and political world of contemporary Europe enabled him to infuse his own art with a combination of tradition and innovation. Working within the context of multidirectional influences, Ensor had attempted to reconcile his conflicting allegiances to the avant-garde in Belgium, to his Flemishness, and to his English patrimony. Physically removed from the mainstream, his art nevertheless speaks pointedly and often caustically about that mainstream, so much so that a great deal of it was rejected by his closest peers.

Ensor himself helped to perpetrate the myth of his insularity and indifference, as when he observed, "I have happily confined myself to the land of mockery where everything is brilliant but violent masquerade."[2] He often described his personal situation with tongue in cheek; although he spoke glowingly about himself, "I will tell everyone about the beautiful legend of Me, of the universal Me," he added a qualifier, "of Pot-Bellied Me . . . ,"[3] which spoofed his self-proclaimed importance. When it came to his art, his explanations hinted at hidden truths, "Everyone knows that I can draw correctly when I want to."[4] But his pronouncements were also calculated to confuse: disavowing all outside influences on his development, he made his own affirmation suspect by adding a touch of drollery, "I developed freely and not exposed to influences, I ignore the great Gallic schools, the Frankish, the Germanic, the Shabby. . . ."[5]

Ensor did, in fact, borrow widely and from divergent sources, from literature and politics, for example, and from folklore, the fine arts, illustration, and the details of his personal life. This study will deal in large part with those sources, both historical and autobiographical, many of which have been previously overlooked or mentioned only in passing. Unpublished drawings, paintings, and letters will be discussed, as well as examples of published drawings and writings that have never been critically examined in print. Major works such as "The Entry of Christ into Brussels," "The Tribulations of St. Anthony," and "The Cathedral" are dealt with in detail and are shown to contain a wealth of information not before realized.

Any attempt to dispel the mystery surrounding Ensor and to enrich our understanding of his individual works and their relation to his total production can only be part of a continuing effort. The literature on great artists continues to grow,

(Geneva: Weber, 1981); *Ensor. Dipinti—Disegni—Incisioni* (Milan: Electa, 1981); and *James Ensor* (Zurich: Kunsthaus Zurich, 1983).

[2] Paul Haesaerts, "Quand James Ensor peignait *L'Entrée du Christ à Bruxelles,*" *Oeil* 131 (November 1965): 82. Unless otherwise noted, translations throughout the text are mine, often made with the kind assistance of Marilyn Gaddis Rose and Robert Maples. Quotations in the original language appear in footnotes only when the source is difficult to obtain.

[3] Francine-Claire Legrand, *Ensor, cet inconnu* (Brussels: La Renaissance du Livre, 1971), p. 13.

[4] Quoted in *La Plume*, special Ensor ed. (Paris, 1898); also issued separately (Paris, 1899): p. 34.

[5] James Ensor, *Mes Écrits*, preface by Franz Hellens, 5th ed. (Liège: Éditions Nationales, 1974), p. 224.

and future studies will no doubt reveal new insights into the complexities of Ensor's genius and the beauty of his art.

Although references are made throughout the text to the creative activities of a widespread European art community, they are limited, for the most part, to specific links with Ensor's artistic production. The book begins with an examination of the ties between Ensor's art, his family, and the city of Ostend. Ensor's relationships in Brussels, and the cultural and intellectual milieu of that city, are considered, as well as the influence of two major Belgian artists, Antoine Wiertz and Félicien Rops. Literature as inspiration for Ensor's art is the topic of an entire chapter, and references to literary influences appear throughout the text. Ensor's assimilation of religion and history is discussed in Chapter V. And finally, the conundrum of Ensor's lost talent and his own awareness of his failing powers is examined in Chapter VI. In several crucial canvases Ensor addressed this last issue. These brave paintings stand at the watershed of his career, and through them Ensor offered an open and direct line of communication not found in his letters and speeches. In the most unflinching terms he affirmed that his creativity was slipping away, and in recording this decline with sensitivity and feeling, he quietly revealed a great deal about himself and his art.

I

ENSOR'S EARLY LIFE IN OSTEND

AND HIS ISOLATION

The ocean was Ensor's first subject and he returned to it often throughout his career. At sixteen he painted several small seascapes on cardboard, all approximately 7" x 9". Most of them show a narrow focus of dunes, rangy sea grass, and a corner of the ocean. They are somewhat subdued in color and one of them, perhaps the last, is particularly sensitive, with loose, free brushstrokes on sand and sea, and delicate, moving strands of vegetation on windswept dunes (Fig. 1). A reminiscence of that early time suggests the comfort that Ensor derived from the ocean and recalls the small painting "Cabin on the Beach" (Pl. 1): ". . . I was becoming melancholic and wanted to live in a large cabin in front of the sea. I would cover it with pearly shells and sleep there, ideally soothed by the noise of the sea. . . ."[1]

[1] Quoted in Legrand, *Ensor, cet inconnu*, p. 16.

[2] Michael Van Guyck and André Dubar. Ensor may have learned the rudiments from them, but his early landscape style also shows the influence of a group of Belgian naturalist painters known for their plein-airist technique: Louis Artan, Guillaume Vogels, and Hippolyte Boulenger. See John David Farmer, *Ensor* (New York: George Braziller, 1976), pp. 17-18.

As a youth Ensor had studied with two local Ostend artists,[2] but he later repudiated this period of instruction.[3] At seventeen he left his hometown to study for three years at the Brussels Académie Royale des Beaux-Arts. Arriving with great anticipation and optimism, yet overwhelmed with pressure to succeed, he desperately drove himself: "I painted mornings, attended classes in composition in the afternoon, drew in the evening, and at night I mapped out dreams for the future. My teachers, preoccupied, and frowning with disapproval, disparaged me as an ignorant dreamer."[4]

Ensor's early studies from plaster casts and live models make a telling contrast to the sensitive early marine paintings in which he felt relaxed and free to investigate nature. Later, he recalled his reaction to an academy assignment

[3] "They initiated me in a professional manner into the deceptive stereotypes of their gloomy, narrowminded, and still-born trade." Quoted in Paul Haesaerts, *James Ensor*, translated by Norbert Guterman (New York: Harry N. Abrams, 1959), p. 31 (unless otherwise specified, references to Haesaerts will be to this English version).

[4] Ibid., p. 40.

FIG. 1. Ensor. *Dunes of Ostend*, c. 1876.

FIG. 2. Ensor. *Classic Academy Model*, 1878.

that used a plaster cast: "I was told to paint the bust of Octavian, the most illustrious of the Caesars, from a brand-new plaster cast. The snow-white plaster dismayed me."[5]

Whether or not the painting Ensor mentions still survives is uncertain, but a charcoal drawing that Ensor signed and dated "1876" is a typical academic exercise and illustrates the difficulty Ensor had with plaster casts (Fig.2). The drawing is tight and the shading perfunctory in the hair and beard;

in addition, the eyes are strangely detailed for a cast, with dark pupils and smeared charcoal in the white areas. Overall, the visual solution is ambiguous and Ensor's plaster cast appears to contain the obscured depiction of a real man. It is tempting to link this early suggestion of transformation with Ensor's later practice of infusing inanimate masks with piercing, lifelike eyes.

In 1880 Ensor returned to Ostend, where he established a

[5] Ibid.

7

FIG. 3. Ensor *Pears*, 1881.

Answerable to no one in Ostend, Ensor nevertheless continued contact with artistic groups and new acquaintances he had made in Brussels. He submitted paintings for exhibit and was accepted by La Chrysalide in 1881. In 1882 Le Cercle Artistique hung his paintings, which were labeled "turpitudes," and subsequently a petition from its own members demanded that they be withdrawn from the exhibition.[7] For more than a decade following Ensor would fight such establishment criticism, which ranged from petty slander to invectiveness.[8]

Free to experiment, Ensor produced between 1880 and 1882 a number of still-lifes that show a remarkable variation in style and color. In one of his finest paintings from this period (Fig. 3), he worked on volume and perspective using three pears nestled in a dish. The plate and its contents are slightly tilted up and out toward the picture plane, and the oblique angle of the newspaper underneath and its unclear positioning in relation to the table top create a peculiar ambiguity. These explorations and the ease of Ensor's sure brushstroke anticipate Cézanne's later preoccupation with illusion and reality in still-lifes.

Ensor's monumental "Woman Eating Oysters" from 1882 was his most ambitious still-life (Pl. 2). In this painting, which is over seven feet tall, he expanded his interest from objects on a table to a larger concern with those objects in relation to a total environment. The top half of the com-

studio on the top floor of his family's home. He worked there for the next sixty-nine years: ". . . I walked out on that establishment for the near blind without further ado. . . . I have never been able to understand why my teachers were so upset by my restless explorations."[6]

[6] Ibid., p. 41. In a letter to Pol de Mont, Ensor recalled his painting from the years 1877-1880: "I have few works left from this period. Now and again I was dissatisfied. I destroyed those I hadn't finished. . . ." Quoted in *Ensor: ein Maler aus dem Späten 19. Jahrhundert* (Stuttgart: Staatsgalerie, 1972), p. 37.

[7] Haesaerts, *James Ensor*, p. 363. The artists of La Chrysalide, which included Dubois, Vogels, and Rops, have been characterized by Haesaerts as "moderate revolutionaries" (p. 93). Le Cercle Artistique was more conservative.

[8] For example, La Gazette of 1886 described two paintings, including the remarkable "Woman Eating Oysters," as "two veritable examples of outlandish painting." As late as 1894 *Le Patriote* asked of Ensor's art, "That's painting? Come on then! That's excrement" (*Cahiers de Belgique* [1929], p. 35). In a letter of that same year Ensor recalled his reaction to criticism: ". . . I suffered tremendously when people laughed or were horrified and this behavior was generally common among the bourgeoisie. At that time I learned to look down at them and this feeling never completely left me" (*Ensor: ein Maler*, p. 37).

position works well and is painted with considerable skill. In a luminous interior a solitary sturdy bourgeois woman partakes of a meal, surrounded by bottles, half-filled glasses, and dinner plates. On the ample white tablecloth a partly folded napkin drapes over the edge, visually stabilized by the bright yellow lemon next to it. Warm sparkling yellows, reds, and golds vie with the cooler blue and pink reflections in the tablecloth, which in turn contrast with the creamy ivory of the woman's shawl. She eats alone, and the spotless plate opposite her suggests a quiet domestic drama.

The bottom half of the painting is not as successful: a chair and a white shawl seem to be evident in the lower left, but they confuse the composition; further, at the right of the table a large patch of smeared, loose brushstrokes applied in varying thicknesses and in different directions blocks out the woman's form and expands the bulk of the table into disproportion.

With these splotches of paint the picture appears unfinished, and such artistic indulgence would have horrified an academically trained eye. This carelessness may, in fact, have been the reason for the painting's rejection by the Antwerp salon in 1882 and by the avant-garde group, L'Essor, in 1883.[9] Today it is hard to imagine any other reason for its being refused, although perhaps its sparkling color seemed incongruent with its heavy palpable forms. Then, too, in comparison with the popular Alfred Stevens's paintings of elegant women, Ensor's model may have seemed somewhat coarse and too concerned with earthy appetites.

Ensor's indifference to acceptable technique and his rebellion against established practices led him to make daring innovations in picture-making. In later canvases, such as the 1887 "Tribulations of St. Anthony" (Pl. 7), he allowed no restrictions to hamper the creation of a hallucinatory surface thick with scumbled and violent color. His art was problematic with even the most liberal groups, including Les Vingt, the radical organization of which Ensor was a founding member.[10] During the years of its existence, from 1883 through 1893, Ensor was asked to withdraw numerous works that others in the group felt were particularly offensive and shocking. Yet it was during this period of frequent rejection that Ensor continued to paint his most vital and challenging works.

In 1882 Ensor painted a still-life quite unlike his others from that period. Entitled "The Ray," it recalls Chardin's famous eighteenth-century depiction of the same subject, although Ensor's is simpler in design: a stingray and a small fish have fallen out of an overturned basket and lie on a pile of straw at the edge of a table (Fig. 4).[11] The painting's realism seems reactionary for Ensor, and its conservative style may have been meant to ensure the picture's acceptance and to counter the attacks directed against his more innovative experiments. Yet Ensor's compositional arrangement and

---

[9] Ironically, the word "l'essor" has several meanings, all suggestive of free and open inspiration: "flight," "soaring," "progress," "impulse," "life," "vigor." In 1884 Ensor submitted the painting to the Brussels salon where it was rejected for its "lack of form" (Farmer, *Ensor*, p. 21).

[10] For the literature on Les XX and its predecessors consult Jane Block, "Les Vingt and Belgian Avant-Gardism, 1868-1894" (Ph.D. dissertation, University of Wisconsin at Milwaukee, 1980). Also by Block, "Les XX: Forum of the Avant-Garde," *Belgian Art 1880-1914* (New York: The Brook-lyn Museum, 1980), pp. 17-40. Francine-Claire Legrand, *Le Groupe des XX et son temps* (Otterlo: Rijksmuseum Kroller-Muller, 1962); Madeleine Octave Maus, *Trente Années de lutte pour l'art belge, 1884-1914* (Brussels: Librairie L'Oiseau bleu, 1926); Jean Warmoes, "Les XX et la littérature," *Cahiers van de Velde*, no. 7 (Brussels, 1966), pp. 19-42.

[11] The inspiration for the painting may have originated with a small snapshot of a stingray lying at the top of a fisherman's basket. It can be found in the Ensor archive, Musée des Beaux-Arts, Ostend.

Fig. 4. Ensor. *The Ray*, 1882.

sensuous painting of the body of the ray belie the painting's obvious conventionalism. The ray reclines in a precarious position, its head and side protruding over the table's edge from a bed of shining golden straw that seems to crackle with electricity. Pink-coral tones infuse the perimeter of the ray with warmth, and soft brushstrokes radiate outward toward those edges from the center of its milky white body.

The ray lies exposed, yet its thin, poisonous tail is alert and pointed directly into the large, open mouth of the wicker basket. In combination with this rigid tail, the flat, pliant body attracts and repels at the same time. It is tempting to postulate that Ensor chose to paint the ray not only for its association with an acceptable artistic tradition, but also because of the personal appeal that the creature had as an image of potential danger, even in its vulnerable captive condition.[12]

In the next year, 1883, Ensor painted "The Rower," a picture that along with several others of the same year, contains the suggestion of autobiographical content (Fig. 5). It is an enigmatic canvas, boldly executed with thick, free brushstrokes and a compelling composition. Filling the foreground and middleground of the painting is a rowboat that holds a single occupant. Whether or not he is a fisherman is uncertain; he may be rowing out to the sailboat that, partly obscured by fog, makes a spectral appearance in the middle distance. Over his right eye a patch is suggested, and a cord across his forehead seems to hold it in place. The painting's heavy harmony of colors, dark blues and greens, is lightened somewhat by the glowing yet cool yellow oar, and by the swirling amorphous forms of red and blue painted on the back of the rower's boat and on the lapels of his predominantly black clothing.

Detached from his surroundings and preoccupied, the rower rows his boat, pointed toward the open sea, but slowly and haltingly, with a single oar. Whether consciously intended or not, the painting could well stand as a metaphor for Ensor's own solitary condition in 1883: alienated and alone, Ensor abandons the mainland and rows in the direction of the open sea; rejected and criticized, he seems destined to follow the Flying Dutchman, who according to legend was condemned until Judgment Day to sail the seas against the wind.[13] Huysmans's last lines from *À Rebours*, published the following year, follow Ensor's visual observation: "Lord take pity on the Christian who doubts, on the sceptic who fain would believe, on the galley-slave of life who puts out to sea alone, in the darkness of night, beneath a firmament illumined no longer by the consoling beacon-fires of the ancient hope."[14]

Ostend was dependent upon the sea for sustenance, through both its fishing and its tourism, and Ensor was dependent upon Ostend for the roots of his art. He loved his city of narrow streets flanked by high buildings standing like vertical slats in a tall wooden fence, and he loved its light, often filtered through an atmospheric haze over the North Sea. Ensor was born on the rue Longue in April of 1860, and he lived there until 1917 when he moved to 27, rue de Flandre, his uncle's former home and the artist's residence until his death in 1949. The rue de Flandre feeds into the main boulevard that holds the coastline bathing beach. Today a sign on the wide, stone ocean walk announces his house a half-block away.

His mother, grandmother, and aunt were Flemish shopkeepers in a store below their apartment. Souvenirs, Oriental curios, and carnival masks were sold to the summer tourists who swelled the otherwise insular city. The seasonal change was schizoid: nine months of uneventful regularity, which could well have been described with Sinclair Lewis's phrase, "where dullness has been made god," broken only by the

---

[12] Belgian folktales linked stingrays with the devil, as in Tyl Ulenspiegel's tale in which a live ray falls from a fisherman's cart and is mistaken for the devil (Charles De Coster, *The Glorious Adventures of Tyl Ulenspiegel*, translated by Allan Ross Macdougall [New York: Pantheon Books, 1943], p. 337).

[13] The Flying Dutchman was also the name of a phantom ship seen near the Cape of Good Hope. A form of the story was used by Richard Wagner in his opera *Der fliegende Hollander*. In recalling the years from 1877 to 1880 Ensor wrote of his fascination with Wagner: "This extraordinary genius influenced and strengthened me. . . ." Letter to Paul de Mont in *Ensor: ein Maler*, pp. 36-37.

[14] *Against the Grain*, translated, with introduction, by Havelock Ellis (New York: Three Sirens Press, 1931), p. 339 (the title has also been translated as *Against Nature*, e.g., in the translation by Robert Baldick).

FIG. 5. Ensor. *The Rower*, 1883.

12

FIG. 6. Ensor. *Baths at Ostend*, 1899.

FIG. 7. Ensor. *Sleeping Woman*, c. 1882.

traditional Belgian holiday carnivals, and three months of mass hysteria when vacationers filled the beaches. Ensor was to treat the subject of summer madness in his later art when he depicted this annual wave of self-indulgent strangers as caricatures intent on perverse activity (Fig. 6).

During the long winter months the women in Ensor's household appeared to hibernate. For the energetic Ensor, who had chosen to come home, this inactivity may have

been a constant source of irritation, tempering his enjoyment of his surroundings and reminding him of an underlying repressive atmosphere. He documented their constant sleep in numerous poses (Fig. 7), sometimes with heads thrown back and mouths slack and fallen open. Above one depiction of Ensor's aunt he printed his description of her condition with the mocking words "Faire des Grimaces," "Make Faces" (Fig. 8). Later he was to add fantasy to those kinds of draw-

FIG. 8. Ensor. *Portrait of the Artist's Aunt*, c. 1883.

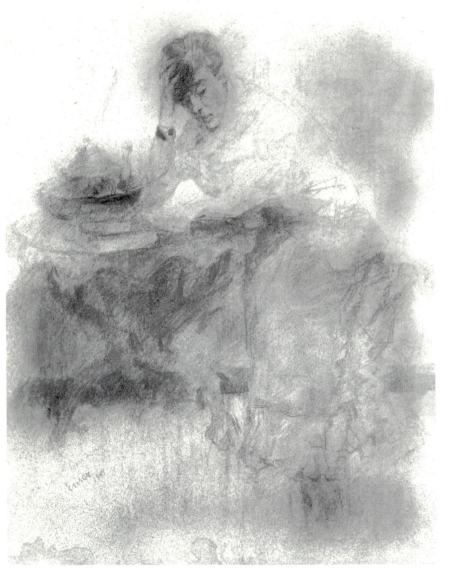

FIG. 9. Ensor. *Portrait of the Artist's Sister*, 1881.

ings, as in "The Old Woman Asleep" from 1893, which recalled Goya's "Sleep of Reason" and showed Ensor's aunt or grandmother unperturbed by the demons who surrounded her and nudged at her shoulders.

Ensor's younger sister, Marie, called Mitche, was a beautiful woman who was shown in similar, but more flattering poses (Fig. 9). A series of oil paintings from the early 1880s, among them "Somber Lady," "Afternoon at Ostend," and "Woman in Distress" (originally known as "Troubled"), document her home life and illustrate the growing sense of entrapment and suffocation she felt. In a little-known painting from 1880 Mitche sits in profile with her shawl drawn around her shoulders; her eyes are closed, her mouth slightly open, and her hands rest in her lap (Fig. 10). The background is indistinct, a wall of smeared brushstrokes, but the weight of her body and its position sideways against the chair imply more than simple sleep. In fact, its title, "The Convales-

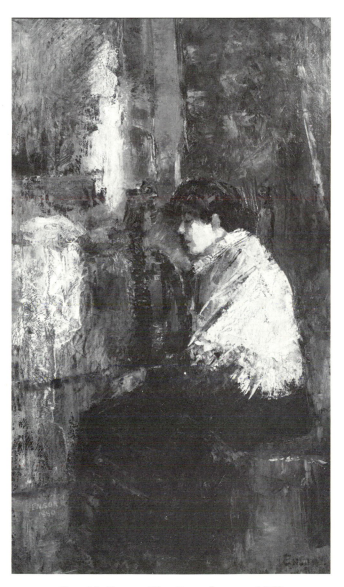

FIG. 10. Ensor. *The Convalescent*, 1880.

FIG. 11. Ensor. *Portrait of Mitche*, 1883.

cent," hints at the numerous illnesses that plagued the female members of Ensor's family.

Mitche was involved in a physical, as well as emotional, rebellion. She often disappeared for several days at a time, then she would return home briefly and run away again.[15] Although her unhappiness with her environment is evident in most of Mitche's portraits, an unusual painting from 1883 shows her in a somewhat different mood (Fig. 11). It is a three-quarter view of her upper torso, and a large corsage of

[15] Haesaerts, *James Ensor*, p. 65.

FIG. 12. Ensor. *Pair in an Open Landau*, 1883.

FIG. 13. Ensor. *Intrigue*, 1890.

flowers is pinned on the open-necked bodice of her gown. It is Ensor's most sensuous portrait of his sister, and the palpable thickness of the paint accentuates the density of her body. In that same year, in an ink sketch on a letter, which includes the phrase "with Mitche," he portrayed her riding in an open carriage, a delightful caricature, tall and thin like Ensor, and obviously happy (Fig. 12).

For the most part Mitche seems to have seen herself trapped in the company of older women and destined to become like them. Perhaps as the ultimate gesture of escape, in 1892 she married a Chinese salesman whom she had met in their

store. Abandoned that same year, she returned home with a daughter, Alex, and never left again. Libby Tannenbaum and Francine-Claire Legrand have suggested that the monumental painting entitled "Intrigue" (Fig. 13) is Ensor's biting comment on the newlyweds: the bride, with corsage and wedding bouquet, and her companion, with almond-shaped eyes and top hat, appear with a fat attendant who carries an oriental doll and points at the groom. Ensor dated the work 1890, but its obvious biographical reference—and we know that Ensor took liberties with some dates—implies a date of 1892 or later.[16]

[16] Libby Tannenbaum, *James Ensor* (New York: Museum of Modern Art, 1951), p. 83, and Legrand, *Ensor, cet inconnu*, p. 80.

In an unfinished drawing Ensor may have shown Mitche with her beautiful child (Fig. 14). Only a closed eye and the nose and mouth of her face are shown as she cradles the sleeping curly-haired infant in her arm. This sketch has been placed in the middle of a page between a piece of furniture, a large sideboard cropped on the left, and a small image on the right, an ugly old woman with hanging breasts. The ephemeral beauty of this fragment of mother and child contrasts sharply with the heavily carved sideboard and the grotesque caricature of old age.

Ensor felt partly responsible for his sister's unhappiness, although he never explained why. His relationship with her was complex and no doubt encompassed great love and some resentment as well. At one point he wrote, "My sister ruins herself and I have to assist. . . ."[17] It appears that in his art the drawing with her daughter Alex as a baby may be the only depiction executed after Mitche's return, despite the fact that Mitche and Ensor lived together in the same house until her death in 1945. Mitche's daughter did escape. At fifteen she left to marry, and, although she kept in contact with her mother and uncle, she never returned home.

Throughout the years Ensor's involvement with his female relatives was linked with responsibility and guilt. Letters to friends complained of crucial time lost from his art and spent attending to their needs: "I am surrounded by the sick. My mother is in bed, my sister also. My aunt is helpless and I should comfort and nurse all the patients."[18]

Ensor was dependent upon his mother for financial support

FIG. 14. Ensor. *Mitche with Child*, n.d.

and he lived with her until her death in 1915. His last portrait of her shows her on her deathbed, emaciated and white-skinned, with her mouth hanging open in a pose pointedly reminiscent of those earlier sketches of sleeping relatives (Fig. 15). A statuette of the Virgin, her head bowed in mourning, appears on a carved pedestal to the right, but most distinctive is an imposing arrangement of medicine bottles

---

[17] Quoted in Francine-Claire Legrand, "Les Lettres de James Ensor à Octave Maus," *Bulletin des Musées Royaux des Beaux-Arts de Belgique* 15 (1966): 17.

[18] Legrand, "Lettres": 24. In 1909 he recalled those early years and the toll they took: "Yes, I worked a lot, especially between 1881-1882 and there! The sufferings, anxiety, and the daily worries are harmful to my work.

Sometimes when I'm thinking of my troubles a frightful hopelessness takes hold of me and I curse people a great deal. I would have made so many interesting things; I like work but everything conspires against me and, nearly every day when I want to set to work, somebody comes to pull me from the easel for some trivial task" (Legrand, *Ensor, cet inconnu*, p. 22).

FIG. 15. Ensor. *The Artist's Mother in Death*, 1915.

FIG. 16. Ensor. *Portrait of the Artist's Father*, 1881.

standing on a table in the foreground, where they work as an effective barrier between Ensor and the body of his mother.

Ensor's father was an outcast in this house dominated by women. Although born in Brussels, he was an English subject, and his parents had been independently wealthy. In marrying a native of Ostend, a daughter of lace merchants, Ensor was marrying below his class. After the birth of his son he had left Belgium for the United States, choosing to look for work as a civil engineer just at the time when Amer-

ica was involved in civil war. Forced to return to Ostend and to accept his wife's charity, he began to drink heavily. His alcoholism became the subject of great local amusement, causing Ensor to complain bitterly, "The bourgeois used to enjoy getting him drunk; we have suffered greatly for it."[19] Yet Ensor's father was cultured, musical, gifted in drawing, and able to read and write in several languages. In a reminiscence Ensor described him as ". . . truly a superior man,"[20] and it was he who encouraged his son's interest in art. Ensor

[19] Ibid. Frank Patrick Edebau quotes Ensor's explanation for his father's alcoholism: "He was really a superior man, finally preferring (quoting Paul Claudel on Verlaine) to be drunk rather than to be like the rest of us" ("James Ensor and Ostend," in Farmer, *Ensor*, p. 10). Edebau also described the family conflicts: "His mother, who was continually complaining about

her husband, tried to set the son against his father, while his aunt kept harping about the state of her health, and his sister made frequent pleasure trips, deserting the others in their mounting panic. All this created a terribly depressing atmosphere. . . ." (Ibid.).

[20] Quoted in Legrand, *Ensor, cet inconnu*, p. 15.

FIG. 17. Ensor. *The Artist's Father in Death*, 1887.

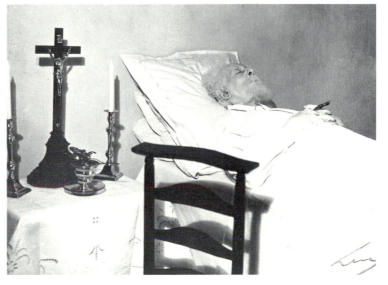

FIG. 18. *Photograph of Ensor in Death*, November 1949.

painted his father's portrait in 1881, showing him engrossed in a book as he sat in a blue armchair (Fig. 16).

In discussing the bourgeois society in Ostend, Jean Stevo described the suffocating atmosphere and the peculiar smells of the city. Clannish, petty, and mean, it was a society in which Ensor's mother and her relatives were at home, but in which Ensor's father could not survive:

There was a faded side, mean, a stinginess, also an odor. That was a simenonien climate, that of secret Ostend, where one lived poorly in the kitchen cellar which always smelled a little of gas and boiled fish, where one gossiped, where one served hot and sweet-smelling cups of coffee, with bad hu-

mor, with sullenness, with suppressed spite. . . . Because, at Ostend, there were cliques. . . .[21]

An 1887 drawing Ensor made of his father in death (Fig. 17) can be compared with a photograph of Ensor on his own deathbed in 1949 (Fig. 18). The physical similarities are striking, and David Farmer has noted that Ensor would have been well aware of the close resemblance between his father and himself.[22]

Ensor expressed his physical and psychic link with his father in two paintings and a drawing in 1882 and 1883. "The Drunkards," from 1883, is a simple painting with an

[21] Jean Stevo "Ensor l'Ostendais," *L'Art Belge* (December 1965): 12.

[22] Farmer, *Ensor*, p. 25.

FIG. 19. Ensor. *The Drunkards*, 1883.

obvious message (Fig. 19). Two workers sit at a table with a liquor bottle and a glass. A second glass has rolled onto the floor under the table, swept away by the collapse of the man on the right. Behind them a sign advertises a farm for sale through bankruptcy proceedings. It is a large painting, over five feet in length, and its simple composition and direct treatment make it a striking statement of concern and sympathy for the disastrous effects of alcoholism.

In that same year Ensor's use of carnival masks in a paint-ing established a precedent for an important corpus of work that was to deal with such motifs in later years. "Scandalized Masks" depicts a confrontation in simple terms (Pl. 3). In a bare room a single lamp illuminates the wall with a rich, warm light. Seated at a small table on which a half-filled bottle of liquor rests, a man in a smiling mask places his hands on the table top and looks up at a masked woman who has just entered the room and still holds the doorknob of the opened door. Her mask includes round, blue glasses and she wears a high-peaked, white hat with a blue ribbon tied in a bow.

Eighteen eighty-three seems to have been a year in which masks became a popular motif in a number of literary and artistic compositions.[23] Perhaps Ensor was aware of Odilon Redon's 1883 drawing from Edgar Allan Poe's "Masque of the Red Death" and found there some inspiration for using masks. More remarkable, however, is the similarity with Redon's charcoal and crayon drawing, "Interior with Skeletons" (Fig. 20), which Huysmans reviewed after seeing Redon's 1883 exhibition.[24] In this "fantaisie macabre," as Huysmans called it, a skeleton is seated at a table and holds a tall glass. A wine carafe and two plates appear on the table and a lamp hangs above the scene. From a doorway at the right a second skeleton appears, holding back one side of the curtain while the other section hides most of its bony figure. In later years Ensor was to use skeletons as subjects in paintings and prints, but in this instance it is the situation, the element of surprise and confrontation, that makes Redon's drawing similar to Ensor's "Scandalized Masks." Furthermore, Redon's composition, the view of the room, and the scale of the figures and their placement add notably to the comparison.

Marcel De Maeyer has suggested that, because of its early date and the fact that Ensor did not begin to develop fantasy motifs until at least two years later, "Scandalized Masks" was meant simply as a genre painting:

FIG. 20. Odilon Redon. *Interior with Skeletons*, c. 1882.

This painting is . . . essentially a "slice of life." The mask has not yet acquired the complex symbolic value that it will have. It only seems like a realistic representation of a disguise. . . . The entire situation is expressed with a vigorous realism, and the carnival-like disguise itself contributes to emphasizing the picturesque and accenting it.[25]

He concludes by observing: "Nothing permits the interpretation of this work in the perspective of Ensorian art such as it will be five years later. . . ."[26]

[23] In 1883 Félicien Rops illustrated Barbey d'Aurevilly's *Masques Parisiens*, and the sculptor Zachary Astruc created "Le Marchand des Masques," a bronze statue of a youth holding a collection of masks of famous creative men, including a portrait of d'Aurevilly. See Robert Pincus-Witten, *Occult Symbolism in France: Josephin Péladan and the Salons de la Rose-Croix* (New York: Garland 1976), p. 193 and fig. 63.

[24] *Le Symbolisme en Europe* (Paris: Musées Nationaux, 1976), p. 179, fig. 182.

[25] Marcel De Maeyer, "Derrière le masque: L' Introduction du masque, du travesti et du squelette comme motifs dans l'oeuvre de James Ensor," *L'Art Belge* (December 1965): 20.

[26] Ibid. Farmer agreed with De Maeyer, observing that it was not until 1886 that Ensor's mature style used "familiar objects at the service of fantasy. This approach became a means of venting his feelings through the abstraction and distortion of events in his own life" (*Ensor*, p. 26).

FIG. 21. Postcard of Ensor drawing *Le Buveur*, c. 1882.

Yet the painting can be seen to hold much more significance. Ensor's drama refers to his father's alcoholism and the tensions evident within his family.[27] An unpublished drawing, entitled "The Drinker" (Fig. 21), can be seen as an important step in the development of the idea that culminates in "Scandalized Masks":[28] a man dressed also in black, wearing the same kind of black hat as the man in the painting, sits at a small table on which a bottle of liquor stands. One of his arms leans on the table, while the other rests on his right leg. We cannot see his eyes, which are covered by the hat's brim, but the downward tilt of his head, the protruding lower lip, and the weight of his body as he leans forward suggest an introspective mood; the half-filled bottle adds the probability of an alcoholic revery.

A work painted the previous year and entitled "The Sick Tramp" showed a man dressed similarly to "The Drinker." In the "Tramp," which was destroyed during World War II, a man was seated on a chair next to a coal stove. His feet were propped on the stove's platform and he clasped his hands between his knees as he looked out at the viewer. Although it is uncertain that the title referred to a condition related to alcohol, "The Sick Tramp" and "The Drinker" form an interesting series with the "Scandalized Masks."

Libby Tannenbaum has observed that the tramps and drunkards Ensor painted were not merely members of the lower classes but rather were "outcasts from any class and represent Ensor's first insistence on man at his most abject and inglorious."[29] Ensor's father, as an outcast in Ostend and as an alcoholic who was to die from exposure and alcoholism

[27] This observation was first made by Libby Tannenbaum, *James Ensor*, p. 50.

[28] The drawing's present location is unknown, but a postcard that reproduces it along with its title can be found in the archives at Ostend's Musée des Beaux-Arts. Frank Edebau believes it dates from the early 1880s.

[29] Tannenbaum, *James Ensor*, p. 44.

on the streets when he was just fifty-two,[30] belonged with that large group of outcasts.

It is a representative of this group, then, rather than Ensor's father, who appears in "Scandalized Masks." It may have been too painful for Ensor to paint his father in such a confrontation; in fact, the smiling mask, with its huge nose, gives its wearer an air of childish embarrassment, as if he has been caught by the standing figure in a compromising, or perhaps even a predictable, situation.

Ensor's spare symbolism creates an atmosphere of mystery that has a literary counterpart in the writings of his friend Maurice Maeterlinck, the Belgian Symbolist who was to praise Ensor's art in the 1899 tribute issue of *La Plume*. The painting's title adds to this sense of mystery. "Masques scandalisés" may refer to shocked or scandalized masks, but, according to one Belgian authority, "when a mask frightens someone in Belgium, it's said that it 'scandalizes.' "[31] Thus the true sense of the word may refer to a frightening confrontation, as well as to the original meaning of a shock to one's sense of propriety.

"Scandalized Masks" has been described as a "scène conjugale," with the standing female figure identified as Ensor's maternal grandmother, who continued to take part in carnival activities despite her advanced age:

The cane of a shrew with blue glasses prepares to chastise the patience of a long-nosed, stupefied husband. This old lady, with features hardened by miserliness, wasn't she an effigy of the maternal grandmother . . . who became hardened with age: about 60 at carnival she still went out masked and disguised?[32]

A description of the painting's mood follows with the observation that "an irrational fear escapes from this canvas. . . ."[33] It is difficult to be specific about the elements that determine this "irrational fear," but one reason for this feeling may lie with the masked woman and her intrusion into the man's solitary space. A 1947 monograph on Ensor described her as "the horrible old one of our nightmares and of our childhood fears. The Macaco sorcerer with its sickly and deceitful smile, who weakly extends the hand, but surely to grab you. . . ."[34]

The object in her hand, which she grasps firmly, is not a cane, as it has been described above, but rather a horn that can be played in the carnival festivities. Perhaps the horn's use ultimately goes back to that long tradition of noisemakers meant to ward off evil spirits in pagan religious rites, but it is significant to recall that, in the poetry of the French Symbolist Jules Laforgue, the horn announces death.[35] As Ensor was well aware of Symbolist literature, and he transformed some of its philosophical implications to work within the context of his own art, it is possible to suggest a similar analogy: for the seated figure the opened door and icy blue outside world reveal an intruder, who, although she comes in corporeal form, is reminiscent of Maeterlinck's later spectral harbinger of death.[36]

---

[30] Ibid., p. 50.

[31] Jollivet Castelot, *Croquis scientifiques et philosophiques* (Paris: Durville, 1912), p. 321. Chap. 29 is devoted to Ensor.

[32] Lucien Schwob, *James Ensor* (Ostend: n.p., 1963), p. 136.

[33] Ibid.

[34] Jean Stevo, *James Ensor* (Brussels: Éditions Germinal, 1947), p. 20.

[35] See William Jay Smith, ed. and trans., *Selected Writings of Jules Laforgue* (New York: Grove Press, 1956), p. 88. On a sheet of sketches Ensor

included a horn in a disembodied hand drawn between the heads of two sleeping female figures (his mother and aunt?) and the face of a man who, with eyes closed, holds his open hand over his mouth and nose (Collection of Mlle. Julienne Boogaerts, Brussels; reproduced in Tannenbaum, *James Ensor*, p. 48).

[36] For example, in such dramas as "The Intruder" from 1889. Maeterlinck's link with Ensor, as well as the influence of other Symbolists, is discussed in Chapter IV. Libby Tannenbaum has noted this quality, "The

It was also the year 1883 in which Ensor realized the appropriateness of and potential for fusing the drama of his own family situation, with its mean and sordid details, with the longstanding Belgian tradition of holiday masquerade. The implications of this fusion were both personal and universal.[37] The mask, which is used to hide one's identity, is a vehicle for escape. Once in place it is also a cover for indiscriminate behavior. In Ensor's painting the carnival remains a viable exercise in indulgence, practiced by the old woman and, by implication, accepted by church and community. Ironically, for the seated man, the mask fails to hide or protect. Trapped by his pathetic life and his vulnerable hidden self, Ensor's surrogate father will not escape death.

The female mask, with its distinctive blue glasses and pointed hat, may be a construction from Ensor's imagination: there is no evidence that it ever really existed. However, the large-nosed mask is similar to a mask with a pointed nose found among other masks in Ensor's apartment. These two masks will reappear in Ensor's later work and take part repetitively in its drama as members of his personal family of masks.[38]

We have seen that in the years from 1881 through 1883 a number of Ensor's paintings were distinctly autobiographical or family related: "The Somber Lady," "Woman in Distress," "The Drunkards," "The Rower," and "Scandalized Masks." One painting from 1886, "Les Enfants à la Toilette" or "Children Dressing" (Pl. 4), should be discussed in the context of these early works. Not only does it relate to Ensor's series of indoor family scenes from the early 1880s, but it also can be seen as having profoundly personal implications for Ensor and his family.

In a canvas almost four and a half feet tall, Ensor created a bedroom interior; in fact, the green and red patterned rug, tall curtained windows and blue and rose-colored wallpaper suggest Mitche's bedroom from the 1882 "Woman in Distress." A warm golden light floods the interior, filtering through shades and reflecting the orange-pink glow of curtains on the nude bodies of two young girls:

Despite the large windows, no exact source of light is indicated; it is diffused everywhere. . . . A timeless, restful effect is achieved, yet because of the flowing, transparent curtains and the simplicity of the children's gestures, the

---

whole scene exists in an aura of some mysteriously intimate evil" (*James Ensor*, p. 48). Ensor may have meant the painting in part as an appeasement for his fear that his alcoholic father would die; when he exhibited it at Les XX the full title was "Masques scandalisés raillant la mort" ("Scandalized Masks Mocking Death").

[37] It was in 1883 that Josephin Péladan established one of the requisites for the Symbolist esthetic when he wrote in the May issue of *La Jeune Belgique* describing the battle of the sexes as "man, puppet of woman, woman, puppet of the devil" (Reprinted in Josephin Péladan, *Les Maîtres contemporains: Félicien Rops*, 1st ed. [Brussels: Callewert père, 1885], p. 58).

[38] One last observation, which may give further evidence of the painting's ominous mood and provide pointed historical, as well as personal, meaning to the work, was suggested to me by Penelope Mayo. She observed that the

masked man has been posed in a situation similar to that of the figure that symbolizes the Carnival King on early tarot cards. He is the first trump and originally was called the Juggler (in more modern packs he became the Magician or Magus and sometimes stood behind the table). The Carnival King reigned during the pre-Lenten season when drinking, entertainment, and merrymaking were his occupations. With his death at Lent a new king would reign. On the cards he is shown on the last day of carnival, seated at a small table having his final meal before he is sacrificed. Brueghel had dealt with such matters in "The Battle between Carnival and Lent." If such an association were meant by Ensor, then the masked carnival figure standing in the doorway brings death. For an illustration of this card and an explanation of its role in the carnival procession, see Gertrude Moakley, *The Tarot Cards, Painted by Bonifacio Bembo for the Visconti-Sforza Family* (New York: The New York Public Library, 1966), p. 58.

scene remains innocent. The figures' gentle nudity is surrounded by the light like a cocoon.[39]

Ensor's nudes fuse with the golden light of their environment in a manner reminiscent of J.M.W. Turner's interiors at Petworth Castle,[40] or of Whistler's effects in "The White Girl" (1864) and "The Artist in His Studio" (1867-1868).[41] And Ensor's figures establish a physical and spiritual relationship with the room that anticipates by almost twenty years Vuillard's and Bonnard's similar experiments with mood, color, and composition.

Francine-Claire Legrand has called "Children Dressing" the "most beautiful of the bourgeois interiors,"[42] but, although the overall mood of the painting is one of gentle revery and natural innocence, an element of mystery can be perceived. Legrand alludes to it in her discussion of Ensor's use of symbolism, although her reference is to the universal implications of the Symbolist movement: ". . . (it is) the most symbolist also, in the sense that the evocation of mystery is the very heart of Symbolism, and where the most simple mystery, a confrontation of bodies stripped of protective disguises, rejoins the Symbolism of creation."[43]

Physically revealed, yet protected within their surroundings, these young girls are also trapped in their hermetically sealed interior, with no view of the outside world and a mirror reflecting only the room's boundaries. Jean Stevo has described Ensor's ability to use light and the role that closed blinds play in protecting his interiors from the outside world:

Closed awnings filtered a suffused and magical light which gives to each thing its poetry and restores to it its aura of mystery. Sensitivity of filtered light. Silence and secrecy of lives, of little lives, of provincial life behind closed awnings. Closed faces. . . . It was always summer outside, the sun was shining in strong and vibrant rays. . . . All closed awnings. Cloth awnings: symbolic barrier between the street and the studio.[44]

A clue to this particular painting's sense of mystery lies with Ensor's depictions of the two nudes. Although both are clearly adolescents, their poses suggest two distinctly different perceptions of their own bodies. The girl on the left seems unaware of her nakedness: she sits in a relaxed and casual manner on a chair in front of a window, her left foot stretching to meet the floor, while her right leg crosses over her left knee, and her hands rest on her right leg and foot. Her body is seen almost frontally, and her thick waist and undeveloped chest suggest the body of a ten year old. The other girl stands in the middle of the composition in a seductive pose. The verticality of her body is accentuated by the tall, thin mirror that hangs above the bureau directly behind her. The back of her head is reflected in that mirror, as is the corner of a framed painting and a red object, perhaps a piece of furniture, directly across the room.[45] There is the suggestion of a slight swelling in the outline of her breast as this nude twists her body slightly, her left arm reaching across her chest to grasp the handle of a white pitcher. Her rounded stomach exaggerates the curves of her back and

---

[39] *Belgian Art 1880-1914* (New York: The Brooklyn Museum, 1980), p. 92.

[40] Observed by A. H. Cornette, "James Ensor," *La Revue de l'art ancien et moderne* 62 (1932): 22.

[41] Legrand, *Ensor, cet inconnu*, pp. 55-56.

[42] Translated and quoted in *Belgian Art, 1880-1914*, p. 92.

[43] Legrand, *Ensor, cet inconnu*, p. 55; translated in *Belgian Art 1880-1914*, p. 92.

[44] Stevo, *James Ensor*, p. 14.

[45] The object may be Mitche's bed, which appears red in the "Woman in Distress."

FIG. 22. Ensor. *Portrait of Ensor's Mother*, 1882.

buttocks as she stands in contrapposto with her weight falling on her right leg.[46] She appears somewhat older than her companion, both physically and in the way she holds her body. Gert Schiff has reacted to the painting's aura of sensuality by calling it Ensor's most erotic work.[47]

There is no record of who these young girls were or whether they posed for Ensor. They may have been painted from his imagination.[48] In fact, part of the painting's mystery lies with their identification and their activity. Ensor's title suggests that the girls are getting ready to dress, yet their poses are curiously static and there is no evidence of clothing. Furthermore, although a comb may be lying on the dresser, the pitcher has no washbowl.[49]

Because of the painting's suffused light and warm, hazy atmosphere, its details are difficult to reproduce. The painting has been in private collections in Belgium since it was first purchased, and its public showing in America at the Brooklyn Museum's "Belgian Art 1880-1914" in the spring of 1980 offered this viewer a surprising revelation: in the painting two distinct portraits appear. The dark hair of the seated figure is short or pulled back, and her head is surrounded with delicate brushstrokes suggesting flowers; she has a full round face, a short nose, and full lips. Her eyes appear closed or looking down, and her features bear an unmistakable resemblance to Ensor's younger sister Mitche.

[46] The figure can be seen to relate to the earlier northern tradition in which artists portrayed their female nudes with small apple-shaped breasts and swelling ogival stomachs (for example, Hugo van der Goes and Lucas Cranach). See Chapter VIII, "The Alternative Convention," in Kenneth Clark, *The Nude: A Study in Ideal Form* (Garden City: Doubleday, 1956). The southern classical tradition may have also been in Ensor's mind: the seated girl recalls the pose of the Hellenistic bronze "Boy removing a Thorn," and the standing girl could relate to a number of Greek prototypes.

[47] The description was given in a talk, "Ensor the Exorcist," Guggenheim Museum Lecture Series, February 22, 1977. In an article of the same name

he describes the painting as ". . . the most blissful and luminous in Ensor's youthful oeuvre. It is also the only one that, through the chaste, yet seductive bodies, conveys a certain eroticism," Gert Schiff, "Ensor the Exorcist" in *Art the Ape of Nature: Studies in Honor of H. W. Janson*, edited by Moshe Baraschand and Lucy Freeman Sandler (New York: Harry N. Abrams, 1981), p. 722.

[48] Schiff identifies them as the artist's sister and her companion (Ibid.).

[49] A northern tradition links pitchers or jugs with female imagery; thus a broken jug denotes loss of virginity, as in Brueghel's "Kermesse," or later in eighteenth-century France, in Greuze's "The Broken Pitcher." A pitcher

The standing nude has somewhat longer and lighter hair; it reaches her shoulders, partly obscuring one eye as it falls forward. Her face is considerably longer, with heavy-lidded eyes, a long nose, and full sensuous lips. The face of this nude has a pouting sensuality somewhat anachronistic with her youthful body. It is not the face of an adolescent, but that of a mature woman. In fact, it appears remarkably similar to the face of Ensor's mother as she might have appeared when she was younger. Portraits from 1882 and 1887, an oil painting and a drawing, show her features clearly (Figs. 22 and 23).[50]

Ensor's mother had a strong aversion to depictions of the nude. A friend recalled that she made Ensor aware of her disapproval, reminding him, "If you need proper feminine models—take your sister, your aunt, or me."[51] This painting is the only known depiction of full-length nudes Ensor ever made,[52] and it is possible to reconstruct a situation in which the pressures from his mother's prudery prevented him from using nude models. He may have felt compelled to use the faces of the two woman closest to him in order to give the painting a sense of reality, or he may have wished to include them as a perverse joke. There is also the possibility of a deeper psychological meaning. "Children Dressing" is an intimate scene of provocative nudity, replete with innocence and invitation. With its location in Ensor's own home, its

FIG. 23. Ensor. *Portrait of the Artist's Mother*, 1887.

---

or jug held by a nude female recalls Ingres's "La Source" and suggests the concept of the female as the source of fecundity.

[50] A secondary image appears in the drawing at Mrs. Ensor's right: it is a male figure who may be holding a chalice or long-stemmed cup in his clasped hands. Since 1887 was the year Ensor's father died, there may be an association between this spectral figure and Ensor's deceased father. In any event, his mother's presence is formidable, and the ghostly figure, who bows his head, takes an obsequious position behind her.

[51] Quoted in Stevo, "Ensor l'Ostendais": 13.

[52] An academic drawing found in Ostend's Musée des Beaux-Arts shows

FIG. 24. Ensor. *A Fisherman*, 1880.

The complex and ambivalent feelings Ensor felt for his family—his alcoholic father, his unhappy sister, and his demanding mother—applied in part to his attitude toward the people of Ostend. From his early paintings, such as "The Drunkards" and "The Rower," and from his sensitive drawings of laborers (Fig. 24), it is evident he thought the working class admirable and that he felt sympathy and concern for their condition. His attitude toward the middle class was different; misunderstood, ridiculed, and dismissed as an eccentric by the bourgeoisie, Ensor was to become proficient at mocking their philistinism through his art.

Pale, tall, and thin, Ensor dressed to exaggerate his difference from the short, stocky Flemish people by always appearing in black wearing a tall top hat. He was a strange figure walking alone through the narrow streets of Ostend and on the beach, and his dress and demeanor earned him the nickname "Pierrot la mort,"[53] a characterization that reflected the development of the macabre in his art.

For the most part, the paintings and drawings discussed thus far owe their inspiration to Ostend and Ensor's life there. Yet there were also influences on Ensor from the outside, from his involvement in the city of Brussels and its cultural life. Friendships made there gave him the support and encouragement withheld in Ostend; he was introduced in Brussels to a cosmopolitan world of radical thought and avant-garde creation, and he carried this intellectual stimulation back to his studio in Ostend. The results were an art of increasing sophistication, sometimes caustic in its sarcasm, often witty, and occasionally brilliantly beautiful.

rarefied atmosphere of esoteric mystery, and his mother and sister as models for the faces of the two nudes, it may have been Ensor's personal and erotically charged adaptation of old voyeuristic stories such as "Diana at the Bath" or "Susannah and the Elders."

---

a seated woman wearing a skirt, but nude from the waist up. Otherwise, with the exception of two drawings, Ensor's nude females were caricatures, amusing Venus figures who stood on half-shells or cavorted around a classical herm. The exceptions are discussed in Chapter III.

[53] Legrand, *Ensor, cet inconnu*, p. 13. The writer Camille Lemonnier described Ensor's walk: "the pace of a slow morose Pierrot walking through life with a haunted look" (ibid.).

II

"PECULIAR INSECTS": BRUSSELS; ANOTHER
WORLD REVEALED

Although the cultural milieu of Brussels was to influence Ensor's vision and to expand the artistic boundaries of his art, he was careful to withhold himself from others in order to preserve the authenticity of his personal style. In a telling photograph from 1888 he appears standing aloof within a crowd (Fig. 25); taller than most of the others and the only man dressed totally in black, he also sported the only top hat and beard. Posed in the manner of Napoleon with his hand in his jacket front, Ensor retains the essence of his solitary condition with calculated aplomb.

From the early 1880s he sensed his own greatness and he saved for posterity even the smallest thumbnail sketch, no matter how seemingly insignificant.[1] Often these drawings are on torn scraps of letters, sometimes signed and dated in

[1] In later years he was to feel the same about his writing, and he made every effort to collect all the letters he had ever sent. (See the introduction to James Ensor, *Lettres à André de Ridder* [Antwerp: Librairie des Arts, 1960].)

FIG. 25. *Photograph of Ensor in a Crowd*, 1888.

FIG. 26. Ensor. *Two Waders*, n.d.

retrospect,[2] and in these sketches Ensor is usually the spectator, removed from any action. For example, he is a dark profile standing at the lower right of a page where he watches two young women as they stand at the edge of the ocean wading in the water (Fig. 26). They are shown holding up their skirts and revealing their legs in a pose that might have seemed quite titillating in the nineteenth century. Written under them is the inscription, "signé par moi James Ensor à Ostende."

One family in Brussels was able to reach through the self-protective barrier that Ensor had constructed. Ernest Rousseau was a professor of physics, his wife Mariette, a respected botanist, and their son, Ernest, Jr., although twelve years younger than Ensor, was to become one of the artist's closest friends.[3] Introduced to the Rousseaus in 1879 by Théo Hannon, Mariette's brother-in-law and Ensor's fellow art student at the Brussels Academy, Ensor was to find with them the congenial atmosphere and support, as well as the intellectual stimulation, that he lacked in Ostend.

Blanche Rousseau, a niece of the family, described her first meeting with Ensor and remembered his initial resistance:

I can still see that tall figure, pale in his black clothes, standing alone in a dark corner, and hesitantly extending an elegant hand—and above all, his quick, inquiring glance from those extraordinary eyes, at once shy, provocative, gentle, sarcastic, and shifty, rapidly raised and lowered, while his huge rigid body made an awkward bow. He had the face of a mocking Christ or a nostalgic Satan. . . .[4]

As a meeting place for artists, writers, scientists, and a wide assortment of intellectuals who gravitated there for stimulating discussions, the Rousseau home offered a diversity of interests and unlimited possibilities for Ensor's

---

[2] Libby Tannenbaum mentions the problem that arises with some of Ensor's dates: some drawings and paintings were dated by Ensor years after they were produced (*James Ensor*, p. 104). Further, sketchbooks similar to Kandinsky's housebook were made, perhaps even after the 1920s, and dates were attributed to paintings in retrospect. Tannenbaum observed: ". . . his work is a rich and tangled skein of concurrent styles, and it is often exactly the dating of the extraordinary prefigurations one is most inclined to suspect

that is substantiated by early exhibition catalogues" (*James Ensor*, p. 104).

[3] Ernest Rousseau, Jr. (1872-1920) was to follow in the footsteps of his mother, Mariette, who published *Florule mycologique des environs de Bruxelles* with Elisa Bommer in 1884 (Gand: C. Annoot-Braeckman). Between 1906 and 1920 he edited fifteen volumes of *Annales de biologie lacustre* (Brussels: M. Forton).

[4] Haesaerts, *James Ensor*, p. 81.

development: "The Rousseaus were on the whole inclined to anarchism and atheism, but the persons who frequented their home held the most divergent opinions."[5] There Ensor encountered the brothers Reclus, who have been described as "enthusiastic geographers as well as notorious anarchists";[6] he was also introduced to Félicien Rops, whose art was to become significant for his own production and to Eugène Demolder, whose writing was to affect him.

The Rousseau home was at 20 rue Vautier, located near the museum of natural history, as well as near a museum dedicated to the nineteenth-century Romantic painter Antoine Wiertz: "The strangeness of these museums, one of which contained all sorts of oddities of nature—gigantic prehistoric monsters and miniscule monsters of the insect world—and the other, oddities collected by the eccentric Wiertz, amused and intrigued Ensor."[7] Legrand has pointed to the influence of natural scientists, mathematicians, and especially to Mariette Rousseau's microscope on Ensor's art, ". . . the infinitely small, and the invisible, the subconscious creating new fields of experience."[8] Stored within Ensor's fertile imagination, these influences would help to shape the fantastic creatures that were eventually to dominate a large part of his artistic production.

The patriarch of the family, Ernest Rousseau, was an admired and respected academic who was well liked by all who knew him.[9] In 1887 Ensor produced a tribute to his host, a

---

[5] Ibid., p. 80.   [6] Ibid., p. 81.   [7] Ibid., p. 80.

[8] Legrand, *Ensor, cet inconnu*, p. 19; also quoted in translation in Farmer, *Ensor*, p. 18. Farmer added that "images found in his later drawings and paintings are probably directly attributable to this experience" and that Ensor "seems never to have forgotten or failed to find visual stimulation in anything . . ." (*Ensor*, p. 18). Legrand also mentioned that Mariette and her brother-in-law were amateur antiquarians, collectors of Chinese bibelots and porcelain (*Ensor, cet inconnu*, p. 19).

[9] Haesaerts, *James Ensor*, p. 80. Rousseau was chancellor of the Université

FIG. 27. Ensor. *Ernest Rousseau*, 1887.

simple, yet monumental etching in which Rousseau's massive body is shown in three-quarter length (Fig. 27). Rousseau appears as a tower of strength, a black-coated dense figure surrounded by open space. Yet Ensor seems to have had subtle problems with the realization of the image: a close examination of the print reveals that the right hand is incomplete and both arms are suggested rather than implicitly defined. Although the face is carefully detailed, it is turned in profile and the eye is lost in the dark shadow of a bushy eyebrow. The outline of Rousseau's coat disintegrates from sharp edges into fuzzy areas of cross-hatching, and a thick chaotic scribble of strokes attaches Rousseau's body to the paper in the lower left corner.[10]

The year in which Ensor made this portrait may have had a significant bearing upon the tentative aspects of its realization for it was the year in which Ensor's father died. Ensor's drawing of his father on his deathbed shows distinctive thick rough strokes connecting his face to the corner of the paper (Fig. 17), and these repetitive scribbles are similar to those in the corner of the Rousseau etching. The physical resemblance Ensor showed in his depictions of the two men is striking. Ensor's feelings for Rousseau may have related to his feelings for his father, and the artist's hesitation with the peripheries of Rousseau's formidable presence in the print adds credence to that possibility. As we have seen, when Ensor finally died in 1949 he had become a veritable *doppelgänger* for his father (Fig. 18).

The Rousseau etching may, whether consciously or not, have been meant as a tribute to a surrogate father figure, a strong, supportive, and caring man whose love could help console Ensor for the loss he felt with the death of his real father.[11] In any event, the print had a special meaning for Ensor: he kept the first one pulled from the plate, and in a letter written in the 1890s he recalled that it was one of only five prints that remained in his collection.[12]

The deep regard Ensor also felt for Mariette is evident in a lightly sketched 1889 drawing where she is shown in profile as an attractive, smiling woman reading a book. A microscope stands on a table at the right, while over her head, as a watchful protector, the faint outline of a painting reminiscent of a Fra Filippo Lippi "Madonna and Child" appears.[13] Apparently Mariette gave Ensor the warmth and encouragement he failed to receive from the women in his own family. A photograph reproduced in Haesaerts' biography shows her standing next to the young Ensor, leaning toward him as he sits on a chair. According to Haesaerts, she regarded him as her protégé: she bought his works and she cheered him when he was depressed.[14] Ensor often stayed at the Rousseau home for weeks at a time, and he had a room there in which to work when he was in Brussels.[15]

Legrand has suggested that Mariette, nineteen years younger than her husband, might have meant a bit more to Ensor than a supportive maternal figure.[16] She quotes a reminiscence from Blanche Rousseau, who recalled a passage from

---

libre between 1884 and 1886; I have been unable to discover why he held the post for only two years.

[10] The plate went through four states, described by Auguste Taevernier in *James Ensor, Catalogue illustré de ses gravures, leur description critique et l'inventaire des plaques* (Ghent: N. V. Erasmus, 1973), p. 47.

[11] Rousseau had shown his support by buying Ensor's paintings when no one else would have them. In the late 1880s he rescued Ensor's "Bourgeois Salon" after it had hung in the Ostend casino with a for sale sign for six

or seven years (See Tannenbaum, *James Ensor*, p. 95).

[12] *Ensor: ein Maler*, p. 43.

[13] Reproduced in Legrand, *Ensor, cet inconnu*, p. 97.

[14] Haesaerts, *James Ensor*, p. 344.

[15] Ibid., p. 81.

[16] "No doubt he was vaguely smitten with Mariette Rousseau" (Legrand, *Ensor, cet inconnu*, p. 19).

PLATE 1. Ensor. *Cabin on the Beach*, 1877.

PLATE 2. Ensor. *Woman Eating Oysters*, 1882.

FIG. 28. Ensor. *Peculiar Insects*, 1888.

a poem, "Amorous Caprices," which was read aloud one evening when Ensor was present: "A beetle clung to a hedge, sad and thoughtful; he had fallen in love with a fly! O! fly of my heart! Be the bride of my choice. Marry me, don't reject my love: I have a stomach of solid gold. . . ."[17]

This melodramatic description, with its amusing reference to the possibilities of unrequited love in the insect world, and its link with Mariette's profession, was appropriate for Ensor's own situation. It became the subject of a wry etching in which Ensor revealed his close affinity with the beetle in the poem. "Peculiar Insects" (1888) shows Ensor as a beetle while Mariette is depicted with the long graceful wings and tail of a dragonfly (Fig. 28). She appears in profile and gazes intently at Ensor, whose eyes look down-

[17] Ibid.

33

FIG. 29. Ensor. *The Garden of Love,* 1888.

34

ward.[18] Ensor took the etching through five states, and in an earlier version the print had followed the literary description more closely, with Mariette shown as a fly with shorter wings and without the long tail. In the second state a small, grotesque figure was included at the window of the house on the right and the smaller beetle was added at Ensor's left.[19] It has been suggested to me that this little beetle, a miniature of Ensor, but without a distinctly human face, reveals Ensor's wish for a child. And perhaps the strange figure at the window suggests that Ensor felt someone within the Rousseau residence might have become aware of his feelings about Mariette.[20]

It seems to be Mariette again who appears in Ensor's painting of the same year, "The Garden of Love" (Fig. 29). There, one woman has been depicted more clearly than the rest. She wears a large, round hat with a thick, dark outline around its brim and it forms a halo around her head. Her identification as Mariette becomes even more plausible when the figure next to her is considered: a tall, mustached, large-stomached man who resembles Ernest Rousseau.[21]

In 1890 Ensor included Mariette in an amusing painting that satirized a recurring confrontation at the Rousseau home

FIG. 30. Ensor. *Ensor and General Leman Discussing Painting*, 1890.

(Fig. 30). In a small, wooden panel Mariette stands between Ensor and General Leman, a military professional who had

---

[18] In 1880 Baudelaire's preface to the Belgian writer Léon Cladel's *Les Martyrs Ridicules* included a reference to two lovers as "insects amoureux" (*Les Martyrs Ridicules: Roman Parisien* [Brussels: Henry Kistemaeckers], p. 7). Later in the text, ". . . Musette, what a fine fly . . ." (Ibid., p. 198). Anthropomorphic insects had a long tradition in the nineteenth century. P. J. Béranger's songs, such as the 1810 "La Mouche" were popular, and the Flemish journal *L'Uylenspiegel*, produced by Félicien Rops, included the poem, "Les Galanteries d'une mouche," in an 1856 edition (no. 38 [October 19, 1856]: 3). For a discussion of insect and animal literature that includes examples by Balzac, Georges Sand, and Charles Nodier, see Pierre Jules Hetzel, *Scènes de la vie privée et publique des animaux*, 2 vols. (Paris: J. Hetzel et Pauline, 1842). The cover page includes an illustration by Grandville that shows a beetle with a top hat and rapier. Included in the text is

Paul de Musset's "Les Souffrances d'un scarabée" (pp. 113-114).

[19] See Taevernier, *James Ensor*, pl. 46, pp. 119-121.

[20] The English translation for the print's title has always described it as "Peculiar Insects." I believe a more appropriate translation of Ensor's meaning for "*singulier*" would be "Rare Insects," a sense that originates in Old French and Latin and emphasizes the remarkable or extraordinary as rare or precious rather than strange or odd. See *The Compact Edition of the Oxford English Dictionary* (New York: Oxford University Press, 1971), p. 2834.

[21] "The Garden of Love" was also the title of an 1888 etching. Three couples are shown in an outdoor setting, and, although they are difficult to see distinctly, all three men resemble Ensor (See Taevernier, *James Ensor*, pl. 63).

frequent and violent quarrels with Ensor about art.[22] It is a simple caricature of reality, yet highly symbolic and cleverly charged with sexual innuendo. Leman, dressed in military uniform, wears a sign with Masonic emblem on his bald head, which is encircled by a puny wreath of leaves. He lights a toy cannon as he points it directly at Ensor, who retaliates with a giant bristly paintbrush and an index finger which stops up the cannon's mouth. Ensor is dressed in red, with long spiky feathers attached to the top of his head. His palette carries the names "Ensor Leman." It also holds a large red area of paint that, while it uses the palette's outline for the overall suggestion of its shape, makes its own distinctive statement by closely resembling a giant phallus and testicles pointed directly at Leman.

Dressed in neutral gray, Mariette gazes with passive resignation away from the scene at hand. Ensor's giant brush intrudes upon Leman's space and the artist's stoppage of the cannon may have caused it to backfire; Ensor's phallic palette not only gestures toward Leman, but it also extends its influence over the lower body of Mariette. Adamant and unyielding in his opinions, Ensor depicts through his painting his own virile response to masculine military prowess.[23]

Although Ensor was welcomed into the Rousseau family's life and was regarded with warm affection, someone within that circle may have felt resentment over his presence. Blanche Rousseau discussed a photograph from the family's collection that had been altered by blackening the image of Ensor: "I have a photograph of Ensor in front of me. It's a family group. Someone blackened his image, but I succeeded in removing the stain. . . ."[24] She did not discuss who tried to obliterate Ensor from the group, or why, instead she paid tribute to Ensor's persistence through a romantic description of the artist in a state of transformation, moving out from the darkness to which he had been relegated: ". . . The mocking figure appeared to me, all white, strange among the others, different, as if from another world, as if to say: 'Yes, it's me, you haven't been able to hide me; I was there, here I am.' "[25]

Given Ensor's deep regard for Mariette, an undated pen and ink drawing in Antwerp's Musée des Beaux-Arts is a disturbing image (Fig. 31). It is a rough sketch in which Ensor stands at the left, a smiling, emaciated figure. In his hands he holds an oversized clyster, and he extends it toward the figure opposite him, a large skeleton with clawed hands and feet who, like Ensor, also wears a top hat. Between them a crucifix rises from the top of an elongated shape that could be meant to suggest a large rock or a draped object of some sort. At the base of this phallic protuberance, connected to the heavily shaded area on the right, Ensor printed the words "Madame Rousseau!"[26]

Thick smears of black ink, perhaps applied with a brush,

[22] Haesaerts, *James Ensor*, p. 111. Leman was to become a Belgian hero for his defense of the Liège fortress in 1914. See Maurice des Ombiaux, *Le Général Leman* (Paris: Blond & Gay), 1916.

[23] Combined with Leman's profession, the Masonic emblem, linking Leman with Masonic principles such as the abstract belief in a "Great Architect of the Universe," can be seen as spoofing organizations that claim the improvement of society as their goal. It is notable, though, that it was the Masons who founded the University of Brussels in 1834 to counteract the influence of the Catholic University at Louvain. Mariette, whose head tilts slightly toward Leman, is connected through her profession and her husband to the University of Brussels and approved academic life. Two drawings of the scene exist, one in pencil, one with colored crayon, and there is also a copy of the painting. Although the copy is dated 1890, its marked inferior quality suggests a date after 1900. The pencil drawing does not contain Mariette's image; on the back Ensor wrote "Le Général Leman et J. Ensor discutant peinture en 1890." See Gisèle Ollinger-Zinque, *Ensor by Himself*, translated by Alistair Kennedy (Brussels: Laconti, 1977), figs. 48-51.

[24] "Ensor Intime," *La Plume* (1899): 28.

[25] Ibid.

[26] The photograph from A.C.L., Brussels, has cropped the exclamation point; it appears in the drawing in Antwerp's Musée des Beaux-Arts.

obfuscate the face of the skeleton and boldly define its body, parts of the crucifix, and its base. In comparison, Ensor's figure is formed from a few light, linear strokes of a pen. Despite his large weapon, he appears no match for the strong form of the skeleton, who has wings or wears a cloak, and whose clawed hand almost touches the crucifix as he stands his ground with virile aggressiveness.

A crucifixion, combined with the image of a skeleton, Ensor's frail form, and a clyster—all these images are emphatically linked with Madame Rousseau's name, which ends in an exclamation point. It is a fascinating drawing, but one can only speculate as to its exact meaning. It may have been a visual exorcism, meant to free Ensor from a romantic wish that, given the situation, could never have led to any satisfying resolution, and that in fact held the possibility of embarrassing discovery. Or perhaps the drawing referred to Ensor's fear that he might lose Mariette to death. An 1829 lithograph by the French painter and illustrator Louis Boulenger contains a winged skeleton and a crucifixion, and carries a similar implication (Fig. 32).[27] Part of a series illustrating Victor Hugo's *Les Fantômes*, the Boulenger print shows a young woman being bodily dragged away by a skeleton while another woman tries to save her. At the far right, emerging from the darkness and in the same proportion to the figures as is the crucifix in Ensor's drawing, Christ's body appears on the cross. Ensor, holding the giant clyster as weapon, may be ready to battle Death to save Mariette, thus paralleling the rescue attempt in the Boulenger print.

There seems little doubt, however, that Ensor's depiction of himself as a smiling, puny figure with a useless weapon was meant to reveal the powerlessness of his own situation. The clyster recalls a prototype in Gustave Doré's illustra-

[27] See Aristide Marie, *Le Peintre Poète Louis Boulenger* (Paris: H. Floury, 1925), p. 30.

FIG. 31. Ensor. *Death and a Doctor By a Gravestone*, n.d.

32. Louis Boulenger. *Dead at Age Fifteen, Beautiful, Happy, and Adored*, 1829.

tions for Book IV of Rabelais's *Gargantua and Pantagruel*, in which the author has a sorcerer cure the giant Bringuenarilles with a giant-sized instrument. Book IV deals with satires on various professions and institutions, as well as on human traits, and Doré's illustrations for the text were published in numerous editions from 1854 on.[28] Ensor may have added the enema in part as a sardonic reference to the medical profession's medieval beliefs in the wide-ranging powers of that treatment.

From the late medieval development of the skeleton figure, often wielding a giant scythe and identified as "The Triumph of Death," or winged and flying through the air, through numerous examples of the skeleton as participant in the Dance of Death, and as a fiddler and horn player,[29] skeletons have appeared often in art to remind us of our mortality. In the nineteenth century the use of skeleton imagery was still prevalent, and any number of examples could have influenced Ensor's development: mid-century prints by Alfred Rethel and Rudolphe Bresdin come to mind, and even closer to Ensor through nationality and acquaintance was Félicien Rops's use of the motif. Ensor borrowed widely and adapted the appropriate sensibility to fit each specific, intended vision. For example, in an 1888 drawing Ensor has a skull playing a horn;[30] Hans Kurth was to employ the same theme in 1900, but both depictions relate back to examples such as Daumier's 1871 vision of a skeleton with flowered hat, seated on a rock and playing pipes (Fig. 33).

FIG. 33. Honoré Daumier. *Peace, an Idyl*, 1871

Ensor's 1896 engraving "Death Pursuing the People" (Fig. 34), an apocalyptic image in which Death flies above the narrow streets of a Belgian city crowded with fleeing figures, recalls Karl Gottfried Merkel's 1850 winged skeleton "The Pest-Death" (Fig. 35).[31]

---

[28] For Doré's illustrations see *Doré's Illustrations for Rabelais; A Selection of 252 Illustrations by Gustave Doré* (New York: Dover, 1978). A quotation from Rabelais's *Gargantua* (Book I, Chapter 57) appeared on the heading of *Uylenspiegel's* title page.

[29] For a lengthy discussion of the skeleton within the context of the dance of death, see Veronique Filozof, *Der Totentanz: La Danse macabre* (Basel: Pharos-Verlag, 1976).

[30] Reproduced in Farmer, *Ensor*, fig. 83. This work, in which Ensor included the stem of a cello as well, has been incorrectly labeled "Skeleton Playing a Flute."

[31] A similar flying figure holds up a large banner in Charles Meryon's 1854 print, "The Old Gate of the Palace of Justice, Paris," Loys Delteil, *Catalogue Raisonné of the Etchings of Charles Meryon* (New York: W. P. Truesdell, 1924), fig. 19.

FIG. 34. Ensor. *Death Pursuing the People*, 1896.

FIG. 35. Karl Gottfried Merkel.
The Pest-Death

Ensor's birthplace made the skeleton a particularly viable motif. Ostend is famous in history as the site of a devastating three-year siege inflicted by the Spanish at the beginning of the seventeenth century. Belgian casualties numbered over 130,000, and remains were still being uncovered well into the twentieth century.[32] Human skeletons found on the beaches and in the town itself became as familiar as the driftwood that lay partly buried in sand. Photographs from 1892 show Ensor and his young friend Ernest Rousseau, Jr. staging a lighthearted mock fight on these very dunes, using human arm and hand bones as weapons.[33]

[32] For a complete history of Ostend consult Robert Lanoye, *L'Épopée ostendaise* (2d ed.; Ostend: Erel, 1971). In the Spanish war of succession Ostend was occupied by the allies under Marlborough. In 1745 Louis XV took the fortress there after a siege of eighteen days, and in 1794 it again fell to the French, who held it until 1814. The fortifications along the beach were demolished in 1865, five years after Ensor's birth.

[33] Reproduced in Haesaerts, *James Ensor*, pls. 1 and 2, p. 348.

FIG. 36. Ensor. *The Sad and Broken: Satan and his Fantastic Legions Tormenting the Crucified Christ*, 1886

Marcel De Maeyer pointed to the skeleton's first appearance in Ensor's work in the 1886 drawing "The Sad and Broken: Satan and His Fantastic Legions Tormenting the Crucified Christ" (Fig. 36). While one skeleton flies through the air, others, robed, cluster around the cross, and still another has climbed the cross and physically attacks Christ's body.[34] De Maeyer observed that it was not until 1888, in etchings such as "My Portrait in 1960," that Ensor fully

[34] Marcel De Maeyer, "De genese van masker—, travestie en skelet-motieven in het oeuvre van James Ensor," *Bulletin des Musées Royaux des Beaux-Arts de Belgique* 10 (1963): 77. The drawing is fourth in a series of six entitled "Auréoles." They are treated in depth by Auguste Taevernier in *Le Drame Ensorien: Les Auréoles du Christ ou les sensibilités de la lumière* (Ghent: N. V. Erasmus, 1976). A drawing from 1886 entitled "The

FIG. 37. Ensor. *Ensor and Death*, December 25, 1887.

defined the artistic parameters that would govern his particularized use of the skeleton,[35] but on December 25, 1887 Ensor drew a winged skeleton along with his self-portrait on a letter to Octave Maus. The drawing reveals Ensor's already very personal association with that symbol (Fig. 37).[36]

At the left of the page Ensor is shown being led from his bed, which stands complete with a tiny, smiling head peering from one bedpost and a chamber pot underneath. Ensor's face and body are shown in silhouette, but the thin-pointed beard and wispy hair are similar to those in Ensor's self-portrait in the "Madame Rousseau!" drawing. Here also he shows himself as a wry creature. Small strands of hair curve upward from his head, and, together with a long ink line that moves from the back of his head down past his shoulders, they suggest a delicate headdress. The translucent sleeves of his nightshirt billow outward to form a series of rounded shapes. Ensor appears frail and tentative, perhaps even somewhat feminine, especially in contrast to the larger figure of the skeleton, which wears a top hat and grins at Ensor as it gestures toward a scene in the distance. The skeleton appears much like a man of the world showing off his sophistication to a shy, reluctant companion. The scene that the skeleton reveals is small and somewhat difficult to decipher: in the distance below a large cathedral with a tall spire is identifiable; small figures seem to raise their arms toward heaven; and boats filled with other gesticulating figures are visible to the left of the church. In the sky, at the upper right of the

---

Artist Decomposed" shows Ensor as a skeleton, but Ensor had drawn over the original self-portrait at a later date (Farmer, *Ensor*, p. 25 and fig. 71). It was during 1887-1888 that Ensor began to add skeletons and masks to earlier works. See De Maeyer above, or the French version, "Derrière le masque": 17ff.

[35] De Maeyer, "De genese van masker": 77.

[36] See Maus, *Trente Années*, p. 32, and Legrand, "Lettres": 30, and pl. III.

page, a figure with raised arms, perhaps Christ, stands in the clouds. On one level the scene recalls Christ being shown the temptations of the material world by the devil, a subject Ensor developed in the next year in an etching entitled "The Temptation of Christ."

The date of the letter, Christmas day, would suggest the appropriateness of a reference to Christ. But the skeleton also represents Death, and Ensor has been taken from his bed by that creature.[37] The text of the letter is only one sentence, "Why didn't you write me about what happened at the last meeting?" and refers to the activities of Les XX, of which Ensor was a dedicated member, suggesting that he was unable to attend. During the 1880s he had suffered lengthy bouts of illness; for example, letters from 1885 and 1888 complained of his confinement and inactivity and this may have been the reason he was unable to travel to Brussels in 1887.[38]

In the drawing, then, Ensor has been led from his sickbed on Christmas day by Death, who gestures with glee toward the church and civilization below. The view is probably toward Ostend, since the cathedral there is directly across from the boat basin. An abyss is suggested by pen lines that form a sharp cliff above and below the letter's date. Whether intentionally or not, the little stick figures, with their raised arms, recall the symbolic posture of mourning figures used on black-figured Greek geometric amphora showing attendants at a funeral. Between the figure of Christ in the clouds and the skeleton, a long, dark mark appears. It may simply be an accidental brushmark, but perhaps it can also be seen as necessary to the drawing—a "divine missile" aimed at Death and sent by Christ as a reprieve for the ailing artist. In any event, the sketch is sensitive and poignant and successfully elicits sympathy for Ensor's difficult condition.

Mortality had been on Ensor's mind: his mortality and the mortality of a work of art. In an 1886 letter he had lamented his fragility and he had seen art as suffering from a similar fate. He offered as an explanation for his newfound interest in etching this reasoning:

I'm twenty-six years old. . . . I am not happy. Ideas of survival haunt me. Perishable pictorial material upsets me; I dread the fragility of painting. Poor painting exposed to the crimes of the restorer, to insufficiency, to the slander of reproductions. Yes, I want to speak for a long time yet to the men of tomorrow. I want to survive and I think of solid copper plates, of unalterable inks, of easy reproductions, of faithful printing, and I am adopting etching as a means of expression.[39]

[37] For a discussion of the wide use of the theme of death and the artist, and a bibliography, see Sharon Latchaw Hirsh, "Arnold Böcklin: Death Talks to the Painter," *Arts Magazine* 55 (February 1981): 84-89. Also consult Hans H. Hofstatter, *Symbolismus und die Kunst der Jahrhundertwende* (4th ed., Cologne: Du Mont 1978).

[38] Legrand identifies the drawing as, "an allusion to the illness Ensor spoke about in letter 11" ("Lettres": 30). The Ensor museum at Ostend contains a letter from June of 1885 in which Ensor answers a dinner invitation with the warning that although his health is finally returning he can't eat or drink and doesn't know what causes his illness. A letter from the beginning of 1888 includes, "I've been in bed for four weeks, gravely ill and don't know how it will end" (Legrand, "Lettres": 31); and a letter from February of that year mentions a two-month illness ("Lettres": 33).

It is worth noting that a pale inscription in the upper left of the drawing on the letter reads "Ensor 88," a date he must have inscribed in retrospect. It is curious that in dating the drawing Ensor neglected to look at the letter's date, but, in reacting to the image he had drawn, he may have been recalling his illnesses in 1888. This combination of illness with a reference to a figure of Death adds credence to that suggestion for the "Madame Rousseau!" drawing.

[39] Letter to Albert Croquez (1934), quoted in Hubert Juin, ed., *Histoires étranges et récits insolites* (Paris, Livre Club du Librairie, 1965), p. 14. His graphic work was produced between 1886 and 1904 and includes 133 etchings and dry points as well as some lithographs. 1888 was a particularly

FIG. 38. Ensor. *My Portrait in 1960*, 1888.

Ensor's sense of humor was one of his most endearing traits, particularly when he turned inward and mocked the precariousness of his own situation. In 1888 he showed himself as a skeleton, a fey creature wearing tiny slippers, in an etching entitled "My Portrait in 1960" (Fig. 38). One hundred years old and disintegrating, he reclines on a bed, or perhaps on the floor; next to him a favorite personal symbol appears, a spider, while at his feet three tiny snails wait. His skull still sprouts curly strands of hair, as in the other self-portraits

just discussed, but now they recall with irony that death will destroy the full curly locks of which he was once so proud.[40] For contemporary viewers, the etching's title gives the work a heightened sense of the present. It is as if Ensor were speaking personally to us from across the years and affirming with poignant humor the common link we all share, the effects of time that will eventually unite us.

In 1889 Ensor again represented himself as a skeleton (Fig. 39), but this time the mood and spirit are completely alien

fruitful year with Ensor etching fifty-five plates. This output is made all the more remarkable when his monumental "Entry of Christ into Brussels" (1888) is considered.

[40] Strands of hair sprout from the skulls of three skeletons in the final

plate from the late fifteenth-century "Nuremberg Chronicle," in which the three skeletons dance playfully while another plays an oboe. Reproduced in Edward Lucie-Smith, ed., *The Waking Dream: Fantasy & the Surreal in Graphic Art 1450-1900* (New York: Alfred A. Knopf, 1975), fig. 19.

FIG. 39. Ensor. *My Portrait Skeletonized*, 1889.

FIG. 40. Photograph of Ensor, 20 rue Vautier, Brussels, 1889.

to the 1888 etching. A photograph of Ensor standing in front of the Rousseau home, leaning with one arm on a ledge, while his other hand is placed in his jacket pocket, was used as inspiration (Fig. 40). The first state of the plate shows Ensor's normal features; in the second and third states his eyes and hair remain, but the beard and flesh have been removed from his face. There is none of the light humor from ''My Portrait in 1960''; instead the corporeality of Ensor's hands and his suited body give the etching a grotesque physicality that, combined with the skull's cold eyes and grimacing jawbone, produces a distinctly macabre effect.[41] There is an additional observation to be made, and it intensifies the unsettling atmosphere that pervades both the photograph and the print. In the photograph a secondary image emerges from the darkened glass in the interior of the home: it appears to be Mariette, whose face looms next to Ensor's. In the print her countenance has disappeared and a skull has been substituted, superimposed upon the background crosshatching at the lower left edge of the windowsill.

Later in the 1890s, Ensor would use a photograph of him-

[41] Perhaps late medieval tomb sculpture, which emphasized the body's fragility by depicting partly decomposed corpses, may have been inspiration for Ensor's etching (Reinhold Heller kindly offered this suggestion). For discussion of a similar motif that has appeared as church sculpture, see Chapter III, p. 81 and n. 61.

FIG. 41. Ensor. *Skeleton Painter in His Studio,* c. 1896.

46

self in his studio (Fig. 113) and transform himself into a skeleton again for "Skeleton Painter in his Studio" (Fig. 41).[42] Ensor would also appear as a skeleton in a drawing entitled "The Artist Decomposed,"[43] but in these two works there is a somewhat lighter touch with Ensor's skeleton. Large, round eye sockets contain the luminous whites of eyes in the painting, and in both works Ensor's suited body is delineated with cursory outlines suggesting caricature.

Ensor's juxtaposition of a skull with a living body in the 1889 etching has a prototype in an engraving from the sixteenth century that reproduced Titian's drawing "Death in Armor" (Fig. 42).[44] There a robust figure stands in a protective coat of armor, one gloved hand holding aloft a helmet with large elegant feathers. The skeleton's throat and neck are fully covered by a wide band of lace that makes the skull exist as an integral living part of the virile body. The old Italian inscription, "Etiam Ferocissimos Domari/Per Feroce Che Sia Convien Esser Domato," refers to the "taming" of "ferociousness." There is no evidence that Ensor saw this print, but it becomes a perfect model for the particularized mood of disturbing palpability that Ensor conveyed. Further, its reference to a self-portrait links Ensor's identification with a skeleton to a tradition developed by one of the most illustrious artists of the past.

There were specific Belgian adaptations of the skeleton that would have stimulated Ensor's interest in the motif. Antoine Wiertz used it to recall the passage of time and the inevitable loss of youth and beauty in his 1847 painting "La Belle Rosine."[45] The Belgian Charles Simonon had shown a skeleton standing before an open doorway and gesturing to

Fig. 42. Titian. *Death in Armor*, n.d.

a startled male figure in an 1811 drawing that would become the subject of a poem in 1832, "LI SPERE."[46] Similar in style to Simonon was Redon's 1882 drawing of "Interior with Skeletons" (Fig. 20) and an 1885 charcoal of a skeleton that stood with one hand on hip and the eye sockets of which appeared to contain living eyes. The skeletons of Félicien

[42] For a thorough examination of this painting, consult Lydia Schoonbaert, "Schilderend geraamte van James Ensor," *Jaarboek van het Koninklijk Museum voor Schone Kunsten,* Antwerp (1973): 321-337.

[43] Reproduced in Farmer, *Ensor,* fig. 71.

[44] The engraver and date are unknown. See Lucie-Smith, *The Waking Dream,* p. 21, n. 29.

[45] Brussels, Musée Wiertz. Reproduced in Farmer, *Ensor,* p. 15, fig. 5.

[46] Liège, Collection Daniel Droixhe.

FIG. 43. Léon Frédéric. *Studio Interior*, 1882.

Rops, whose influence on Ensor was significant in diverse ways, will be included in a discussion of Rops in the next chapter; for now another Belgian, Léon Frédéric, is worth considering for an unusual five-foot canvas he painted in 1882. Entitled "Studio Interior," it shows a skeleton wrapped in a transparent drape and held on the lap of the nude artist (Fig. 43). Evening clothes are piled on a chair in the background and a palette and brushes are placed on a chair in the right foreground. A paper on the floor carries a clearly printed message, "le beau et le laid sont des conventions."

Frédéric was four years older than Ensor, and in 1880 he joined L'Essor, where Ensor could have met him. In 1882 he won the first of many gold medals with a Realist painting entitled "Chalk Merchants," and he was to become famous for his Realist depictions of Belgian peasants and for his fanciful, allegorical Symbolist canvases of masses of rosy-skinned children. His son remembers him explaining that "Studio Interior" was a painting intended for a special salon of parody, an exhibition entitled "L'Art zwanze."[47] "Zwanze" meant "joke" in Brussels patois and its use implied strong mockery or farce. The idea originated with an exhibition in 1870, but the next exhibitions did not occur until 1885 and 1887 when they were organized by L'Essor.[48] Frédéric first showed in the zwanze exhibition of 1885, but the entry titles don't suggest that he included "L'Interieur." Given the painting's date it seems unlikely that it could have been intended for that exhibition.

There has been no satisfactory explanation for the painting; it has been called "an enigma" and "an exquisite night-

[47] *Belgian Art 1880-1914*, pp. 102-103.
[48] Jacques Van Lennep, "Les Expositions burlesques à Bruxelles de 1870 à 1914: l'Art zwanze—une manifestation pré-dadaiste?" *Bulletin des Musées Royaux des Beaux-Arts de Belgique* 19 (February 1970): 127.

PLATE 3. Ensor. *Scandalized Masks*, 1883.

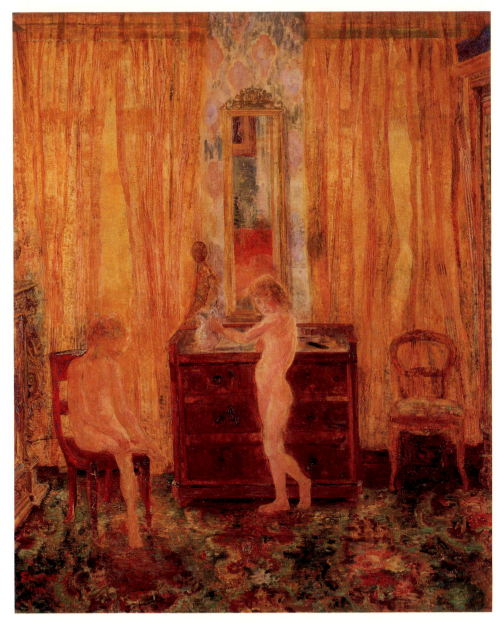

PLATE 4. Ensor. *Children Dressing*, 1886.

mare."[49] Further, it has been observed that the painting's technique is "notably different from the brighter, more brittle brushwork of his allegories" and that there was an intention of "elegance."[50] Certain peculiar details in the painting have been overlooked, however, and they appear to be specific symbols: the stalks of corn that lie on the floor and float over the upper part of the skeleton's frame and above the head of the artist, and the golden stars imprinted on the material covering the skeleton. It would seem to this viewer that a key to the painting's fascination may lie with a relationship to practices of the occult. Frédéric's nudity and his strange, wrapped companion have been joined in an intimate relationship that is visually shocking. The scene would make sense as a depiction of the artist involved in some mysterious ritual; Sâr Péladan's tribute to artists comes to mind: "Artist, you are priest. . . . Artist, you are king. . . . Artist, you are Magus. . . ."[51]

The painting's secrets may never be explained, but its obvious irony, a nude artist seated like a ventriloquist with a silent skeleton spokesman, combined with a written message that may be meant to invert the meanings of beauty and ugliness, also make it appropriate for an exhibition of Belgian "l'art zwanze."

Like Frédéric's skeleton, the skeletons in Ensor's paintings wear coverings, and they inhabit interiors that often suggest the artist's surroundings.[52] Ensor's paintings of skeletons also seem to contain a hidden message, something specific that the viewer cannot quite decipher, but which contains

FIG. 44. Ensor. *Skeletons Fighting for the Body of a Hanged Man*, 1891.

the substance of the picture's *raison d'être*. "Skeletons Fighting for the Body of a Hanged Man" (Fig. 44) is such a painting. It is the skeletons that control their surroundings in Ensor's painting, but, as in the Frédéric canvas, there is a written message: the prize over which they battle is the body of a

[49] *Belgian Art 1880-1914*, p. 103.   [50] Ibid.

[51] Quoted in Robert Pincus-Witten, *Occult Symbolism*, p. 105 (from the Catalogue du Salon de la Rose-Croix, 1892). Péladan, who had a following in Belgium and who used works by Rops and Khnopff as frontispieces for his novels, had been involved, before his founding of the Rosicrucian Order of the Temple and Grail, with what has been described as a "magico-

kabbalistique" association (Francine-Claire Legrand, *Symbolism in Belgium*, translated by Alistair Kennedy [Brussels: Laconti, 1972], n. 49).

[52] E.g., in the 1889 "Skeletons trying to Warm Themselves," skeletons dressed in loose clothing gather around a stove on a platform in a bare room that recalls the room in which Ensor posed his "Sick Tramp." "Skeletons . . ." is discussed in Chapter IV.

human with a sign around his neck bearing the word "civet." "Civet" is a dressed hare and it can still be found, with its sign of identification, placed for sale in the windows of butcher shops in Ostend.

One of the areas neglected in Ensor literature is his interest in *zwanze* humor and how it may have affected his art. Van Lennep has noted that Ernest Rousseau "had a special taste for *la zwanze*,"[53] and Ensor may have been introduced to that kind of Belgian humor at the Rousseaus. Van Lennep draws a connection between the philosophy of the anarchists frequenting the Rousseau home and *zwanze* philosophy:

... anarchy was generally a revolution "zwanzeur." In a general way, no doubt one will get a better understanding of the climate of the burlesque exhibition in remembering that anarchy could, on a social level and in a general way, be placed in parallel with the artistic overthrow of an age.[54]

In 1887 Ensor exhibited in "L'Art zwanze" and he chose to present a religious theme, a "Study for Christ Walking on the Sea," which may be the oil on canvas signed and dated 1883.[55] His choice brings up the question of intent: did Ensor mean the painting as a mockery of religion; did he intend instead a parody of another artist's painting, as was often the case with *zwanze* art;[56] or did he mean to mock both? There is also another possibility; in discussing the relationship between Ensor and the image of Christ, Francine-Claire Legrand writes: "... Christ is the anarchist symbol, but Christ, in Ensor's work, personifies Ensor himself."[57] Thus the painting, which shows a rainbow and the small radiant figure of Christ pointing toward that phenomenon and almost subsumed within the colors of the sea, may

be Ensor's tribute to Christ as historical anarchist and Ensor-Christ as contemporary anarchist and saviour. Whatever the case, the ideas underlying *zwanze* humor were crucial to Ensor's development in the mid 1880s and later in his art, when he used mockery, farce, and insult fully in pointedly anarchist works.

The influence of *zwanze* humor is subtly suggested in a painting entitled "Squelette regardant des Chinoiseries" (Fig. 45). Oriental-style paintings and fans fill the walls in an interior in which a skeleton wearing bright yellow socks sits in a high-backed chair and studies a book of Oriental prints. De Maeyer has used infrared to show that the original conception of the painting had been altered: in the original canvas from 1885 there was no skull at the bottom left of the painting, and a man, rather than a skeleton, sat in the chair.[58] Ensor's use of oriental motifs, his rich color, and the solitary figure gives the painting an air of cloistered sumptuousness that recalls Whistler's 1865 "La Princesse du Pays de Porcelaine," in which the figure sits surrounded by oriental objets d'art. With the substitution of a skeleton, the comparison becomes pointedly ironic: in 1886 Ensor wrote Octave Maus that to invite Whistler to exhibit with Les XX was "to walk toward death."[59]

Curiously, Whistler's influence on Ensor seemed to have been evident in the early 1880 "Woman on a Breakwater" (Fig. 46), in which a flattened, decorative, pictorial surface, orientalized costume with umbrella, and touches of elegant, soft color paid homage to Whistlerian reveries while still maintaining a Flemish sensibility. By 1882 such concerns had disappeared when another painting of "The Breakwater," a pure seascape, stressed the elemental forces of nature,

---

53 Van Lennep, "Expositions": 132.
54 Ibid.   55 Ibid., p. 140.
56 Ibid., p. 139.

57 Legrand, *Ensor, cet inconnu*, p. 76.
58 Marcel De Maeyer, "Derrière le masque": 25-26.
59 Legrand, "Lettres": 25.

the palpable materiality as well as the mystery.[60] After this point Ensor turned north to Turner for an investigation of light more sympathetic to his development of an increasingly Belgian vision.

In his 1886 letter to Maus Ensor's reference to Whistler was based on his belief that Whistler's painting was no longer new and exciting and that it was not worth including in an exhibition of avant-garde art: "Why admit Whistler? His painting is already moldy and musty, he is known and known again, what art and new principle can he bring to us?"[61] In that same letter Ensor admitted his fiercely northern bias that outsiders should not be asked to exhibit with the Belgian group: "Why admit foreigners? Aren't there any more young in Belgium? Are we the last young ones?"[62] In an adamant postscript, he concluded with further evidence of his nationalism: "With a great deal of pain I would see Les XX lose their virginity, their nationality, and perhaps their personality in falling into the grasp of the unscrupulous."[63]

Ensor was reacting to the widespread belief that Belgium was a provincial backwater, that Paris was the center of

[60] Reproduced in Haesaerts, *James Ensor*, p. 308, fig. 57. It is worth noting that with a very few exceptions, such as the "Woman on the Breakwater," the solitary human figure in Ensor's paintings was generally defined within the confines of an interior. Despite his fondness for landscape and his genuine love of the sea, Ensor's human subjects are alienated from nature.

[61] Quoted in Legrand, "Lettres": 25. It appears that Ensor held an unpopular opinion. Les XX did invite him back for a second exhibition and Whistler was to maintain his prestige; by the late 1880s he was a cult figure in England and France. In 1884 the French writer Huysmans began a critique of the salon of 1884 with five and half pages praising Whistler in *La Revue indépendente*, where Huysmans explained that Whistler's unpopularity with the bourgeois was a result of their own ignorance (1[1884]: 106-112).

The 1885 *L'Art moderne* carried an article on Whistler (no. 37 [September 13, 1885]: 294ff) and his "Ten O'Clock Lectures" were translated into French by Mallarmé and appeared in 1888 in *L'Art moderne* and *La Revue indépendente*.

[62] Quoted in Legrand, "Lettres": 25.   [63] Ibid.

FIG. 45. Ensor. *Skeleton Studying Chinoiseries*, 1885.

51

FIG. 46. Ensor. *Woman on the Breakwater*,
1880.

ment of French developments. . . . Flemishness meant melancholy, darkness, directness, and above all, coarseness. . . .''[65]

If Ensor felt Whistler unsuitable because of his nationality and because his art was retardataire in the 1880s, he felt contempt for the younger Georges Seurat's painting ''Sunday Afternoon on the Island of La Grande Jatte'' shown in Les XX's 1887 exhibition and heralded as a modern masterpiece. Ensor's response was finished in 1888: the monumental ''Entry of Christ into Brussels,'' a painting even larger than Seurat's and a view of brutalized contemporary Belgian society that was in direct contrast to the French artist's Parisian landscape of classless utopia.

It was not only Seurat's Frenchness and his naively optimistic subject matter that infuriated Ensor, but his technique as well, which Ensor repudiated as cold and lifeless. He must have been furious when after Seurat's exhibition with Les XX a number of Belgian ''pointillist'' pastiches appeared, for example, Henry van de Velde's 1889 ''Twilight'' and Théo van Rysselberghe's 1890 ''Family in the Orchard.''[66] Rysselberghe, a talented painter who excelled in portraits, continued to be influenced by Seurat and as late as 1903 paid him tribute by painting a large group portrait, ''The Reading,'' in the pointillist style.

The 1887 *zwanze* exhibition had used Impressionist and Pointillist theories as the brunt of some of their most irreverent jokes,[67] but Ensor's objections were deadly serious and they related to his own philosophy of art:

I have condemned the dry and repugnant processes of the pointillists already lifeless for the light and for art. They

political and cultural creativity and life elsewhere was but a second-rate existence.[64] Dore Ashton has described the avant-garde art world in Brussels as struggling to keep up with Paris: ''The art students . . . recognized that Belgian art trailed in the wake of Paris, and they longed to find some national identification while yet participating in the excite-

[64] See Jean F. Buyck, ''Antwerp, Als Ik Kan, and the Problem of Provincialism,'' in *Belgian Art, 1880-1914* (New York, The Brooklyn Museum, 1980), pp. 71-80.
[65] Dore Ashton, ''James Ensor's Re-Entries,'' *Arts Magazine* 51 (March

1977): 137.
[66] Reproduced in *Belgian Art, 1880-1914*, pp. 155 and 147. For a discussion of the response to Seurat's work, see Jane Block, ''Les XX,'' pp. 27-28.
[67] Van Lennep, ''Les Expositions burlesques'': 139.

coldly and methodically apply without sentiment, their dotting between correct and cold lines, only arriving at one aspect of light, its vibration, without coming to give its form. . . .[68]

He concluded by repeating the image of death he used to describe Whistler's art, "All the rules, all the canons of art vomit death. . . ."[69]

Ensor's criticisms of Impressionism and Pointillism were meant to illustrate his own Belgian artistic viewpoint, which stressed a creative interpretation of one's surroundings through a spontaneous, emotional response to subject matter. In a letter he asked why Belgian painters treated form and line as though they were timid sculptors; why did they not go for an inner vision and why did they despise light and the distortions that could be created with line?[70]

What Ensor was attempting was to create a Belgian sensibility of radical modernity, one that would incorporate the influences of a great Belgian past and speak in a manner totally alien to the artistic sensibility coming from France.[71] His task was made especially difficult by Belgium's internal conflict. During the active years of Les XX, particularly between 1886 and 1888, Belgian life was disrupted by a rift that threatened to erode the foundations of its culture and destroy the vitality of contemporary creativity. The problem was political; it involved French- and Flemish-speaking natives, growing French-language supremacy in the nineteenth century, and a resultant chauvinistic Flemish reaction.[72] Baudelaire wrote of this division in the notes for his pamphlet, "La Pauvre Belgique," and he observed that not only were there different language communities of Flemings and Walloons, but there was competition between cities, such as Antwerp and Brussels, respectively Flemish and French speaking. In art, as competition to the Brussels-based Les XX, an Antwerp art circle was formed in 1883 that called itself "Als Ik Kan," "The Best I Can Do."[73]

Ensor's relations with the members of Les XX were often strained, and his personality, difficult at times when he was opinionated and argumentative,[74] made him extremely unpopular with some of its members. Initially he had agreed to allow foreigners to exhibit with Les XX, but in later years

[68] Quoted in Frédéric de Smet, "James Ensor," *Gand Artistique: Art et esthétique*, no. 12 (December 1925): 254-257.

[69] Ibid., p. 257. Ensor used this phrase more than once in discussing his art theory. Also consult Florent Fels, *James Ensor* (Brussels: Weisenbuch, 1958), p. 15.

[70] Letter to Pol de Mont, ca. 1895, quoted in *Ensor ein Maler*, p. 37.

[71] An article in *L'Art moderne* addressed these issues in 1884. It lamented the tendency of young Belgian writers to take inspiration from foreign influences and recalled the great Flemish literary and artistic tradition of Henri Conscience, Georges Eekhoud, Rubens, and Van Dyck ("Nos Flamands," *L'Art moderne*, no. 27 [July 6, 1884]: 217-219).

[72] French had been in use as the national language since the Revolution of 1830 when the Flemish and Walloon provinces threw off the Dutch rule and founded Belgium. Flemish consciousness grew gradually and there was an increasing effort to gain equal footing for Flemish culture. By 1883 Flemish was obligatory in secondary schools of Flanders and by 1886 Belgian money was printed in both Flemish and French. For a thorough discussion of the problem see Andrew Jackson Mathews, *La Wallonie, 1886-1892: The Symbolist Movement in Belgium* (Morningside Heights: King's Crown Press, 1947), pp. 43-52. Today the problem of language is even more acute; for example, many Flemish Belgians refuse to speak French as a matter of principle and Flemish pride.

[73] See Buyck, "Antwerp, Als Ik Kan," pp. 71-80. Ensor was probably familiar with the writing of Charles Verlat, an academician who became the director of the Antwerp Academy in 1885. Although Verlat was associated with Flemish ideals, he had urged young Belgian artists to assert themselves as a group, and he warned against the growing influence of French art, advocating "the preservation of a native tradition in painting . . ." (Buyck, p. 73). Jan Van Eyck used the phrase "Als Ik Kan" on the Ghent Altarpiece; thus the group associated itself with an ancient and venerable tradition.

[74] For example, Ensor's strong dislike of Alfred Stevens, an older realist painter popular for his formulaic portraits of pretty Belgian women, led Ensor to a vicious diatribe in which he described Stevens as "a national

FIG. 47. Ensor. *Demons Taunting Me*, 1888.

54

acted favorably to his first exhibit: "Among new arrivals, James Ensor seems full of promise and has attracted attention. His sketches reveal an attentive observation to the effects of light and air, a finesse in producing certain tonalities, and an extraordinary lack of banality for a beginner."[83]

In 1885 *L'Art moderne* praised his still-lifes and interiors with a poetic description of his early painting that may have been written by Octave Maus, who was one of the art reviewers between 1884 and 1893: ". . . of the still-lifes and of the interior of James Ensor, which have unforgettable charm. His painting is a treat. Nothing clashes in these harmonies, which sing to the eyes like a symphony charms the ear."[84]

These positive reviews were reactions to Ensor's early work, the luminous still-lifes, seascapes, and interiors. From 1886 on, when Ensor's art was to develop in a direction utterly free from constraint in technique and subject matter, his audience became increasingly limited. Two Belgians were influential in this shift in artistic emphasis. Both were older than Ensor, successful artists who belonged to two different generations. The first, Antoine Wiertz (1806-1865), died when Ensor was five years old. Wiertz had been the most celebrated Belgian Romantic. He had lived in Paris between 1829 and 1832; he traveled to Italy with a Prix de Rome; and he returned to Belgium to paint huge, romantic canvases and macabre paintings with themes of death, madness, and de-

monic possession.[85] Wiertz's studio was to become a museum after his death; there, near the Rousseau home, Ensor studied his art and his writings, both of which influenced Ensor's production after 1886.

Wiertz also influenced Félicien Rops (1833-1898), the most admired and respected Belgian artist Ensor knew. In 1860, the year of Ensor's birth, Rops was twenty-seven years old. Even then he had already gained a measure of success for his witty illustrations for *Uylenspiegel*, an eight-page weekly he had founded in 1856.[86] In 1862 Rops left for Paris to study with Braquemond and Jacquemart. A list of his good friends and acquaintances reveals that through the years he had become involved with the Parisian literary avant-garde: Flaubert, Mallarmé, the Goncourt Brothers, Baudelaire, Huysmanns, Verlaine, Mirbeau, and Villiers de l'Isle-Adam.

Rops was the epitome of the successful Belgian and he returned to his homeland often. He exhibited with La Chrysalide and Les XX and it was through the latter that Ensor met Rops. The Belgian writer Eugène Demolder also ensured contact, since Demolder was Rops's son-in-law and Ensor's friend. Ensor would have known Rops's work without any personal contact, however; his illustrations appeared regularly in books by leading Symbolists such as Péladan, Mallarmé, Villiers de l'Isle-Adam, and his art was frequently reviewed in periodicals and newspapers.

As sources of inspiration, the art of Wiertz and Rops is

---

[83] Jean-François Portaels in *L'Art moderne* (June 5, 1881): 107; quoted in Farmer, *James Ensor*, p. 20.

[84] ". . . des natures-mortes et de l'interieur de James Ensor, qui ont des séductions inoubliables. Sa peinture est un régal. Rien ne détonne dans ces harmonies qui chantent aux yeux comme une symphonie charme l'oreille" (*L'Art moderne* [February 8, 1885]: 42).

[85] Consult Alfred Mockel, *Antoine Wiertz* (Brussels: n.p., 1946); H. Colleye, *Antoine Wiertz* (Brussels: La Renaissance du Livre, 1957) and Philippe

Roberts-Jones, "L'image irréaliste chez Antoine Wiertz," *Bulletin de la classe des beaux-arts, Académie Royale de Belgique* 59, nos. 2-4 (1977): 55-63.

[86] The word "Uylenspiegel" comes from the Flemish, "Ik ben u lieden spiegl," shortened to "Ik ben ulen spiegl," "I am your mirror." Cultural reviews, political commentary, and lively dialogue, as well as satire and caricature, made *Uylenspiegel* a "mirror" reflecting the character of mid-nineteenth-century Belgian life.

highly significant for Ensor's development, and Ensor himself lists Rops and Wiertz as two of "The Classic Dozen," the Belgian artists whom he most admired.[87] But it is in the

manner of interpretation that we can appreciate Ensor's own creative genius, and the debt to Wiertz and Rops then becomes not only comprehensible, but laudable as well.

[87] Ensor, *Mes Écrits*, p. 49. He begins with Wiertz and mentions Louis Dubois H. Boulenger, Henri De Braeckeleer, and several others. With the exceptions of Rops and Wiertz, these Belgians are honored by Ensor more for their nationality than for their specific importance to the development of his oeuvre.

III

OF SIRENS AND FALLEN ANGELS: THE LURE
OF WIERTZ AND ROPS

The extent of Félicien Rops's influence on James Ensor's art has elicited some controversy. At one extreme Rops's art has been dismissed as unimportant for Ensor;[1] at the other it is claimed that Ensor copied Rops, "trait for trait, in his etchings, in his paintings, in his writings."[2] There is a meaningful position between these two viewpoints, but what has been missing in discussions of Ensor's debt to Rops are specifics rather than generalizations. Although Legrand has suggested that Ensor's winged skeletons came from Rops,[3] and Babut Du Marès connected Rops's "reversed" Hamlet, a reclining skeleton holding a human head (Fig. 49), with Ensor's etching of "My Portrait in 1960" (Fig. 38),[4] many of the key comparisons have been neglected. Both phases of Rops's production were important for Ensor: the light, quick touch of

early illustrations for *Uylenspiegel,* and the later prints of dark, satanic sexuality. These influences are crucial to all aspects of the younger artist's development, to his paintings, prints, and drawings. Furthermore, the links between Rops and Ensor were strengthened by Rops's debt to Antoine Wiertz, and Ensor's debt to Wiertz as well. Although of different generations, the art of these three Belgians is entangled in a complex and fascinating interweaving of multileveled adaptations of themes, symbols, and techniques. Thus, to neglect Ensor's debt to either Rops or Wiertz is to ignore a significant aspect of his artistic formulation and a crucial reason for the change in style and content in his art after the mid-1880s.

In Brussels Wiertz is honored by a wide street that bears

---

[1] Dore Ashton has remarked, "Historians prefer to remember the undeniable influence of Rembrandt, and to deny the influence of Ensor's countryman, Félicien Rops, whose fashionable erotic prints seem to them trivial" ("James Ensor's Re-Entries," *Arts Magazine* 51 [March 1977]: 138).

[2] Babut Du Marès, *Félicien Rops* (Ostend: Erel, 1971), pp. 144-145, quoting

the Ostend painter Jean-Jacques Gailliard.

[3] Legrand, *Ensor, cet inconnu,* p. 86.

[4] *Félicien Rops,* n.p., with the inscription, "Ensor gravura plus tard avec un même ésprit moqueur, 'Mon portrait en l'an 1960.'"

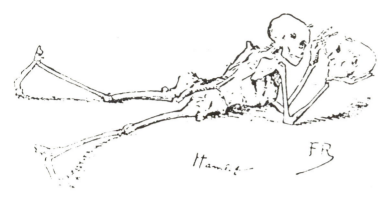

FIG. 49. Félicien Rops. *Hamlet*, n.d.

his name, as well as by the Musée Wiertz, a building that was formerly the artist's country residence and studio. Bought by the Belgian government after the artist's death, the museum's property is completely enclosed by two streets: the rue Wiertz and the rue Vautier. The rue Vautier was the address of Ensor's close friends, Ernest and Mariette Rousseau, and Ensor would become familiar with the Wiertz museum in 1879, when he first began visiting the Rousseaus.

During Ensor's formative years, continued public interest in Wiertz was reflected by the government's gift to his memory: in 1881 a bronze monument to Wiertz was erected in the Place de la Couronne, a few blocks south of the Wiertz museum. The museum was entered through a large iron gate and the main room was Wiertz's studio, an impressive hall two stories high with a barrel vault ceiling. There Wiertz painted his gigantic canvases of straining life-size figures in religious, mythological, and fantastic settings, and today they still fill the huge walls: "The Contest of Good and Evil," "The Triumph of Christ," "Contest for the Body of Patroclus," and "A Giant on Earth," in which the huge leg of Polyphemus is shown trampling Ulysses' men.

The adjacent rooms were of normal proportion and the walls held smaller paintings, oil studies, and drawings. Among these works were Wiertz's dramatic depictions of insanity, suicide, and witchcraft. Wiertz's love of the macabre interested Ensor more than his style, which vacillated between an academic blend of neoclassic romanticism in the large canvases and theatrical melodramatic realism in some of the smaller ones. There are a few very small sketches, however, such as "The Triumph of Christ" (Fig. 50) and "The Revolt of Hell Against Heaven" (Fig. 51), that had a pointed impact on Ensor, both through subject matter and through the technique of using thick paint strokes vigorously applied with energetic motion to create a surface alive with tense, palpable excitement. Ensor was also to develop his own distinctive method of applying paint, which through its surface and color would pulsate with radiant energy and movement. His 1889 "Fall of the Rebel Angels" (Fig. 52), in which bodies formed from smeared strokes join with force lines, creates a swirling energy reminiscent of Wiertz.

Wiertz's oil sketch, "The Apotheosis of the Queen" (Fig. 53), has been called his masterpiece, and it has been observed that, "an almost mystical sense of exultation seems to have inspired this vision, which intermingles both men and the elements."[5] Approximately 3' x 2' in size, the sketch is painted on paper and framed with a semicircular top. It was originally planned for completion as a gigantic painting 150 feet tall. Wiertz envisioned that the final version would be displayed in the public square in front of the Royal Palace during Brus-

[5] Legrand, *Symbolism in Belgium*, pp. 33-34. Also see Roberts-Jones, "L'Image irréaliste," esp. p. 62.

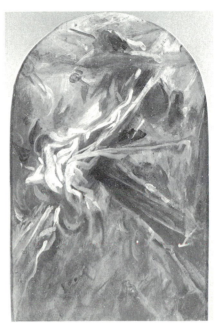

FIG. 50. Antoine Wiertz. *The Triumph of Christ*, n.d.

FIG. 51. Antoine Wiertz. *The Revolt
of Hell Against Heaven*, n.d.

sel's Silver Jubilee celebration in 1856: "Under the light of a brazier a mass of human figures surge impetuously forward toward a spiraled column, the summit of which disappears into the clouds, symbolizing the path of the virtuous leading to heaven."[6] Torches burn, smoke and shafts of sunlight fill the air, and banners unfurl with the names of cities—Anvers, Gand, Bruges—as hordes of people cheer from a Roman-style amphitheatre and crowd the foreground in a swirling surge of movement. They pay tribute to their beloved queen, Louise-Marie, whose name is visible on the base of the column, a pastiche of spiraled Roman columns like those sculptured with the exploits of Trajan and Marcus Aurelius.

Ensor adopted this concept—a huge crowd gathered in a claustrophobic mass to pay homage to a ruler—in his 1888 "Entry of Christ into Brussels," in which he also included banners with easily readable descriptive labels. An etching

[6] Legrand, p. 34.

61

FIG. 52. Ensor. *The Fall of the Rebel Angels*, 1889.

from that same year, "Capture of a Strange City" (Fig. 54), has a closer sense of the spatial ambience of the Wiertz sketch, however, with tall elephant-headed columns on one side and elaborate architectural details including statues and a tall column surrounded by a burst of radiating light.

Ensor's strong debt to Wiertz is suggested by the fact that the only monograph on an artist found posthumously in Ensor's collection of books was Louis Labarre's 1867 second edition of *Antoine Wiertz; avec des lettres de l'artiste.*[7] The signature on the inside reads "J Ensor" in handwriting unlike the artist's, and its inscribed date, although difficult to decipher, may be 1874, suggesting that the book originally belonged to Ensor's father, or may have been a gift at that time to his fourteen-year-old son.

Wiertz was to influence Ensor in a significant way other than his art: as a writer of scathing commentary.[8] In 1859 Wiertz published a brochure in which he compared human beings to the animal and insect world. Entitled "Peinture mate," which was both a reference to mat painting and a pun on "mate" as deadly or dull, Wiertz viciously attacked

humanity as a group and as individuals: "Odious pile! Vile toads, vile serpents, packs of insects inflated with envy, of bestiality and meanness—stupid crowd, from what muck do you arise? . . . Don't do anything for this ungracious crowd. . . . suffer this man and he'll spit in your face."[9] Ensor developed his own talent for vulgar verbal descriptions that paralleled some of his more insulting caricatures in art, as in 1896 when he wrote with ironic fervor, "M. Stevens knows how to quickly shoot a greenish spurt of civette wind."[10]

Wiertz's "ungracious crowd" would occupy Ensor in a number of significant art works, and at one point in the diatribe of "Peinture Mate" Wiertz observed: ". . . he who grubs about a swamp resigns himself to listening to the frogs croaking about him."[11] Ensor was to use the frog and Wiertz's "insects inflated with envy" in his own descriptive motto, "Les suffisances matamoresques appellent la finale crevaison grenouillère," "The hot air of windbags always makes them burst like frogs."[12] This description became the last line of several of his published speeches and essays,[13] and, when a monograph was planned on Ensor, the artist wrote

[7] It appears that Ensor, or someone else with access to his belongings, carefully selected this collection. For the most part, what remains are books published after 1900, with handwritten inscriptions from the authors praising Ensor. They celebrate his friendships in the literary world and acknowledge him as an artist beloved of writers. This collection has never been published; it is stored in cartons in the Ensor archive at the Musée des Beaux-Arts in Ostend. Mr. Frank Patrick Edebau, then director of the museum, graciously allowed me to document its contents. The appendix of my dissertation contains the complete list ("James Ensor's Transformations of Tradition: A Study of His Life and Art During the Creative Years 1877-1899," Ph.D. dissertation, State University of New York at Binghamton, 1982).

[8] For a discussion of Ensor's writing in and of itself, see Paul Haesaerts, "Stridences et bigarrures des écrits d'Ensor," *L'Art Belge* (December 1965): 32-40.

[9] "Amas odieux! vils crapauds, vils serpents, tas d'insectes gonflés d'envie,

de bêtises et de lâcheté, foule stupide de quelle fange sortez-vous? . . . Ne faites donc rien pour cet homme et lui cracher à la face." Quoted from *"Peinture mate par M. Wiertz," Uylenspiegel*, no. 22 (July 3, 1859): 1.

[10] Ensor, *Mes Écrits*, p. 27. Civet is the odor that comes from the anal glands of a civet-cat.

[11] ". . . celui qui défriche un marais se resigne à entre les grenouillères coasser autour de lui" ("Peinture mate par M. Wiertz": 1). Roberts-Jones mentions a frog Wiertz sculptured as a youth, "so truthful that it startles . . ." ("L'image irréaliste": 56).

[12] Translated by Paul Haesaerts; see Evelyn Schlumberger, "Project for a Film on James Ensor," *Réalités*, December 1970, p. 85. Frank Edebau offered his translation, "The self-conceit of prigs makes them burst in the end like a blown-up frog," in an interview with me in Ostend in October 1977.

[13] See *Mes Érits*, "Les Frères Stevens" (1896), p. 28; "Un Bronze ostendais à placer" (1903), p. 48; "Réflexions sur quelques peintres et lanceurs d'ephemères" (1911), p. 20; and "Interview" (1921), p. 72.

FIG. 53. Antoine Wiertz. *The Apotheosis of the Queen*, 1856.

FIG. 54. Ensor. *Capture of a Strange City*, 1888.

the author requesting that his famous line be included on a blank page at the beginning of the book.[14]

Wiertz claimed that "Peinture mate" was written in response to an exhibition of German drawings that he found deplorable,[15] but in 1859 he had also developed a strong hatred for the French and for Paris, which he described as "ulcer of civilization, den of demons,"[16] after a poor critical response to his paintings in the Paris salon of 1859. He may have been reacting in part against a general belief in French cultural superiority,[17] as Ensor was to do later with Les XX,

[14] Ensor, *Lettres à André Ridder*, p. 29.

[15] "Peinture mate par M. Wiertz": 1.

[16] Quoted in Paul Fierens, *L'Art en Belgique* (Brussels: La Renaissance du Livre, n.d.), p. 448.

[17] David Farmer has observed that Baudelaire's travels to Brussels in 1864,

64

when he sought to negate the pressures of French influence on Belgian painters.

For Félicien Rops France was a second homeland, and he developed strong ties there that influenced his art. There was an obvious change from the early years, when he reflected Belgian culture and literature in his illustrations for *Uylenspiegel*, and his later work in graphics, which could easily be described as decadent, and which reflected a sophisticated Parisian sensibility. The quick, nervous line of Rops's early illustrations captured the earthy energy of the Belgian bourgeois and peasant. Two lithographs from 1858, "Printemps" and "Garde Civique" (Figs. 55 and 56), give the viewer a high vantage point from which to observe the crowd below.[18] In "Printemps" the crowd escapes from the narrow city streets in mass exodus from what the sign in the middle characterizes as an "unhealthy town." In an unleashed torrent of springtime sexuality, Belgians fill the countryside with raucous fighting, drinking, dancing, and loving. In the upper left kegs are emptied, and, perhaps in a tribute to the drinking of Belgian beer and Brussel's famous Mannekin-pis, Rops shows a man urinating in front of a shocked woman. At the top, right of center, a platform has been erected and a trio of musicians play drums, bass, and horn. On the lower right a huge snail watches this encroachment upon its peaceful countryside.

"Garde Civique" contains banners and flags and, at the bottom right, a marching militia, drummers, and a tall drum

FIG. 55. Félicien Rops. *Printemps*, 1858.

FIG. 56. Félicien Rops. *Garde Civique*, 1858.

"confirmed that the apparent lack of art in Belgium was a sad truth: Only painters of lowly themes existed there, all specializing in narrowly prescribed areas of subject matter and content" (*Ensor*, p. 15).

[18] Rops's oeuvre is reproduced in Maurice Exteens, *L'Oeuvre gravé et lithographié de Félicien Rops*, 4 vols. (Paris: Pellet, 1928). For "Printemps," also see *Uylenspiegel*, no. 14 (May 9, 1858); for "Garde Civique," *Uylenspiegel*, no. 20 (June 20, 1858).

major. Handsome in his uniform and posed in a dramatic parade gesture, the drum major attracts several housewives, who in their excitement appear to forget all about their own children.

In Ensor's "Entry of Christ into Brussels" (Fig. 57) a parade leader also appears at the bottom of the composition, but he is transformed into a coarse, bloated monstrosity who gives visual expression to Ensor's dictum about blown-up frogs. Although Ensor's "Entry of Christ" owes important debts to other sources (see Chapter V), the *Uylenspiegel* lithographs, with their tilted, high viewpoint, crowding figures, banners, marching soldiers, musicians, and stage performers, illustrate a distinctive and memorable Belgian "slice of life" that must have impressed Ensor with its originality and verve.

An early lithograph and an etching by Rops (Fig. 59) of comic bathing scenes can be compared with an oil painting on panel by Ensor entitled "The Call of the Siren" (Fig. 58). It is signed and dated "Ensor 93" and shows the artist with his hair wildly unkempt and his arms crossed as if to protect his chest. He is dressed for the beach in a striped swimming shirt and he gingerly descends the steps of a bathing cabin. Eagerly awaiting with outstretched arms is the well-endowed, undulating figure of a woman, perhaps Augusta Boogaerts. She was the saleswoman Ensor had met in 1888 and with whom he maintained a relationship until his death. Ensor nicknamed her "the Siren," an appropriate description for a female creature from the sea, but also a significant

characterization explained by one Ensor biographer as an association with the "woman demon companion of the fallen angel from the book of Enoch."[19]

Ensor's painting and a Rops etching are amusing to compare for their differing masculine heroes and female accomplices. "Reactive Belgian Hand Towels" shows a bathing cabin pulled into the sea (Fig. 59). Inside, a bare-chested muscular swimmer towels himself off, assisted in his task by an adolescent who wipes his stomach.[20] More similar in spirit to the Ensor is an illustration from an 1856 issue of *Uylenspiegel* entitled "Déballage," or literally, "display of goods for sale at bargain prices" (Fig. 60).[21] Two bathers meet in the sea: a plump woman with her arms close to her body twists away from the encounter. According to the legend below the print she complains to herself, "Darn! the Marquis de Finoel and I'm without a corset!" The emaciated male, with striped shirt and hair dripping with water and seaweed, mutters, "Hang it! The Duchess de Crupet and I don't have my padded suit!"

At Ostend Rops's observations of bathers could often be pointedly cruel, as in one particular beach print that carried the explanation, "A hideous, big nose came forth from the midst of the waves."[22] In an article entitled "The Baths, Ostend," Rops related how Nadar accompanied him there and was astonished by the huge crowds crammed on the beach.[23] What followed was Rops's description of various body types and a phrase reminiscent of Ensor's later beach

---

[19] Ollinger-Zinque, *Ensor by Himself*, p. 41. Also see Louis Réau, *Iconographie de l'art chrétien*, vol. 1 (Paris: Presses Universitaires de France, 1955), p. 121, where "La Sirene" is linked with "mermaid."

[20] The sex of this assistant is difficult to identify; at first I thought it was female, but in fact it may be male. At the top of the print, turned upside down, are three separate depictions of cupids, "L'Amour-orchestre," "L'Amour-harpiste" and "La Muse en crinoline." This part of the print doesn't seem to have any specific connection with the main area, but since love,

or at least eroticism, is involved, there may be a tangential association through the hand towels, which as "reactive Belgian hand towels" may tend to be responsive or to react to stimulus.

[21] *Uylenspiegel*, no. 28 (August 10, 1856). In that same issue a long article on Wiertz appeared entitled "Fantaisie Artiste" (4ff).

[22] See *Uylenspiegel*, no. 27 (August 2, 1857), p. 3, "Un éffroyable pif sortit du sein des flots. . . ."

[23] *Uylenspiegel*, no. 30 (August 23, 1857), pp. 1-2.

Fig. 57. Ensor. *The Entry of Christ into Brussels*, 1888.

CHAPTER III

FIG. 58. Ensor. *The Call of the Siren*, 1893.

scenes in which grotesque shapes cavort and gambol un-selfconsciously (Fig. 6): "... nothing saddens more than the shameless deformities that crowd the waves with skeletons, baldness, atrophies, and hypertrophies."[24] The article ends with Nadar's scornful protest that "there are always women who have the appearance of wanting to refuse what you don't even dream of asking them."[25]

In Ensor's "Call of the Siren" his depiction of a woman bather follows the cruel caricatures of Rops, as well as Rops's written description of Nadar's misogynist observation. The

[24] "... rien n'attriste plus que la laideur impudente qui remplit les vagues de squelettes, de calvitiés, d' atrophies et d'hypertrophies" (Ibid.).

[25] "Il y a toujours des femmes qui ont l'air de vouloir vous refuser ce qu'on ne songe pas à leur demander" (Ibid.).

FIG. 59. Félicien Rops. *Essuie-Mains
Réactifs Belges*, n.d.

FIG. 60. Félicien Rops. *Déballage*, 1856.

woman is a grotesque female whose face carries a vapid expression and whose eyes do not even look directly at her ostensible prey. Ensor's self-portrait, however, is a more sensitive depiction: his protected chest, his gingerly placed step, and his unruly hair make his feelings of vulnerability and fear of submission almost touching. Ensor may be the fallen angel, but he has shown himself as an unwilling victim of temptation. This painting came in the year after a key work, "The Consoling Virgin," in which Ensor kneeled in obeisance to his holy female comforter and his palette served as a partial shield for a frayed paintbrush penis (Fig. 61).[26]

Ensor commented upon his sexual insecurity in a number

[26] Legrand, *Ensor, cet inconnu*, p. 78 and Diane Lesko, "Ensor in his Milieu," *Artforum* 15 (May 1977): 62.

FIG. 61. Ensor. *The Consoling Virgin*, 1892.

of works (see Chapter VI). One might compare Rops's self-image in this regard with the radically different self-image presented by Ensor. Rops used a palette to reflect his potency, as an artist and as a man, in a print entitled "La Peinture Erotique." This "erotic painting," meant as a self-portrait of sorts, shows an erect phallus and testicles encircled by a palette and brushes and crowned above with a laurel wreath floating in the air. A lively eye regards the scene below from a triangle radiating beams of energy. A banner, which floats around one end of the triangle, carries the inscription, "I see you, little rascal!!!!"[27] In its third state the print became a diptych and included a voluptuous female nude torso and a skeletonized female head. The inscription on that side of the plate, "Tout passe! Tout casse!" may imply that time destroys desire, both in regard to female beauty and male potency.

As early as 1868 the Goncourt brothers had expressed the well-known misogynist rantings that were to permeate late nineteenth-century European literature and art. In discussing Rops, they remarked: "Rops is truly eloquent in depicting the cruel aspect of contemporary woman, her steel-like glance, and her malevolence toward man, not hidden, not disguised, but evident in the whole of her person."[28] Any number of Rops's etchings could have been in mind, and Rops continued to produce erotic etchings with female as murderer and castrator throughout his long career.

Ensor's 1888 etching entitled "L'Écorché" shows two women who are skinning a male figure tied to a cross (Fig. 62).[29] One of the women is similar in spirit to some of Rops's

[27] Reproduced in Exteens, *L'Oeuvre gravé*, no. 732.
[28] Quoted in Mario Praz, *The Romantic Agony*, translated by Angus Davidson (2d ed., London: Oxford University Press, 1951), p. 369 and John Milner, *Symbolists and Decadents* (New York: E. P. Dutton, 1971), p. 115.
[29] Reproduced in Taevernier, *James Ensor*, pl. 57. Taevernier entitles the

more vicious females: she is nude except for black stockings or tall boots and a holster around her waist. She pierces the chest of her victim with a large knife and blood gushes down to his groin. Her companion, dressed in a skirt, faces the victim, and a mace or club becomes an extension of her right arm. The background contains a number of parallel lines moving in different directions, and at the edge of the ground line several masked faces appear. A head also rests at the top of the cross. The body of the flayed man lacks palpable form, and he could also be masked, but there is an intensity of feeling that is almost pathological and that suggests a personalized depiction of cruel torture and sadistic murder.[30]

In 1886 Ensor had made an attempt to deal with physical torture in an extremely rare etching entitled "The Flagellation" (Fig. 63).[31] Barely visible at the bottom of the print and only occupying one-fifth of the page, it shows nude females whipping the figure of Christ while soldiers armed with lances look on. The upper part of the print shows the design of a cathedral portal; Ensor worked that part of the plate into a more complete state than the lower section, and its palpable form contrasts sharply with the ghostly images in the scene below.

Jacques Janssens relates that, according to one Ensor biographer, Firmin Cuypers,[32] there was a cache of erotic draw-

work "L'Écorché," but "flaying a convict" is his English translation. There are two states and most of the engraving was executed in dry point.

[30] In 1899 Ensor would produce another etching of a similar subject, "Queen Parysatis Flaying a Eunuch"; see Taevernier, *James Ensor*, pl. 116. This image first appeared in 1887, therefore earlier than "L'Écorché," as a small vignette in Ensor's drawing, "The Temptation of St. Anthony" (fig. 99).

[31] Reproduced in Taevernier, *James Ensor*, p. 39, pl. 8.

[32] For Cuypers see *James Ensor: L'Homme et l'oeuvre* (Paris: Écrivains Réunis, 1925) and *Aspects propos de James Ensor* (Bruges: A. G. Stainforth, 1946).

FIG. 62. Ensor. *Flaying a Convict*, 1888.

71

FIG. 63. Ensor. *The Flagellation*, 1886.

ings that Ensor made after 1918 and which he kept hidden: "All the sexual games . . . the games of pleasure and flesh, display themselves there in voluptuous and lewd scenes, that the ensorienne libido suffuses with a vaporous sensuality."[33] Paul Haesaerts stated that these small pictures were destroyed by "sacrilegious hands."[34] Unfortunately, no description of these works is available, but it would not be surprising if their inspiration came in part from Rops's explicitly lascivious etchings.

What remains of Ensor's erotica in a public collection is a line drawing found in Antwerp's Musée des Beaux-Arts (Fig. 64).[35] Another line drawing of a nude shown at her toilette in four consecutive poses may be the same woman (Fig. 65). A model need not have been used for the woman in the chair, but if it was it may have been Augusta Boogaerts. She was the only woman, besides the female members of his family and Mariette Rousseau, with whom he formed a lasting, close relationship. Although one writer claimed Ensor was a "piêtre amoureux,"[36] a poor or pitiful lover, it has been reported that for a number of years he did take Augusta to hotels in Brussels.[37] In fact, in 1905 Ensor

[33] Quoted in Jacques Janssens, *James Ensor* (Paris: Librairie Flammarion, 1978), p. 80.

[34] Ibid.

[35] An erotic pastel was reproduced in Phyllis and Eberhard Kronhausen, *The Complete Book of Erotic Art*, vol. 1 (New York: Bell, 1978), p. 104, fig. 18. Its title reads "Orgy Scene by James Ensor (France) [sic], pastel." The collection is undocumented and the provenance is not mentioned, therefore the attribution should be open to question. In style it relates to the light soft colorful caricatures Ensor occasionally produced in the 1920s, but the amorous activities of the group are far more explicit than those we usually see reproduced in Ensor literature.

[36] Legrand quotes René Lyr from *Carnet de souvenirs* (unpublished, Brussels: Succession René Lyr), in *Ensor, cet inconnu*, p. 21 and p. 102, n. 37.

[37] Legrand, *Ensor, cet inconnu*, p. 21 ("Ensor occasionally took his lover to Brussels; they went to the Hotel de Namur, a very modest inn where

FIG. 64. Ensor. *Satyr*, n.d.

FIG. 65. Ensor. *Four Nudes*, n.d.

painted himself and Augusta in a double portrait, seated in a hotel room.[38]

Ensor's "Nymph Embracing a Herm," ca. 1920 (Fig. 66), is a light caricature similar in its main figures to Rops's "Hommage à Pan," an etching of dark, demonic sexuality, which was originally a frontispiece for Joséphin Péladan's 1885 *Curieuse* and then engraved by Bertrand and published in 1900 (Fig. 67). But in the Ensor the scene is crowded with

numerous amusing vignettes: rosy nudes, a curly-haired flapper-picador with sword, a boar in the upper left, plump buttocks in the upper right, a bacchus gnome with a wine glass, and a coarse old man who vomits forcefully, aiming his spray at the groin of the statue. Ensor may have been making a comical historical allusion. It has been reported that phallic worship had existed in Belgian communities, as well as in areas of France and Sicily into the nineteenth century, and

Ensor paid his bill in pictures, then, after 1905, to the Hotel de Wavre, Place du Luxembourg").

[38] The painting is discussed in Lesko, "Ensor in His Milieu": 62, and in Chapter VI of this study.

FIG. 66. Ensor. *Nymph Embracing a Herm*, c. 1920.

FIG. 67. Félicien Rops. *Hommage à Pan*, 1900.

74

FIG. 68. Félicien Rops. *La Médaille de Waterloo*, 1858.

FIG. 69. Ensor. *Skeletons Playing Billiards*, 1903.

that there was an ancient statue of Priapus at Antwerp.[39] Accordingly, phallic worship may even have been the original inspiration for Brussels seventeenth-century Manniken-pis,[40] whom Ensor wanted to dress as an artist and to whom he alluded in his 1887 self-portrait etching of "The Pisser."[41]

It was mentioned in an earlier chapter that Ensor used Rops's motif of the skeleton as one of many sources of inspirations for his use of that symbol. Mirabeau had pointed out that Rops was always reducing people to skeletons[42] and Rops reminisced about Baudelaire: "Our first meeting was

[39] John Gregory Bourke, *Scatalogic Rites of All Nations* (Washington, D.C.: W. H. Lowdermilk, 1891); (reprinted, New York: Johnson Reprint, 1968), p. 431, n. 1.

[40] Ibid., "The prevalence of phallic worship all over Flanders should be adverted to in the mentioning of the 'manniken' of Brussels" (p. 166). "[It] . . . may have superseded some long since forgotten diety . . ." (p. 165).

[41] In general the Manniken-pis can be seen to represent Belgium's spirited resistance to outside influences, and it is significant that Ensor linked that

figure with the painter: "I ask you for a painter's costume for the Manniken-pis. . . . Long live Manniken-pis, the splashing baron, the mascot of bold painters, the tiny god ogled by our sisters . . ." (Ensor, *Mes Écrits*, pp. 211-212). Ensor had spoken those words in a 1929 speech, "Discours aux masques loyaux et autres," and his choice of the words "le baron cracheur," the splashing baron, is amusing and pointed, since 1929 was the year in which Ensor was awarded that honor and made baron by King Albert.

[42] Cited from *La Plume* by Philippe Roberts-Jones, *Beyond Time and*

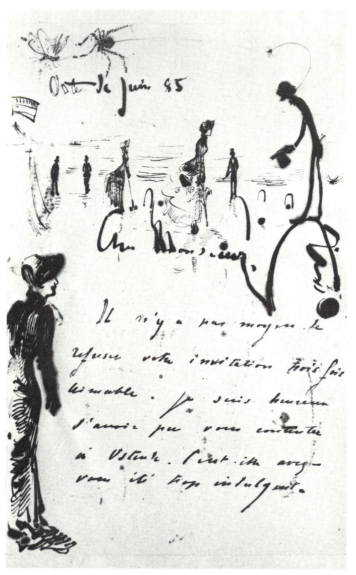

FIG. 70. Photograph of an Ensor letter, 1885.

encompassed by a strange love, a love for the primary christallographic form and a passion for the skeleton."[43]

Skeletons appear early in Rops's work, in the upper right of his 1858 cover for Charles De Coster's *Flemish Legends*, where the supine body of a skeleton has fallen victim to a skeletonized vulture, and in the bottom right, where a skeleton holds an emblematic shield with the banner "Nul ne feut contre moi." In the 1876 lithograph "The Waterloo Medal" the dead soldiers are skeletons arising from a graveyard (Fig. 68). They grab, press, and gesticulate in a staccato manner of energy and movement, and their persistence precludes any self-righteous glorification of hero and country, despite what the title of the print might imply.[44] In Ensor's 1903 "Skeletons Playing Billiards," Rops's animation of the skeleton is made to serve Ensor's own sense of irreverence (Fig. 69). Skeletons walk up walls, shoot pool upside down, and fly through the air. They show a sense of community in an exclusive club that has reduced its membership to the "bare bones" of a select elite.[45]

Ensor's illustrated correspondence was also inspired by Rops. A letter dated "June 85" showed croquet on the beach (Fig. 70). At the left a tent appears, a small boat sails by, and below, a large female figure dominates the page. On the right Ensor's silhouette stands on a giant wicket and he doffs his

Place; Non-Realist Painting in the Nineteenth Century (Oxford: Oxford University Press, 1978), p. 167.

[43] Quoted in Legrand, *Symbolism in Belgium*, p. 35.

[44] Hoffmann discusses the Rops print and links it to Gillray in "Notes on the Iconography of Félicien Rops," *Burlington Magazine* 123 (January-June 1981): 210.

[45] The inscription reads "à Mme Lambotte, en souvenir des parties de billard." Emma Lambotte, wife of Dr. Albin Lambotte, became Ensor's friend in the early 1900s. She was an amateur painter and art critic who bought his paintings. See Georges Hermans, "Un 'Cahier Ensor' d'Emma Lambotte," *Bulletin des Musées Royaux des Beaux-Arts de Belgique* 20

top hat toward a feminine profile. Other male figures with top hats stand nearby. A long strand of web that echoes the wicket's shape connects Ensor's neck to the body of a spider. Above the date, a huge spider follows closely behind its prey, a large winged insect, either a darning needle or a butterfly.[46]

Rops's undated etching for a poem entitled "The Fan" probably served as a prototype, most obviously for the cropped female figure at the left, who holds a croquet mallet and looks toward the male and female figures who stand near the shore (Fig. 71). The fan, an aid for flirtation and sexual entrapment, was used by Mallarmé as the subject for several poems[47] and may have inspired this particular poem. The illustration shows the fan three times: twice in a woman's hand held near her face, and once metamorphosized into the fluttering wings of a beautiful butterfly seen at the lower left of the composition.

Ensor's letter was addressed to a M. Van Cutsem in Blankenberge. In it he speaks of paintings he had worked on since their visit: flower paintings, a seascape, and a self-portrait. Then he answers an invitation to dinner with the warning that although his health is returning, unhappily he will be a wretched table companion. He will not eat or drink and he doesn't know what causes his difficulty.[48] If there were a connection between the content of the letter and Ensor's

FIG. 71. Félicien Rops. *L'Eventail*, n.d.

(1971): 85-121, in which her letters to the artist are reproduced. Lydia Schoonbaert has compared Ensor's drawing with an 1899 work by the Japanese artist, Kawanabe Kiosa. See "Gazette des Beaux-Arts en The Studio als inspiratiebronnen voor James Ensor," *Jaarboek van het Koninklijk Museum voor Schone Kunsten*, Antwerp, 1978: 217.

[46] Also reproduced in Frank Patrick Edebau, *La Maison de James Ensor* (Brussels: Connaissance, 1957), p. 7.

[47] *Stephane Mallarmé: Oeuvres complètes* (Paris: Bibliothèque de la Pléiade, 1945), pp. 57-58, 107-110.

[48] This letter is located at the Ensor Museum in Ostend. I am indebted to Mr. Frank Edebau for supplying me with a typed text.

drawing, one could make a lighthearted guess at "malaise d'amour," but in point of fact Ensor complained of illnesses in numerous letters during the next few years.

It is tempting to postulate that the woman Ensor greets on his letter and the dragonfly his spider chases are meant to suggest a specific person. Since he had not yet met Augusta Boogaerts in 1885, Mariette Rousseau comes to mind, especially because she appears later as the dragonfly in two of Ensor's 1888 prints, "Peculiar Insects" (Fig. 28) and "Small Bizarre Figures."

In 1884 Ensor had drawn a spider connected to the back of his neck by a curving line in a letter to Octave Maus. There Ensor stood alone, with his hat held in his hand as in the 1885 drawing.[49] The text of the letter reveals that Ensor couldn't go to Brussels, but that he had several suggestions about who should be included in Les XX's exhibition.[50]

From Grandville and Griset to Dostoyevsky and Kafka, insects have been associated with human beings in nineteenth-century art and literature.[51] In 1880 and 1881 Odilon Redon drew spiders with human faces in the middles of their bodies[52] and in 1866 Mallarmé wrote of ". . . the center of myself, where I cling like a sacred spider to the principal threads already spun from my mind."[53]

Gisèle Ollinger-Zinque described the spider as trying to escape Ensor on the 1884 letter, "it symbolizes the worries and despair that plagued Ensor at the time he wrote this letter."[54] This explanation seems questionable in light of the 1885 drawing where it is clear that the spider pursues a dragonfly or butterfly. Since Ensor doffs his hat in both, one might suppose that the spider has been freed from the hat that hid it when the hat was on Ensor's head, but rather than a negative symbol, the spider can be seen as Ensor's playful, personal symbol for an aspect of himself, a symbol much like Whistler's butterfly.

One of Ensor's most intimate statements of self-revelation is a painting entitled "Self-Portrait in a Flowered Hat" (Pl. 5). Although it is dependent upon a number of sources, none is more crucial than the debt to Félicien Rops. It is signed and dated 1883, but Marcel De Maeyer has shown that the felt hat was added in 1887 or 1888.[55] Rubens' famous hatted self-portraits have often been mentioned as the prototypes for this painting, as well as for Ensor's 1899 version, "Self-Portrait Surrounded by Masks" (Fig. 72).

The "Self-Portrait in a Flowered Hat" shows Ensor at his most appealing: the gaze is direct but gentle, and the head tilts downward slightly. The mustache curls upward toward soft, brown eyes, while the large coral-colored feathers fall in a soft arc framing his face. In a 1977 article in *Artforum*, I suggested that the flowers surrounding the headband are a reference to flower symbolism as an equation with sexual maturity, thus linking Ensor with Rembrandt's "Flora" and Antoine Wiertz's "Rosebud."[56] Ensor used flowers with sim-

---

[49] Although the letter is not dated, Ollinger-Zinque states that it was written between October 12 and October 19, 1884 (*Ensor by Himself*, p. 101, fig. 15).

[50] Besides several Belgians, including Toorop, Mellery, and Meunier, he requested that the Impressionists Degas, Monet, Renoir, Sisley, and Pissarro be included (Legrand, "Lettres à Octave Maus": 21).

[51] Grandville (1803-1847) was the forerunner in envisioning a world populated with bizarre anthropomorphic plants, insects, and mollusks. See Pierre Jules Hetzel, *Scènes de la vie privée et publique des animaux* (Paris: J. Hetzel et Paulin, 1842), but Darwin's theories popularized such investigations through his 1859 *Origin of the Species*.

[52] "The Weeping Spider" (ca. 1880) charcoal, 19½" x 14¾", Amsterdam, private collection, and "The Spider" (1881) charcoal, 22½" x 17¾", Paris, The Louvre.

[53] Quoted in Guy Michaud, *Mallarmé*, translated by Marie Collins and Bertha Humez (New York: New York University Press, 1965), p. 51.

[54] Ollinger-Zinque, *Ensor by Himself*, p. 101.

[55] "Ensor au chapeau fleuri," *L'Art Belge*, special Ensor number (December 1965), 41-44.

[56] "Ensor in His Milieu": 62.

FIG. 72. Ensor. *Self-Portrait Surrounded by Masks*, 1899.

Fig. 73. Félicien Rops. *Diaboli virtus in lumbis.*

ilar suggestion in several paintings of women, among them the commissioned 1889 "Portrait of an Old Woman Surrounded by Masks," in which the association of flowers with sexual availability became a personal insult.[57] In his own depiction long, blue ribbons have been added to the grey hat: they move down the front of the sloping brim in a strange manner, almost like rivulets of rain. Their thin shape and wiggly motion is somewhat similar to Munch's depictions of sperm swimming around the periphery of his "Madonna" pictures.[58]

There is a tradition of linking a flowered or feathered hat with a skeleton. In sixteenth-century German prints, Death wears a large multifeathered felt hat, and a skeleton wears a feathered hat in Grandville's interpretation of "Death and the Woodcutter," seen in the 1838 "Fables de la Fontaine." In Daumier's 1871 lithograph of "Peace, an Idyll," a skeleton plays pipes and wears a flowered hat (Fig. 33) and even Titian's "Death in Armor" holds a feathered helmet in its hand (Fig. 42). The hat Ensor used in his 1887/1888 painting can still be seen in his apartment over the tourist shop in Ostend: it is flowerless, but with a long coral-colored feather. When I took a photograph in 1977 it had been placed atop a skull, which rested upon an Oriental vase.

Why did Ensor add the flowered and feathered hat to his self-portrait in 1887 or 1888? I propose that it was an act inspired by a Rops print, "Diaboli virtus in lumbis," the 1887

[57] Ibid. Farmer relates that she was his hairdresser's mother (*Ensor*, p. 26), and Tannenbaum states it was commissioned to be executed from the photograph of the man's dead wife (*James Ensor*, p. 109).

[58] A comparison with the later painting shows that by 1899 there has been a change of mood and Ensor envisions himself as a different man. He wears a stiff dark red hat with ungainly red-pink flowers and an upturned brim. From the hat band a red feather curls upward and away from a mottled, pasty face. Ensor's eyes have become piercing but lifeless, and their cold gaze suggests his awareness of his position within a crowd of grotesques.

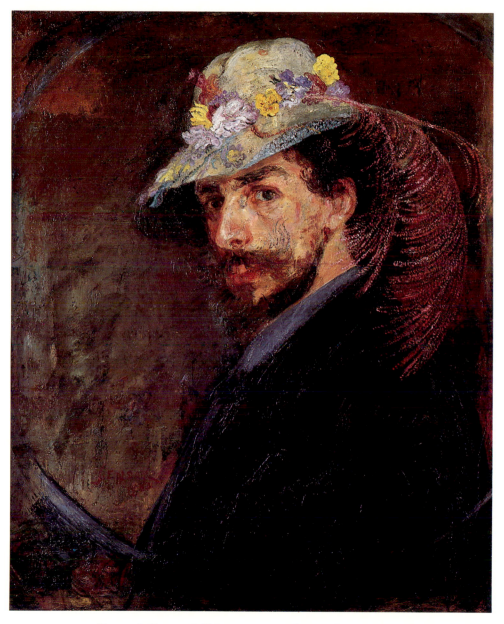

PLATE 5. Ensor. *Self-Portrait in a Flowered Hat*, 1883.

PLATE 6. Ensor. *Skeletons Trying to Warm Themselves*, 1889.

frontispiece for Péladan's *Initiation Sentimentale* in *La Dé-cadence latine* (Fig. 73).[59] There a female figure is seen from the back, her round, full buttocks enhanced by a tight, black corset. Flowers are intertwined in her hair, but the upper part of her body is skeletal and wings sprout from her shoulder blades. She stands on a pelvic bone that can be seen as a giant insect with outstretched wings, and she carries a bow and arrows in a quiver. At the end of her skeletal arm she holds aloft a severed head wearing a soft, feathered hat. The face is youthful and darkly handsome with a short, pointed beard and upturned mustache. Its features record a frozen expression of surprise and horror.[60] The pelvic bone is the foundation from which this female rises, her magical powers hiding her evilness and transforming the lower part of her body into a voluptuous promise that belies its ultimate goal: decapitation-castration. The inscription from St. Augustine, which in free translation reads "The loins are the strength of the devil," leaves no doubt about Rops's message.

The combination of physical flesh and a revealed skeletal structure dates back to the Middle Ages and depictions of "Frau Welt," who can be found on the south portal of the Cathedral of Worms, where her lovely frontal view is coun-tered by a back view of a body eaten by maggots and crawling with toads.[61] She is a seductress promising beauty and happiness and delivering only decay and death. In an 1881 drawing entitled "At the Corner of the Street," Rops showed a female skeleton dressed in evening clothes luring a male victim by hiding her skull under the provocative stare of a beautiful mask.[62]

There is the suggestion of this combination in the nude female figure from the "Initiation Sentimentale" print, although it is only the upper part of her body that is bare bone. Its fleshy posterior relates to Wiertz's titillating painting of satanic instruction, "The Young Sorceress," which shows a Rubenesque young witch blindfolded and clasping a broom-stick between her legs, while an old hag consults a manual, and excited faces in the background watch the incantation (Fig. 74).[63] Rops had taken inspiration from that rear view for the 1895 "Little Sorceress" (Fig. 75), in which a nude figure with broomstick in position between her legs stands before an open book, her body encased in a black corset like the one worn in the 1887 print.

Ensor's self-portrait with its soft, feathered hat bears a remarkable resemblance to the severed head and hat in Rops's

[59] Exteens, *L'Oeuvre gravé*, no. 516. Edith Hoffmann discusses the print in "Notes": 213 and 218: "The book was published in 1887, but the picture must have been invented much earlier, for Rops mentioned it in an undated letter to Noilly as a possible frontispiece for the *Album du Diable*, which they planned to publish after the completion of *Les 100 légers croquis* (1881)" (Exteens, p. 218).

[60] In Rops's "Modernité" from 1883 (Exteens, *L'Oeuvre gravé*, no. 332), a woman holds up a platter with the head of a bespectacled man; a ribbon connected to the decapitated head has the word "Académie" written across it. In 1896 Ensor would include his own head on a platter with the sign "Art Ensor" in "The Dangerous Cooks," a drawing of Ensor's critics about to dine at his personal expense. See Ollinger-Zinque, *Ensor by Himself*, p. 130.

[61] "Frau Welt, or the Perfume of Decay," in Wolfgang Lederer, *The Fear*

of Women (New York: Harcourt Brace Jovanovich, 1968), pp. 35-43.

[62] Reproduced in Hoffmann, "Notes": 208, fig. 24. Legrand has observed that "Romantics and Symbolists both loved to confront Death by Woman—the latter incarnating the passing pleasures of the senses—in the same way in which Vanities of the 16th and 17th centuries depicted flowers, an hour-glass and a death's head, all in juxtaposition" (*Symbolism in Belgium*, p. 33). Other literature on "Death and Eros" as a theme in art includes Hoff-mann, cited above, and the following: Hofstatter, *Symbolismus*, pp. 177-180; Reinhold Heller, *The Earthly Chimera and the Femme Fatale: Fear of Woman in Nineteenth-Century Art* (Chicago: The University of Chicago, David and Alfred Smart Gallery, 1981); Patrick Bade, *Femme Fatale: Images of Evil and Fascinating Women* (New York: Mayflower Books, 1979).

[63] An article on the painting by E. Pittore, "La Sorcière de M. Wiertz," can be found in *Uylenspiegel*, no. 36 (October 4, 1857), pp. 2-3.

FIG. 74. Antoine Wiertz.
La Jeune Sorciere, 1857.

FIG. 75. Félicien Rops.
Petite Sorcière, 1895.

tache in emulation of the mustache on the severed head.

A Mallarmé poem may have inspired Rops to depict the head in his print with a soft, feathered hat. As part of the series "Poésies," which Rops illustrated during that same year of 1887, "Le Guignon" ("The Unlucky," or "The Jinx") described a booted, dwarf skeleton crowned with a feathered, felt hat and went on to invoke "the infinity of vast bitterness."[64]

Eighteen eighty-seven had been a crucial year for Ensor. It was the year his father died and the year he drew himself being led from bed by a winged skeleton on the Christmas day letter. It was also the year in which he worked on his mocking painting of "The Entry of Christ into Brussels," and a time of rejection by his peers in Les XX. The severed head in Rops's print could have attracted Ensor by its facial similarity to his own appearance and by its pointedly appropriate punishment. In the year 1888 he met Augusta Boogaerts and the year that he included Mariette Rousseau in "Peculiar Insects," the etching inspired by a love poem of a beetle and a fly.

Whether overpainted in 1887 or 1888, it is the flowers and the ribbons that make "Self-Portrait in a Flowered Hat" distinctly Ensor's: they speak positively for his sexuality and his availability, and although all the warnings from Rops and Wiertz and countless others are acknowledged, they are quietly countered by the sensitive, sincere expression of one who had come of age in 1887, not only as an artist, but as a person open to all experience as well.

1887 print. Not only had Ensor added the hat to an earlier portrait, but he had also altered his face by adding flamelike bluish brushstrokes that curled upward from his brown mus-

[64] "Et ce squelette nain, coiffé d'un feutre à plume / Et botté, dont / l'aisselle à pour poils vrais des vers, / Est pour eux l'infini de la vaste / amer-

tume." *Mallarmé*, introduced and edited by Anthony Hartley (Baltimore: Penguin Books, 1965), p. 10.

IV

LITERATURE AS INSPIRATION FOR ENSOR'S ART

In J.-K. Huysmans's novel *À Rebours* (1884), the protagonist Des Esseintes showed his contempt for and defiance of conventional society by retreating from physical reality. Suffering from frequent illness and eschewing travel, he immersed himself in literature and created reality on his own intellectual terms in a mental world of rarefied experience that he directed from the interior of his cloistered surroundings.

Ensor was a bit like Des Esseintes in that his own insular lifestyle affected the development of his idiosyncratic art. He scarcely traveled; he was often ill; and it appears that he preferred literature and writing to the companionship and interchange of ideas with other artists.

From Ensor's studio in Ostend a trip to Brussels by train was under an hour; Paris was only a few hours away, and London was easily accessible from Ostend by boat and a short train ride. Yet it wasn't until 1892, after Ensor had already created his greatest masterpieces, that he spent four days in London. Except for two or three quick excursions to Paris and a short journey to Holland to visit the museums of Amsterdam and Haarlem, there were no other trips made outside of Belgium.[1]

In choosing not to travel, Ensor withheld himself from contact with foreign artists. He could have exchanged ideas with the continental avant-garde, as his compatriot and friend Emile Verhaeren did with Rodin, Signac, and Seurat,[2] but he chose instead to remain in artistic isolation. Even at home Ensor's friendships among Les XX and with other Belgian artists were few.[3] It may be that he wanted to keep his art as free from contemporary artistic influences as possible in order to maintain the strength of his own vision. And perhaps, too, his fellow painters were alienated by his opinionated manner and aggressive behavior, as when he attacked Khnopff for what he considered plagiarism of his own painting.

Having isolated himself from other artists, Ensor found

---

[1] Emile Verhaeren, *James Ensor* (Brussels: G. Van Oest, 1908), p. 86.

[2] For example, in letters written in 1889. See Emile Verhaeren, *À Marthe Verhaeren; deux cent dix-neuf lettres inédites, 1889-1916* (Paris: Mercure de France, 1951), p. 149.

[3] Willy Finch, an ardent anglophile, appears with Mitche in Ensor's "Russian in Music." An early friendship with Théo Hannon cooled when Hannon became a critic (Farmer, *James Ensor*, p. 20). Guillaume Vogels, a Plein-airist, was a third friend during Ensor's early years.

his most ardent supporters and friends to be Belgian writers: Emile Verhaeren, Eugène Demolder, Théo Hannon, Maurice Maeterlinck, Georges Eekhoud, Edmond Picard, Octave Maus and Karel van de Woestyne. Ensor continued his relationships with writers up until his death. The books left from his personal collection, poetry, novels and nonfiction, contain handwritten inscriptions to Ensor and they date well into the twentieth century.

In an interview in the month of his death, November 1949, Ensor chose to describe his art as "... very much inclined toward literature. My paintings wander around painting."[4] He had written of his debt to literature in a 1928 letter to André de Ridder, who was planning a monograph on Ensor:

I read, like everyone, and reread the classical writers during the months of expedient slavery spent at the Brussels Academy from 1877 to 1880 and then: Goethe, Cervantes, Dante, Milton, Shakespeare, Schopenhauer, Leopardi, Hugo. . . . Ariosto's "Roland Furioso" amused me greatly.[5]

Balzac, Hoffmann, and Poe are mentioned, the last two with qualifiers:

I had already devoured and strongly tasted the great Balzac. . . . I could read the "Extraordinary Stories" of Edgar Poe, attracted at first by the title of the book. I read Hoffmann, less interesting, and did not like his poorly joined mixtures of reality and fantasy. . . . With regard to Poe, there is only an imaginative Anglo-Belgian sympathy and not an influence.[6]

Ensor approached literature as he did the visual arts, with adamant likes and dislikes: "The writers of the eighteenth century tell me nothing of any worth, their uniform and monotonous style bores and tires me. I no longer read [them]. Certain modern authors have almost nothing to say to me. I hate their style and their tedious opinions. . . ."[7] He thought himself a writer, and it is telling that when his artistic powers weakened, he wrote more. With the exception of his personal letters, the 1882 "Reflections on Art" and the 1884 "Three Weeks at the Academy," his published essays and various "discours" and tributes were written in the late 1890s and into the first four decades of the twentieth century. Words were chosen for their dramatic effect; they could be comic, cruel, or passionate, with dramatic exaggerations of strange-sounding juxtapositions. He loved puns, and occasionally nonsense words appeared, chosen for their strange sounds.[8]

Like an artwork, which is a tangible symbol of communication, the words on a page became for Ensor the expressive symbols he was no longer able to create with paint, charcoal, or an etching needle:

I love to draw beautiful words, like trumpets of light. . . . I adore you, words who are sensitive to our sufferings, words in red and lemon yellow, words in steel-blue colour of certain insects . . . subtle words of fragrant roses and seaweed, prickly words of sky-blue wasps . . . words spat out by the sands of the sea . . . discreet words whispered by fishes in the pink ears of shells . . . evil words, festive words, tornado and storm-

---

[4] "... très porté vers la littérature. Mes peintures se promènent à l'autour de la peinture," J. P. Hodin, "James Ensor: On the Ultimate Questions of Life," *The Dilemma of Being Modern* (London: Routledge and Kegan Paul, 1956), p. 37.

[5] *Lettres à André de Ridder*, p. 56.

[6] Ibid.

[7] Ibid.

[8] Consult Ensor, *Mes Écrits*. Tannenbaum has commented upon Ensor's fondness for strange words, "Ensor apparently never read Swift, and this is a pity; he would have found in the Dubliner even more of himself than he found in Poe; Ensor adored words like 'Houyhnhnm' and 'Brobdingnag'" (p. 118).

tossed words . . . the wise words of children . . . without rhythm or reason, I love you! I love you![9]

In *L'Oeuvre*, Émile Zola maintained that only through language could a certain spirit be maintained that would illuminate a given period.[10] However, Ensor's art succeeded in achieving this end. In reconstructing the wide range of literary influences on Ensor through books, poems, short stories, and articles and reviews in journals, it becomes evident that Ensor's art, although it failed to produce a school of followers, did encapsulate many of the major preoccupations of contemporary life.

Ensor's art reflects a very significant debt to historical and contemporary literature, but his art cannot be called literary in the narrowest sense of the word. Baudelaire had spoken of the arts in his century as supplementing each other, "by lending each other new strength and new reserves."[11] Unlike nineteenth-century painters who transformed a specific literary scene onto canvas and thus related a story visually, Ensor absorbed ideas and descriptions and reflected the spirit of his time. He borrowed widely from his own Flemish literary tradition, from French sources and from English, German, and American writers. These diverse literary interests aided his increasing artistic flexibility: his art has defied pigeonholing into any one given movement; his style has ranged from realism to caricature, from the beautiful to the grotesque, and from appealing poetic nuance to the crude vernacular.

Some literary influences were more important than others; some cannot be proven and may be merely fortuitous coincidence, revealing the shared reflections of an age. For example, an examination of specific literary precedents shows that the work of Balzac and—despite Ensor's disclaimer—Poe had a pointed impact upon Ensor's art, whereas that of other writers, notably Villiers de l'Isle-Adam and Hoffmann, had a less direct impact but clearly influenced the direction of his art. Beyond these individual foreign writers, Belgian literature in general, from the ninteenth-century novelists Charles De Coster and S. Henry Berthoud to Ensor's contemporary Albert Mockel, had a profound effect. In addition, articles in avant-garde Belgian literary periodicals were a constant source of inspiration. Because of the specific nature of these influences, they will not be dealt with in this order. Balzac and Villiers de l'Isle-Adam will be considered first; Poe and Hoffmann follow; and finally, the importance of Belgian writers will be discussed.

Balzac served Ensor as inspiration for an art that dealt with the church as a contemporary institution and with the spiritual despair that surrounded it. As a child Ensor had been introduced to Balzac by his parents, ". . . the great Balzac, the hard working, piercing, and magnificent Balzac, the glorious dreamer, and my father admired him and my mother kept him and myself, I have been reading him since childhood."[12]

Balzac's short story "Jesus Christ in Flanders" is said to have influenced the subject matter of "The Entry of Christ into Brussels,"[13] but the story's impact on Ensor's work is more extensive. Ensor had reminisced about the tale in a

[9] Quoted from Walter Sorell, *The Other Face: The Mask in the Arts* (New York: Bobbs-Merrill, 1973), p. 63.

[10] See Theodore Reff, "Degas and the Literature of His Time," in *French Nineteenth-Century Painting and Literature*, edited by Ulriche Finke (New York: Harper and Row, 1972), p. 197.

[11] Quoted in Jean Seznec, *Literature and the Visual Arts in Nineteenth-Century France* (London: University of Hull, 1962), p. 3.

[12] Ensor, *Lettres à André de Ridder*, p. 56.

[13] Tannenbaum, *James Ensor*, p. 78.

1925 speech honoring the Belgian writer Karel van de Woestyne: "You all know the most delightful of the great Balzac's stories: "Jesus Christ in Flanders."[14] The reference was especially appropriate, for Balzac had been the inspiration for a significant number of Belgian writers, from Charles De Coster to Ensor's contemporaries Camille Lemonnier, Georges Eekhoud, and Eugène Demolder. Balzac's influence on the latter is readily evident in a story about Christianity, "La Cité morte dans l'or," published in his 1893 book, *Les Récits de Nazareth*.[15]

"Jesus Christ in Flanders" has been called Balzac's most complete personal religious statement and an illustration of his attitude toward the church as an institution.[16] The story's narrator explains that he had traveled to Belgium in despair over the French Revolution of 1830. Belgium provided an ironic contrast to France's political situation, particularly as Belgium celebrated its unification in that same year. Furthermore, Balzac chose to write about Ensor's own Ostend as the site of the Second Coming; he had Christ appear on the beach and leave His holy footprints in the sand. Ensor's own insularity was therefore encouraged by the French novelist's reverence for Belgium and for its long northern tradition of personal piety.

In Balzac's story an ugly harridan becomes a beautiful haloed maiden, thus in metaphorical terms transforming the Church as it stood in the nineteenth century back to its golden, medieval age when it inspired art and learning as well as offering spiritual comfort. When the vision fades and the maiden grows old again, Balzac's regret is genuine and militant: "Such was the crisis in which I saw the finest, the greatest, the truest, the most creative of all powers. . . . we must defend the CHURCH!"[17] Balzac had recalled a previous time when there were "thousands of cathedrals," and around them "thousands of people squeezed together, like ants around their nests."[18] Huysmans's *À Rebours* contains similar imagery:

. . . the bourgeois were guzzling like picknickers from paper bags among the imposing ruins of the church—ruins which had become a place of assignation, a pile of debris defiled by unspeakable jokes and scandalous jests. . . . Could it be that this slime would go on spreading until it covered with its pestilential filth this old world where now only seeds of iniquity sprang up and only harvests of shame were gathered?[19]

Ensor reacted to Balzac, as well as to Huysmans, in his 1886 etching, "The Cathedral" (Fig. 76).[20] Following Balzac's and Huysmans's descriptions the masses are squeezed together, and emerging from their midst is a Gothic cathedral

[14] Ensor, *Mes Écrits*, p. 96.

[15] *Les Récits de Nazareth* (Brussels: Ch. Vos, Editor, 1893). Ensor owned a copy that had been inscribed by Demolder, "to my dear JE as a token of sincere friendship" (Ensor archive, Musée des Beaux-Arts, Ostend).

[16] Consult E. J. Oliver, *Balzac the European* (London and New York: Sheed and Ward, 1959), p. 116.

[17] Honoré de Balzac, "Jesus-Christ en Flandre," in *La Comédie humaine: études philosophiques*, Vol. IX (Paris: Librairie Gallimard, 1950), p. 266. The beginning of Balzac's story, rather than this later section, is discussed by James N. Elesh in *James Ensor, The Complete Graphic Work*, Vol. 141 of *The Illustrated Bartsch*, edited by Walter L. Strauss (New York: Abaris

Books, 1982). In this two-volume edition of Ensor's complete graphic oeuvre, Elesh suggests that Balzac's storm at sea served as inspiration for the etchings "Christ Calming the Tempest" (also the title of an oil painting) and "Christ in the Boat" (Vol. 2, p. 68). Also consult Loys Delteil, *Le Peintre graveur illustré (XIX et XX siècles)*, Vol. XIX (Paris, 1925), no. 5. Elesh's fine book was not available when I wrote my text.

[18] Balzac "Jesus-Christ en Flandre," pp. 265-266.

[19] Joris-Karl Huysmans, *Against Nature*, translated by Robert Baldick (Baltimore: Penguin Books, 1959; reprint 1966), p. 219.

[20] Elesh has also observed that Balzac's description may have been utilized for the crowd in "The Cathedral" (*James Ensor*, Vol. 2, p. 68).

FIG. 76. Ensor. *The Cathedral*, 1886.

FIG. 77. Ensor. *The Cathedral*, 1896.

of imposing height. Its twin towers, aspiring toward heaven, are cropped by the top of the page, however, and the building itself, through its delineation by delicate wavering lines, hints at its precarious existence. David Farmer has called it a typical Ensorian statement about society's morality: "... playing off the noble structure of the church—an exalted but rare achievement of mankind—against a group of tiny masked faces. His needle is as meticulously applied to the delineation of the impassive crowd as it is to the skeletal gothicism of the cathedral."[21]

There were actually two different versions of the print: the original plate from 1886 and another from 1896 (Fig. 77 and detail, Fig. 78). The evidence for this second version comes from a letter Ensor wrote in 1897 in which he mentions that he had the "strength to recopy exactly the Cathedral onto a new copper plate."[22] But he went on to observe that the new etching was not exactly identical to the earlier one; that the drawing was less elaborate and the biting was different.[23] In discussing the second plate Taevernier observed that two well-preserved prints suggest that the plate slipped forward in printing and produced "a breathtaking effect of vibration and a duplication of the signature."[24] Since there were at least two of this kind, the implication is that Ensor deliberately experimented. Taevernier suggested this was done to have the church "vibrate in the sparkling light."[25] An alternative is that Ensor was striving for a sense of movement that would better illustrate the church's contemporary state of impermanence. Evidence for this different interpretation lies with an event that appears to have gone undetected in Ensor literature: the year in which Ensor made the new plate was the year that the cathedral in Ostend, the

[21] Farmer, *Ensor*, p. 24.   [22] Taevernier, *James Ensor*, p. 261.
[23] Ibid.   [24] Ibid., p. 257.   [25] Ibid., p. 259.

FIG. 78. Ensor. *Detail of The Cathedral,* 1896.

FIG. 79. Photograph of The Cathedral of Sts. Peter and Paul, Ostend, 1978.

Church of Saints Peter and Paul, was destroyed by fire. In the 1897 edition of Baedeker's *Belgium and Holland* it was reported that the church was in the process of being rebuilt in the Gothic style.[26]

Ensor's new plate can be seen as a memorial to the old church, a view of a magnificent, yet disintegrating derelict before the conflagration. This observation becomes even more obvious after a trip to Ostend and a walk around the rebuilt cathedral. In the print, especially from the first plate, there

is the suggestion of a boat with a tall sail at the left of the church.[27] Ensor's view of the church is from the back, looking toward the east. Therefore, geographically it duplicates the actual location of the cathedral and the boat basins that run north to south at the eastern entrance to the city. In the print the crowd surrounds the back and sides of the church in an area that is now filled with buildings, but a photograph taken randomly from the opposite side (Fig. 79) and a map of the area reveal the similarities to Ensor's print.

[26] Karl Baedeker, *Belgium and Holland* (Leipzig: Karl Baedeker, 1897), p. 4. Elesh has informed me that the first "Cathedral" plate was damaged. A new plate would therefore have been needed if Ensor wished to comment through a print. Baedeker also mentions that a mausoleum was to be erected adjoining the church as a monument to Queen Louise. In 1897 Ensor drew a "Project for a Chapel Dedicated to SS. Peter and Paul," in which the saints

flanked a female figure who was shown in an attitude of prayer, kneeling before a fanciful monument. It has often been noted that the position and pose recall Van Eyck's drawing of St. Barbara.

[27] Wilhelm Fraenger pointed to masts that suggest a distant harbor in his article "Die Kathedrale," *Die graphischen Künste* 49, no. 4 (1926); reprinted in the catalogue, *Ensor—ein Maler*, p. 158.

In "Die Kathedrale," first published in 1926[28] and reprinted in 1932, Wilhelm Fraenger brought up numerous questions about the meaning of Ensor's print. He asked about the marching soldiers in the midst of the people: was this a military parade or a protest? Were the soldiers trying to disperse the crowd; was there a fight for the cathedral's treasure, or were the townspeople assembled for a carnival?[29] Fraenger reasoned that it might be both a military parade and a carnival celebration because of the banners held among the soldiers, the flags hanging from towers, and the costumed people. But he questioned why the people in the foreground were oblivious to the marchers.[30] He concluded that the cathedral was the hero of the work, even though the building was seen as a skeleton, and he also ended with the observation that Ensor would produce the same quintessential, macabre statement in the 1889 etching "My Portrait Skeletonized."[31]

In an article on the cathedral as a contemporary motif, Donat de Chapeaurouge quoted Victor Hugo's *Notre-Dame de Paris:*

The cathedral . . . eludes the priest and falls to the artist's power, the popular covering barely allows one to guess the existence of the religious underpinnings, sometimes a portal, a facade, a church presents a symbolic meaning totally foreign to the creed, or even hostile to the church.[32]

De Chapeaurouge discussed Ensor's print and saw a prototype in Meryon's 1854 etching of "Notre Dame." He concluded with the observation that if we combine the ideas of Hugo with those of Viollet-Le-Duc, who saw the church's importance as crucial for more than religion,[33] we can imagine that Ensor had seen the people in his print as literally holding up the cathedral, but that the building and the people, in their vibrating forms, were working against each other.[34] For Chapeaurouge, Ensor's church was not necessarily a ruin: with its slanting nave listing against the left tower and a right tower that is incomplete, it could be seen as an unfinished building, one that does not work as an organic whole.[35]

There may be a question as to whether Ensor meant to suggest a skeleton, or a shell of a church, similar to its abandoned counterpart in the sand at Ostend, or whether he meant to refer to a new cathedral in the process of being constructed, however inadequately, to replace the old one lost in the fire. What Ensor has succeeded in doing, however, is to transform the materiality of solid stone into a delicate filigree that contrasts sharply with the coarse grotesques below. Tradition, process, and the passage of time are the subjects here.[36] Later Monet will disintegrate stone through the optical magic of light and atmosphere in his "Rouen Cathedral" series, but in those paintings humanity was generally absent. Ensor's theme is closer to the one suggested

[28] Fraenger, "Die Kathedrale": 81-98.

[29] Fraenger, "Die Kathedrale," in *James Ensor-Festschrift zur ersten deutschen Ensor-Austellung* (Hanover: Kestener-Gesellschaft, 1932), p. 54.

[30] Ibid., p. 55.   [31] Ibid., pp. 67 and 68.

[32] "Die Kathedrale als modernes Bildthema," *Jahrbuch der Hamburger Kunstsammlungen* 18 (1973): 163, n. 37.

[33] "The cathedral is not only a church suitable to holy service, it preserves, and preserved even better during the first centuries of Christianity, the characteristic of a sacred tribunal. . . . Assemblies were held there which had a purely political character; it goes without saying that religion almost

always interfered in these large civil or military gatherings" (Ibid., 164, n. 40).

". . . they are above all national buildings . . . symbol of French nationality, the first and the most powerful attempt towards unity . . ." (Ibid., 164, n. 42).

[34] Ibid., 164.   [35] Ibid., 164.

[36] Julius Kaplan suggested that the cathedral may be a metaphor for Ensor's art: "There is no definitive explanation for the etching, but the cathedral may refer to Ensor's own art, lasting through the ages, towering above the organized masses of society . . . as well as the confused activity

in Rodin's "Cathedral," in which two human hands rise and come together in a gesture of enclosure both active and spiritual, and suggestive of the shape of a church.

Balzac's own symbol for the contemporary Church was a withered specter from the cemetery, a female form, hairless and greenish in complexion, with arms that clacked as she moved. The narrator in "Jesus Christ in Flanders" described the first moments of their encounter: "We were seated in front of a firebox in which the ashes were cold . . . [I] tried to guess the history of her life in examining the old clothes in which she wallowed."[37] In that same vision Balzac's protagonist is shown gigantic statues bearing the placards "History," "Science," and "Literature."[38]

Ensor's 1889 painting, "Skeletons Trying to Warm Themselves" (Pl. 6), shows a scene similar to Balzac's description: three skeletons, their clothing ridiculously large and hanging in heavy folds, huddle around a stove on which a sign reads, "Pas de feu" and under it "en trouverez-vous demain?" Two of the skeletons can be identified by their attributes: a violin and a palette representing music and art. Another stands next to an unlit lamp, suggesting that the "Lamp of Truth" no longer shines.[39] As with Balzac's vision, the open door of the stove, the dark lamp, and the sign suggest that the inspiration and encouragement that nurtured cultural growth had been extinguished. Ensor's sign also raised the question of whether it could be rekindled. It is notable that the inactive skeleton, the one who lies on the floor with his boot protruding from under an ochre-colored smock and his skull

resting on the empty woodbox, is linked with the palette and thus becomes a metaphor for the artist.

The painting's size, just over 25" x 18", and its brilliant color, make it a small masterpiece reminiscent of a fifteenth-century Flemish primitive. Various shades of blue, red, ochre, and pink quietly glow and balance each other as they appear in the clothing and on the walls, the floor and the stove. The color contradicts the written message, and despite the sign the base of the stove radiates with a bright orange light. These additions prompted one critic, a contemporary of Ensor, to write in La Plume:

Ah well! They are not cold. The stove is so exactly painted with violaceous red of burning cast iron that they hold out the palm of the hands and they are warm. You are challenged to perceive, on their colored, sketch-like features, an expression of the least disillusionment.[40]

Other elements of ambiguity can be found in the area above the stove and in the identification of the skeleton who enters from the right background. A cross is suggested by the intersection of the stovepipe and a horizontal bar; the latter may be explained as a dark mark on the opposite wall, but below and within the perimeter of the cross the color has been altered and accentuates the central area. In an 1895 etching of the same subject Ensor continued this emphasis by a series of horizontal lines under the cross that were then countered by vertical lines distinguishing the rest of the wall (Fig. 80). A colored version shows the skeleton in the back-

of individuals . . . (Quoted from "The Religious Subjects of James Ensor, 1877-1900," Revue belge d'archéologie et d'histoire de l'art 31-35 [1962-1966]:189).

[37] Balzac, "Jesus-Christ en Flandre," p. 264.

[38] Ibid., p. 266.

[39] In Eugène Demolder's monograph, James Ensor (Brussels: Paul Lacom-

bez, 1892), he described the painting: "In a cold and bare interior, a rusty stove died out. Before him some strange skeletons are squatting, dressed in ill-matched rags: one holds a violin, the second a lantern, and the other a palette. On the stove a joker wrote a quip with chalk" (p. 14).

[40] Louis Delattre, "L'Enfance d'Ensor, peintre de masques," La Plume (1899): 96.

FIG. 80. Ensor. *Skeletons Trying to Warm Themselves*, 1895.

It is tempting to see this outfit as a vestment of some kind, thus associating the figure with the cross over the stove and reminding us of Balzac's influence with his belief that the Church was a responsible party to the century's cultural emptiness.

The three skeletons who surround the stove are at the same time frighteningly alive and comically amusing. Perhaps it is Ensor's use of props that makes us smile: the huge top hat that overlaps the tiny face, the shiny leather boot next to the much used palette, and the violin and the lamp all work to give the painting a connection with material reality. Whatever the case, Ensor has succeeded in making his tragic protagonists endearing while pathetic, and in doing so he has produced an incredible visual pun: through the bare bones of his skeletons he has captured the true essence, the bottom line of our human condition.

In the 1880s religious themes were to become a major preoccupation for Ensor, and following Balzac's lead they were to become inextricably bound to Ensor's attitudes about social and political life in Belgium. His growing self-identification with martyrs like Christ and St. Anthony, as well as with their counterparts, the devil and his demons, made the presence of these figures requisite in his art. Although Ensor continued to use literature as inspiration, his conflict between self and society assumed such a critical form that his art became aggressively irrational and internalized. In a society that he believed to be in danger of total disintegration and in which the church was a shell of its former self, Ensor would speak through an art guaranteed to shock the bourgeoisie—with caricature, with symbolic references to past history, and with increasingly vicious, coarse, and vulgar scatalogical imagery.

Villiers de l'Isle-Adam was influenced by Honoré Balzac,

ground wearing pink; it clasps its hands in front of its chest in what may be an attitude of prayer, and its outfit has a distinctive scallop in the top layer around the hem. In the painting the pink overblouse has an elaborate collar and perhaps a hanging scarf, which is also suggested in the print.

and a sardonic inscription from the earlier writer was included in Chapter 15 of "Claire Lenoir":

Death is a woman,—
married to the human race,
and faithful.—Where is the
man she betrayed?[41]

"Everything I have done I owe to Villiers de l'Isle-Adam," wrote Ensor's friend, Maurice Maeterlinck.[42] In Paris in 1886 Maeterlinck and Villiers had met nightly, and Villiers is said to have read aloud from his *Contes cruels*.[43] With Villier's death in 1890 Mallarmé gave a two-and-a-half-hour soliloquy at the Cercle artistique et littéraire in Ghent, and Maeterlinck was present.[44] Mallarmé had given the same speech in Antwerp, Liège, Bruges, and at Les XX in Brussels, and Ensor might have attended any of these sessions.[45]

In Ensor literature nothing has been made of the similarities that can be found between the work of Ensor and Villiers. Perhaps this is because of Villier's particularized use of language, which suggests Symbolist painting per se: "[Villiers'] overly specific, nearly univocal use of language makes his mannered prose analogous in its techniques to those of contemporary Decadent painting, both Art Nouveau and Symbolist."[46] Yet in reading Villiers's *Contes cruels* it becomes clear that like Ensor, Villiers was capable of two dif-

ferent kinds of artistic expression: an art of mystery and intrigue, occasionally horrific, but with brilliant poetic nuance, and an art of plebeian vulgarity, pointedly critical of the bourgeoisie.[47] These stories alone, which had appeared piecemeal since 1867 and were published together in 1883, make a notable comparison with Ensor's work and point to specifics that may have influenced his direction.

Crowd scenes are described in several of the stories. In "Vox Populi" the square in front of Notre Dame is filled with a teeming mass, vacuous and blind to spiritual values, reminiscent of Balzac's description in "Jesus Christ in Flanders" and suggestive of Ensor's later etching of "The Cathedral" (Figs. 76 and 77). Carnival revelers wear masks in "Le Convive de dernières fêtes," thus both hiding and unleashing their moral degeneracy. Finally, in the historically inspired "L'Impatience de la foule," a cruelly insensitive mob kills a messenger sent by Leonidas, thus guaranteeing the death of the valiant Spartans who were trying to protect their country, and reminding the reader that the crowd victimizes the superior man.

The long story "Claire Lenoir," first published in 1867 and reissued in the 1887 *Tribulat Bonhomet*, has a description of Claire Lenoir that is tempting to link with Ensor. She is an adulteress described as "droll and sinister," and when she dies her pupils reveal the reflection of her husband bran-

---

[41] *Tribulat Bonhomet* (Paris: Librairie Jose Corti, 1967), p. 184. "La mort est femme,—mariée au genre humain, et fidèle.—Où est l'homme qu'elle a trompé?"

[42] Una Taylor, *Maurice Maeterlinck: A Critical Study* (Port Washington: Kennikat, 1968), pp. 77-78.

[43] Bettina Knapp, *Maurice Maeterlinck* (Boston: Twayne, 1975), p. 24.

[44] W. D. Halls, *Maurice Maeterlinck: A Study of His Life and Thought* (Oxford: Clarendon, 1960), p. 22.

[45] Before the Bruges talk, Mallarmé and Pierre Olin, one of the editors of

La Wallonie, went to Ostend for lunch (Mathews, *La Wallonie*, p. 80), where it would have been possible for them to drop in on Ensor.

[46] Marilyn Gaddis Rose, "Villiers de l'Isle-Adam and the Decorative Arts: A Decadent Departure from Symbolism," Third Annual Colloquium in Nineteenth-Century French Literature, Ohio State University, 1977, p. 3.

[47] See Betty Lou Heidelberg, "Narrative Art in the *Contes cruels* of Villiers de l'Isle-Adam," Ph.D. dissertation, University of Minnesota, 1972, p. 39, who observes, "The adverse vision of society is unmitigated. None of the *Contes cruels* present optimistically any strictly human aspect of existence.

FIG. 81. Ensor. *The Domain of Arnheim*, 1890.

dishing the severed head of her lover and howling in a trium-
phant cry. She had hidden behind blue spectacles, "as big
and round as five franc pieces covering her lifeless eyes,"[48]
spectacles curiously like those worn by the standing, masked
figure in Ensor's "Scandalized Masks" (Pl. 3). The name "Lenoir" in Villiers's story refers to Claire's blindness, and it is

possible to imagine Ensor's intruding, masked figure as her
spiritual sister, her opaque glasses hiding eyes that are blind
to any virtues the seated, smiling masked figure may have.

Balzac and Villiers de l'Isle-Adam affected Ensor's art
through idea and metaphor, but the American writer Edgar
Allan Poe was one of the few whose works served as inspi-

A contrast is provided, however, by the stories that direct attention to the
transcendental realm or evoke a mysterious, exotic atmosphere."

[48] This is Huysmans's description, which appeared in his 1884 novel,

Against Nature (p. 304). On the next page Huysmans mentions Villiers's
Contes cruels (p. 305).

ration for literal translation in Ensor's art: Poe's "King Pest" was illustrated by a drawing in 1880 and an etching in 1895; Ensor produced three versions of "The Vengeance of Hop Frog": an etching and a lithograph in 1898 and a painting in 1896; and in 1890 he painted "The Domain of Arnheim."[49] Ensor felt a special affinity with Poe, who was able to create a heightened mood of luxurious mystery and a sense of the incredible with the turn of a descriptive phrase: ". . . I dreamt when I thought about Poe, and like him I liked to daydream of certain nearby landscapes, perfumed with tenderness, even of femininities touched by light and reflected with love."[50]

"The Domain of Arnheim" (Fig. 81) is a canvas heavy with atmosphere and quite beautiful in its brushwork and use of color: the sky is filled with pink and gold and surrounded by blue; trees seem to palpitate with dark energy; and there is a suggestion of a boat on a golden yellow pond scumbled with pink. A magical mist rises in the center of the canvas to join with the middle ground. Legrand described the scene as ". . . remote . . . , magic . . . , a landscape-garden composed for the solitary satisfaction of a delirious imagination, it became, under the capricious paintbrush of Ensor, an open-air theater populated with apparitions."[51]

Poe's story concerns an enormously wealthy man, Ellison, and his desire to plant a landscape-garden that will be an ultimate work of art, since "no such combination of scenery exists in nature as the painter of genius may produce."[52] According to Ellison, despite the fact that we are expected

to regard nature as supreme, there are always defects in even the most enchanting of natural landscapes. These he explains as prognostic of death: The primitive intention of nature fulfills man's sense of perfection in the beautiful and the sublime, but this primitive intention has been frustrated by geological disturbances. These disturbances, then, are the preparations for man's subsequently conceived "deathful condition."[53]

The concluding description of Arnheim, created and made alive through words, ironically reminds the reader of Ellison's original thesis that only through man's art can perfection be attained.[54] Ensor's painting may have been created to carry this thesis one step further, and thus to bring it back to the story's original presumption, that only a painter of genius can create a satisfying landscape:

The boat glides . . . and commences a rapid descent into a vast amphitheatre entirely begirt with purple mountains, whose bases are laved by a gleaming river. . . . Meantime the whole Paradise of Arnheim bursts upon the view. There is a gush of entrancing melody; there is an oppressive sense of strange sweet order;—there is dream-like intermingling to the eye of tall slender Eastern trees—bosky shrubberies— flocks of golden and crimson birds—lily-fringed lakes— meadows of violets, tulips, poppies, hyacinths, and tub-roses. . . .[55]

Poe's "King Pest," a ludicrous story of brutal murder and mayhem, contains a subtitle that may have interested Ensor:

---

[49] Poe's writings had provided the subjects for a series of lithographs that Redon made in 1882, four of which appeared in the exhibition of Les XX in 1886, among them "Le masque de la mort rouge" (Legrand, *Ensor, cet inconnu*, p. 86).

[50] Ensor, *Lettres à André de Ridder*, p. 56.

[51] Legrand, *Ensor, cet inconnu*, p. 86.

[52] Edgar Allan Poe, *The Complete Tales and Poems of Edgar Allan Poe* (New York: Random House, 1975), p. 607.

[53] Ibid., p. 608.

[54] In his introduction to Poe, G. R. Thompson observed that almost everything Poe wrote was qualified by a prevailing irony in which the writer presents us with slyly insinuated mockery of both ourselves as readers and himself as writer (*Great Short Works of Edgar Allan Poe*, introduced and edited by G. R. Thompson, [New York: Harper and Row, 1970], p. 7).

[55] Poe, *Complete Tales*, p. 615.

"The gods do bear and will allow in kings the things which they abhor in rascal routes."[56] Besides Ensor's literal print, which shows King Pest seated at a round table with his grotesque court, sharing with them a huge cauldron while a skeleton hangs overhead, Ensor may have used Poe's allegorical statement as inspiration for an 1888 drawing and a 1904 etching entitled at the top "Plague Here, Plague There, Plague Everywhere" (Fig. 82). The vile conditions suggested in the title are illustrated by thick clouds and a fierce sun-like image in the sky that vomits upon the unsuspecting people below. Ensor's friends and sister are seated on a bench: Ernest Rousseau and to his right, Mitche, the artist Willy Finch, and Mariette Rousseau. These people, dressed in their fine clothing, are surrounded by filthy peasants in tattered rags, one of whom holds a small child. Oblivious to their surroundings, which include a smoking pile of excrement below the bench, the women smile as they enjoy an afternoon outdoors.

Whether Ensor meant the drawing to be critical of his friends and sister remains speculative. The drawing was based on a photograph taken on a trip to Bruges and reproduces the clothing seen there, but it is interesting that the two farthest figures in the photograph, Ensor and a friend of the Rousseaus from Florence, have been omitted from the drawing.[57]

In "Hop-Frog" the hero is a dwarf and the king's jester. When he organizes a masked ball, which the king and his ministers attend disguised as apes, he hangs them from the ceiling above the boisterous courtiers who fail to recognize them. Pretending to use his torch to discover their identity, Hop-Frog burns them to a "fetid, blackened, hideous, and undistinguished mass."[58]

Leslie Fiedler has linked Poe with the abused dwarf, who becomes, in turn, a symbol for all alienated artists: "Only Edgar Allan Poe ever successfully subverted the iconography of ape and dwarf, using it to satirize not the artist, but those who exploited both him and the court jester."[59] Fiedler added a qualifier, however, which suggests he wasn't aware of Ensor's version of Poe's story, ". . . apparently no artist using paint could identify so wholeheartedly with the jester-fool."[60] In fact, the story must have strongly appealed to Ensor's interest in retribution, since his fight against critics and the establishment had been sustained and vicious. Just two years earlier he had commented upon his crucifixion by the critics in the drawing "Dangerous Cooks," in which his head appeared on a platter. In Ensor's print of "The Vengeance of Hop-Frog" a huge multibalconied hall is filled with cheering masqueraders. The king and his retinue burn in the air above a clearing and Ensor's name appears in large letters on the back of a costumed figure who watches the proceedings from the middle of the foreground.[61]

Ensor had acknowledged the writings of E.T.A. Hoffmann, but he claimed that he didn't care for the writer's "poorly paired mixture of the real and the fantastic."[62] Yet some of

---

[56] Ibid., p. 720.

[57] Haesaerts dates the photograph 1889 (*James Ensor*, p. 344), which would have been impossible given the drawing's date. In January of 1888 Ensor could have been reminded of Poe by a lecture on the "Tell-Tale Heart" given by M. Antoine, founder of the Théâtre Libre at the exhibiton of Les XX (*L'Art moderne*, no. 4 [January 22, 1888], p. 30). In 1904 an etching was made of the drawing (Taevernier, *James Ensor*, pl. 127, mistakenly identifies Willy Finch as Ensor).

[58] Poe, *Complete Tales*, p. 509.

[59] *Freaks, Myths and Images of the Secret Self* (New York: Simon & Schuster, 1978), p. 73.

[60] Ibid., p. 75.

[61] See Taevernier, *James Ensor*, for a discussion of the two states of the etching (pl. 112).

[62] *Lettres à André de Ridder*, p. 56.

PLATE 7. Ensor. *The Tribulations of St. Anthony, 1887.*

PLATE 8. Ensor. *The Ray*, 1892.

Ensor's characters seem inspired by Hoffmann's descriptions, such as that of the doctor in "Signor Formica," whose huge stomach and large face with big cheeks, double chin, and bulbous nose recalls several fat men in Ensor's "Entry of Christ into Brussels." In Hoffmann's story an artist was shown as an unappreciated genius maligned by an ignorant academy. Salvator Rosa takes one of his paintings to them, claiming that the artist was foreign and dead. All rejoice in the masterpiece and bemoan the death of such a genius. When the academy learns of Rosa's trick, it is then forced to elect the painter to membership.[63]

Here and there an occasional phrase from Hoffmann calls up Ensor's interests, as the observation in "A New Year's Adventure" that "In the masquerade of life our true inner essence often shines beyond our mask when we meet a similar person. . . ."[64] "Master Flea" contains a description of fantastic insects that even before Ensor, may have influenced Flaubert and the popular novelist Charles De Coster:

Plant-lice, beetles, spiders, slime mold, which had grown to incredible sizes, stretched out their proboscises, walked along on their long hairy legs, and with their jagged maxillae the grayish ant robbers seized and crushed the gnats . . . and in the midst of it all, vinegar eels, eel worms, polyps with a hundred arms, wound in and out among one another, and infusoria peered out from all the gaps with distorted faces.[65]

Many images could be recounted from numerous authors who may or may not have influenced Ensor, but whose particularized viewpoint and descriptive phrases come close to what Ensor was doing with his art. Alfred Jarry is a case in

Fig. 82. Ensor. *Plague Here, Plague There, Plague Everywhere*, 1904

point. *Ubu roi* was first presented as a "spectacle de marionnettes" in 1888 when Jarry was just fifteen,[66] but it wasn't published until 1895 in *César-Antechrist*. There is no evidence that Ensor knew of the play in 1888, but its salacious treatment of human imbecility, gluttony, and lecherousness parallel Ensor's general view of humanity.

It is with Belgian literature, however, that we can illustrate pointed influences crucial to Ensor's development. His strong nationalistic feelings, evident in his fight to withstand foreign artistic pressures, caused him to celebrate his heritage openly through his art. For example, the influence of

[63] *The Best Tales of Hoffmann*, introduced and edited by E. F. Bleiler (New York: Dover, 1967).

[64] Ibid., p. 111.

[65] Quoted from Marianne Thalmann, *The Romantic Fairy Tale: Seeds of*

Surrealism, translated by Mary B. Corcoran (Ann Arbor: University of Michigan Press, 1964), p. 113.

[66] Legrand, "Lettres à Octave Maus," 19.

FIG. 83. Ensor. *Auto-Da-Fé*, 1893.

De Coster, who was a good friend and associate of Félicien Rops, was pervasive throughout Ensor's art. De Coster was born in 1827, six years before Rops. The two of them first met at the University of Brussels, and De Coster's *Flemish Legends*, written between 1856 and 1857, was published in Rops's periodical, *Uylenspiegel*. De Coster is most famous for his epic poem published in 1868, *The Legend of Ulenspiegel*, the comic story of a clever Belgian scamp, Till Eulenspiegel.[67]

Ulenspiegel began tricking people when he was fifteen

years old by holding up a picture frame, behind which he stood to foretell the futures of his susceptible fellow countrymen. Although his burlesque actions were at least partly sanctioned as fun-loving escapades of a high-spirited young man, they served to highlight the gullibility and naiveté of Belgium's people: De Coster's story was actually a thinly disguised history of Belgium during the sixteenth century, when Spain, under Charles V and his son Philip II, ruled the Low Countries.

De Coster's influence on Ensor has been documented in a Flemish text on De Coster by Alois Gerlo.[68] Chapter 5 of Gerlo's book makes comparisons between religion, politics, history, and the carnival, often with specific links between De Coster's written word and Ensor's visual response.[69] He mentions Ensor's 1893 etching, "Auto-Da-Fé" (Fig. 83), which is based upon a small 1891 painting entitled "Philip II in Hell,"[70] and which appears to have been inspired by a specific description in De Coster's narrative: Katheline, a seer and the mother of Nele, Ulenspiegel's love interest, has a vision in which Charles V appears before God and is sentenced to Hell. Nele also has a vision and describes the king as being about fifty-four years old ". . . with a blond beard on a prominent chin, with a mean look in his grey eyes that are all cunning, cruelty and feigned good nature."[71]

In Ensor's composition Philip replaces his father; he stands in profile, a blond, bearded figure with close-cropped hair, flanked by hooded figures, perhaps clergy, and grimacing caricatures. Philip looks toward the latter group, from which swirling smoke arises. The title for the etching gives the

[67] See Charles De Coster, *The Glorious Adventures of Tyl Ulenspiegl*, translated by Allan Ross Macdougall (New York: Pantheon Books, 1944), p. 43.

[68] *Charles De Coster En Vlaanderen* (Antwerp: Uitgevery S. M. Ontwikkeling, 1959).

[69] Ibid., pp. 52-66, and 103-104.

[70] Approximately 4⅜" x 5⅞", oil on panel, reproduced in Haesaerts, *James Ensor*, p. 320.

[71] De Coster, *The Glorious Adventures*, p. 122.

FIG. 84. Ensor. *The Infernal Cortège*, 1887.

punishment an ironic twist, since an auto-da-fé, or act of faith, can refer to the burning of heretics at the stake, or at the very least to the public announcement of the sentences imposed on persons tried by the Inquisition.

Gerlo has noted Ensor's fascination with the Devil and his numerous investigations of that subject. Although Ensor's interest in the theme was provoked by numerous ar-

tistic and literary precedents, one scene in particular in De Coster's story would have caught Ensor's attention: in an attempt to save Belgium from the continued devastation that Spanish rule brought, Ulenspiegel and Nele seek Lucifer to ask his help. In imagery that recalls Gustave Flaubert's *The Temptation of St. Anthony*,[72] De Coster described a hellish battlefield of fighting insects: ". . . well over 100,000 insects

[72] There were three versions of Flaubert's book, the first finished in 1849 and a second shortened and reshaped version in 1856. A few sections of the 1856 version were published in *L'Artiste* in 1856/1857 and the last version

was published in 1874 (Gustave Flaubert, *The Temptation of St. Antony*, translated with an introduction and notes by Kitty Mrosovksy [Ithaca: Cornell University Press, 1981], p. 13).

FIG. 85. Ensor. *The Pisser*, 1887.

larger than Goliaths, armed with swords, with serrated scythes, forks with seven prongs and all kinds of murderous weapons. They fought together with a great din, the strong eating the weak. . . ."[73] Ensor's 1887 etching "The Infernal Cortege" is an early example of similar creatures (Fig. 84). Ensor gave it another title, "Cortege of Devils," and it shows a parade of people and hybrid insects and animal forms, some carrying large, pronged forks, marching up a twisting mountain road accompanied by a band of coarse-featured musicians.[74] Later Ensor would include similar imagery—but in battle—in his historically inspired drawings, "Battle of the Golden Spurs" (1891), "The Rout of the Mercenaries" (1892), and "The Cruel Joke on the Peasant" (1896).[75]

Ulenspiegel should be mentioned in connection with Ensor's famous 1887 etching of "The Pisser" (Fig. 85), even though Callot's engraving of the same subject has always been suggested as the visual inspiration.[76] With the ultimate gesture of condemnation and gleeful hatred, Ulenspiegel ends a confrontation by urinating on his enemies.[77] That Ensor does the same thing symbolically in his etching is suggested by the writing on the wall, "Ensor est un fou," and the crude caricatures that imitate the art of children. Ensor urinates, not to illustrate the inscription, but to show his contempt

[73] De Coster, *The Glorious Adventures*, p. 186.
[74] Taevernier, *James Ensor*, p. 45, notes that the date on the plate is unclear; it may be 1886. Elesh gives the date as 1886 (*James Ensor, The Complete Graphic Work*, no. 9). There is also a drawing of the same subject.
[75] Reproduced in Haesaerts, *James Ensor*, p. 321. Like Brueghel, Ensor produced his version of "The Massacre of the Innocents," a 1913 drawing, possibly also a historical allusion as Brueghel's had been, to the murderous activities performed under the Duke of Alba (also reproduced in Haesaerts, *James Ensor*, p. 321).
[76] Observed in Tannenbaum, *James Ensor*, p. 71.
[77] De Coster, *The Glorious Adventures*, p. 49.

for the graffiti and for the public's ignorance of his art.[78] As we have seen in Chapter III, the popular Belgian statue of the little boy who urinates in the street, the Manniken-pis, is the ultimate prototype for Ensor's etching, and even for Ulenspiegel's act, since that statue can be seen to symbolize Belgium's defiance of outside influences.

In De Coster's 1861 *Contes brabacons*, two stories deal with dreams and supernatural visions: "The Masks," which includes an illustration by Félicien Rops and "The Phantoms." Like Ensor, the protagonist of "The Masks," Hendrik Zantas, is an artist: ". . . genre painter, pale, hypochondriac, phlegmatic, a young, taciturn scholar, searching the corners. . . ."[79] The story takes place on a carnival night; not accustomed to drinking wine, Hendrik gets drunk and has a dream in which he becomes the personification of Satan and directs the affairs of the world: "I am crime, I am evil, it is I who held this dancing rope for you to dance on. God is there, below, among the children and good people, evil is here; choose now, dance or descent."[80] Blanche Rousseau's description of Ensor quoted earlier comes to mind: "He had the face of a mocking Christ or a nostalgic Satan . . . ," and Ensor himself might have felt an affinity with De Coster's artist.

In "The Phantoms" the narrator meets a former painter, an old man called Jerome. Cultured and musical, he plays his violin and conjures up spirits: "Cry, he said, to the phantom, cry: when one of your tears falls on the poet's page, the painter's canvas or the sculptor's marble, it changes itself into a diamond."[81] In speaking of another phantom he explains: "He judges men as they are, tears away all the masks . . . he debated with Rabelais, sang with Jacob Kats, held Molière's quill and Rembrandt's paintbrush . . . he is invulnerable to all wounds. . . ."[82] "The Mad Muse" and her cortege of angels, demons, ghouls, and vampires is also given attention. Jerome describes her as having a million lovers, among them Brueghel, Callot, and Hoffmann and he points to her union with Goethe and its resultant child "Faust," whose godfather and godmother, however, are Knowledge and Reason.[83] His final advice to the narrator and reader promises a reward of patience and love through an analogy that uses the progress a small worm has made in making a miniscule hole in a heavy oak table: ". . . the world will place on his forehead a crown more lasting than that of the kings, the crown of the conquering and glorious Genius."[84] The moral would not have been lost on Ensor, who throughout his creative years failed to win approbation for his art, but who continued to produce prodigiously.

Such stories were a formative influence on Ensor's development and furthered his interest in the fantastic. De Coster had made an artist the protagonist in both works and the stories had dealt with Ensor's own Flemish heritage, the supernatural, the devil, and masks. Further, allegorical personifications of ideas and the genius of famous men were included.

In the year after De Coster's *Contes brabacons*, S. Henry Berthoud also presented the artist as hero in his book *Légendes et traditions surnaturelles de Flandre*, which included the story "Une aventure de Jacques Callot." Berthoud

---

[78] The English cartoonist, Gillray, had included similar stick drawings and inscriptions on the walls in a vicious anti-French cartoon of decapitation and cannibalism entitled "Un petit souper à la Parisienne."

[79] Charles De Coster, *Contes brabacons* (Paris: Michel Levy frères, 1861), p. 154.   [80] Ibid., p. 165.   [81] Ibid., p. 146.
[82] Ibid., p. 147.   [83] Ibid., pp. 147-148.   [84] Ibid., p. 149.

entangles the seventeenth-century artist in a frightening, macabre experience. On a trip to Rome Callot meets a mysterious man who invites him to a party; he is led to a dark house and into a room lit by a single torch and filled with nightmarish horror: lining the walls are strange beings dressed in fantastic clothing and white immobile figures but, according to the narrator, "the most terrible, in the middle, a corpse battered, bloody, mutilated!"[85]

As Callot is pushed toward the cadaver, he falls; urged to rise by the claws of the monster, he cries aloud and rues the fact that his love of painting will be so cruelly sacrificed. Suddenly all activity stops. Callot is asked to prove his claim and he draws a quick sketch. He is enthusiastically embraced by the cadaver, who turns out to be a painter in disguise. In fact the whole room is filled with artists who have disguised themselves for a bit of fun. As a fellow artist Callot is welcomed into the group and offered companionship and hospitality during his stay in Rome. The cadaver recalls his own youth, his early passion for art, and his fight to succeed. He cheers the young Callot with the assurance that with hard work he will one day be famous, and the story ends with a toast to his future success.

The specific influences of Callot's work on Ensor's art have been examined by Libby Tannenbaum. Ensor himself claimed Callot as inspiration,[86] and it is tempting to postulate that Berthoud's story may have caused Ensor to pay special attention to Callot's own images of grotesques and the macabre.

It has been observed that the renaissance of letters in Belgium was, even more than in France, the product of literary reviews.[87] A number of important literary journals were published in Belgium in the 1880s and 1890s. Yet as an influence on Ensor, Rops's earlier journal *Uylenspiegel* must be considered in particular. It was filled with stories on art and literature, as well as political commentary, and it reported on various lectures given in Brussels. For example, in 1860 the French art critic Théodore Silvestre gave lectures on Hogarth and Constable and they were reviewed in *Uylenspiegel*; Silvestre's articles on French artists also appeared weekly in June and July in 1860: Courbet, Ingres, Barye, and others were discussed.[88] Fiction was also published, and a story from an 1863 issue, Léo Lespès's "Ce que disent les meubles," roughly translated as "What the Furniture Says," may have inspired Ensor's development of a small body of work that dealt with a particularized aspect of the supernatural.[89] Like the old Swedish tale of animals who talked on Christmas Eve, Lespès's story tells of furniture that lived and knew all the secrets of its human cohabitants, and on Christmas night it could communicate.

Ensor's "Haunted Furniture" (1885) shows an interior with an elaborately carved chest (Fig. 86). Seated at a large table in the foreground, a young girl looks up and out at the viewer from the book she has been reading; to the left at the end of the table a woman, who appears to be Ensor's sister, Mitche, sits engrossed in her knitting. A clarinet lies in the middle of the table, and a snuffed candle stands at its right edge, along with a vase and several pieces of paper, perhaps some sheet music.

This scene of quiet domesticity is intruded upon by a number of masked faces and skulls that appear at the farthest

[85] S. Henry Berthoud, *Légendes et traditions surnaturelles des Flandres* (new ed., Brussels: Librairie F. De Nobele, 1862), p. 372.

[86] Ensor, *Mes Écrits*, p. 191.

[87] Mathews, *La Wallonie*, p. 12.

[88] Consult *Uylenspiegel*, June 24, 1860, pp. 5-6; July 1, 1860, p. 5; July 8, 1860, p. 2; July 13, 1860, pp. 2-3.

[89] Ibid., no. 39, October 8, 1863, p. 1.

Fig. 86. Ensor. *Haunted Furniture*, 1885.

Fig. 87. Ensor. *Astonishment of the Mask Wouse*, 1889.

104

edges of the composition and seem to press inward toward the unsuspecting females. Directly next to the young girl is a skeleton. Its head and shoulder appear just above the table and its close proximity to the seated figure is made all the more menacing by the girl's oblivious stare. Tannenbaum has observed that the use of shallow space gives the painting a stage-like horizontality that becomes a frequent compositional trick in later mask paintings.[90]

None of the later paintings of masks and skeletons, however, show this strange juxtaposition of real people with grotesques. Marcel De Maeyer has suggested that, although the painting was originally executed in 1885 as a straightforward genre scene, it was repainted sometime between 1889 and 1890.[91] Unfortunately, the painting cannot be examined because it was destroyed in 1940 during the bombing of Ostend. Without the extra figures the composition would seem to be somewhat off balance, with the original two figures at left of center. We shall never know if the right side was overpainted and a figure removed in order to add the masks and skeletons.

The clarinet on the table recalls the horn held in the hand of the masked intruder in Ensor's 1883 "Scandalized Masks" and may again refer to death; the snuffed candle suggests a similar disposition. Both items appear on the floor in the

1889 "Astonishment of the Mask Wouse" (Fig. 87), in which the horn is placed in the mouth of that same masked figure from "Scandalized Masks," and the candle, burning with a thin flame, stands at bottom center of the composition.

The identity of the young girl is not known, although Tannenbaum claimed she was a small cousin living in the Ensor household.[92] A link with the young, nude girl standing at the bureau in the 1886 "Children Dressing" (Pl. 4) would seem possible,[93] but in fact the features of the two are not the same. What is evident is that specters haunt the room, and, although they do not seem to be a part of the furniture itself, their presence, although unnoticed, together with the symbols on the table, make the painting a pointed warning about remaining in that environment. Werner Haftmann sees this kind of imagery as Ensor's own personalized hell: "Ensor's psychosis has all the characteristics of schizophrenia; things take on a hidden significance, the world changes into a weird realm of spectres, peopled by delusions and hallucinations revolving around persistent, obsessive themes."[94]

Closer in actual visual description to the title of "Haunted Furniture" is an 1886 drawing in which Ensor's head and the suggestion of shoulders float out from within the confines of a massive, carved armoire. Now entitled "My Sad and Splendid Portrait," Ensor inscribed the drawing in the

[90] Tannenbaum, *James Ensor*, p. 52.

[91] Marcel De Maeyer, "Derrière le masque": 25. De Maeyer notes that the masks and skeletons are similar to those Ensor painted in the 1889 "Astonishment of the Mask Wouse," and the 1891 "Skeletons Fighting over the Body of a Hanged Man" (23). It should also be noted that the seated skeleton is of the exact same type as those in the 1889 "Skeletons Trying to Warm Themselves" (Pl. 5). The title "Haunted Furniture" did not appear in exhibition catalogues; in fact De Maeyer points to a canvas entitled "Old Furniture" shown at Les XX in 1888 as possibly being the same picture. And in 1891 another title appeared that is also suggestive of the painting in question, "Enfant, jeune fille, masques et squelettes" ("Derrière le masque": 25).

[92] Tannenbaum, *James Ensor*, p. 51. Gert Schiff has identified her as "the artist's sister intent upon her homework under the surveillance of a drowsy, knitting nurse" ("Ensor the Exorcist," p. 722), but in 1885 Mitche's age would coincide with that of the knitting woman (Stephen McGough has come to the same conclusion in "James Ensor's 'The Entry of Christ into Brussels in 1889,'" Ph.D. dissertation, Stanford University, 1981, p. 223, n. 144).

[93] That painting was listed in the 1888 Les XX catalogue just before "Old Furniture" (De Maeyer, "Derrière le masque": 25).

[94] Werner Haftmann, *Painting in the Twentieth Century*, translated by Ralph Manheim, vol. 1 (6th ed. New York: Praeger, 1969), p. 62.

Fig. 88. Ensor. *My Sad and Splendid Portrait*, 1886.

Fig. 89. Ensor. *The Haunted Mantelpiece*, 1888.

lower right "Ensor mon portrait 86" (Fig. 88). Odilon Redon was to use a similar method of juxtaposing the material of reality with the supernatural in a lithograph from 1887 entitled, "A Skull was Revealed by the Gap in the Wall," an illustration for the Belgian writer Edmond Picard's *Le Juré*.[95]

Ensor's transubstantiation in "My Sad and Splendid Portrait" has been sensitively described by Libby Tannenbaum:

. . . the artist superimposes his own brooding image on the great carved chest, as though in that room whose sullen women hibernated in slumber, the restless furniture was by contrast gloomily alive. The furniture and the artist were equally witnesses in this atmosphere from which Ensor was never to have the resolution to remove himself, and there is a sense of this identification in the way he invests the furniture with his own sense of horrors.[96]

The "Haunted Mantelpiece" from 1888 adheres to this description as well, and it includes the heads of two women, one of whom may be napping with her mouth open (Fig. 89). There Ensor's face appears as a light sketch, flanked by a fancy clock and a vase filled with flowers and surrounded by additional details difficult to decipher. In that same year the drawing of a mirror reflected a ghoulish, Satanic presence with bulging eyeballs and horned protuberances arising from its head (Fig. 90). It is surrounded by hybrid sea creatures, a lobster, anthropomorphic fish heads, and females, insect-like, yet suggestive of mermaids. Outside the mirror at the

[95] De Maeyer has commented on the similarity of vision shared by these two artists: "Like Redon, Ensor is fascinated by chiaroscuro and begins to make use of the arabesque. Like Redon, he always takes inspiration from Poe; like Redon, he will soon introduce the mask and skeleton in his work" ("Derrière le masque," 28).

[96] Tannenbaum, *James Ensor*, p. 51. A group of Ensor self-portraits from 1885 and 1886 can be seen as preliminary steps that reveal his development of this motif; reproduced in Ollinger-Zinque, *Ensor by Himself*, pp. 103, 105, 106-107.

FIG. 90. Ensor. *The Devil's Mirror*. 1888.

FIG. 91. Ensor. *Haunted Furniture*, 1888.

left a face in profile looks toward the mirror; perhaps as an ironic reference to Ulenspiegel's mirror, its facial features do not duplicate the reflection. At the right several marine-inspired insect shapes can be seen; their number is multiplied by humanoid faces just outside the mirror's frame on the wall at the right. Such grotesque images will be allowed free rein in Ensor's prints and paintings, as well as his drawings, and Edmond Picard's observation from the 1887 *Le Juré* comes to mind: "Why should there not exist a world made up of invisible, odd, fantastic, embryonic beings?"[97]

"Haunted Furniture" is also the title of an etching from 1888 (Fig. 91). A figure at the lower right stands facing an armoire and watches a skeleton whose gesturing hand and arm appear above its skull and bony shoulder. At first glance the person appears to be a child, but this may be because of the loose clothing and cropped body. Several faint marks near the outline of the face could be a mustache and therefore would identify the figure as Ensor.

The print exists in three states: in the first the mirror encased in the front of the armoire is white; in the second the mirror is shaded and in the third two faces have been added, a mask-like head at the foot of the wardrobe and the head of a strange gnome superimposed over the body of the person in the corner.[98] At the base of the massive cabinet, next to the round foot at the right, a small object appears, suggestive of the body and tail of a lizard or similar creature whose head may be hidden behind the ball. Perhaps this small mysterious being is a symbolic reference to the print's prototype, Bosch's painting of "Pride" from the "Seven Deadly Sins" (Fig. 92). There a woman with her back to the viewer

[97] Used by Redon as the title of an illustration for *Le Juré*. See *The Graphic Works of Odilon Redon*, introduction by Alfred Werner (New York: Dover, 1969), xviii.

[98] See Taevernier, *James Ensor*, p. 71.

is shown admiring herself in a mirror hung on a sideboard and steadied by the hand of a demon whose body is partly hidden behind the furniture, but whose clawed foot and long curved tail are evident.

There were abundant tales of the supernatural in Belgian journals and reviews in the 1880s, and as late as 1897 one could read stories about spirits, monsters, and the Devil, as, for example, in Adolphe Retté's "Idylles diaboliques," published in *La Plume*.[99] Numerous stimulating reviews were born during the 1880s.[100] In fact, *L'Art moderne, revue critique des arts et de la littérature*, began publishing in 1881; at first politically oriented, under Edmond Picard and Octave Maus it extolled the art of Les XX. Reviews of popular authors like Huysmans were featured, as were Belgian writers like Georges Eekhoud, whose "kermesses" appeared in an 1884 issue.[101]

The small review *L'Élan littéraire* began in January of 1885 by mimeographing its editions. In its pages Albert Mockel praised the originality of Ensor and Redon, and in 1886, when it changed its name to *La Wallonie*, it announced an alliance with Paris and the Symbolists, thus strengthening the French cultural connection that had antagonized Flemish Belgians. Emile Verhaeren became its leading poet, although Frenchmen like Paul Valéry were also published, as were prose writers like André Gide. Mockel continued his reviews, which included an 1888 piece on Mallarmé's translations from Edgar Allan Poe.[102]

FIG. 92. Hieronymous Bosch. *Pride*, detail from *The Seven Deadly Sins*, date unknown.

[99] *La Plume*, no. 189 (March 1, 1897). By then the general tone had changed, however. In discussing the "school of 1885," Mathews noted that Retté was "turning the movement into satire" (*La Wallonie*, pp. 7-8).

[100] See the section on the Belgian Renaissance in Robert and Eugenia Herbert, *The Artist and Social Reform: France and Belgium 1885-1898* (New Haven: Yale University Press, 1961), esp. pp. 66ff; also see Mathews, *La Wallonie*.

[101] *L'Art moderne*, no. 26 (June 29, 1884). On the title page *L'Art moderne* explained its *raison d'être*: "To be interested in Art in all its domains: Literature, painting, sculpture, engraving, music, architecture, furniture, costume, etc. It is mainly consecrated to Belgium and follows with a particular interest the manifestations of Flemish art; nevertheless it summarily keeps its readers informed of foreign artistic events."

[102] Mathews, *La Wallonie*, esp. pp. 49 and 61.

La Jeune Belgique published its literary reviews between 1880 and 1897 and its writers were a "Who's Who" of Belgian literature: Maeterlinck, De Coster, Rodenback, Eekhoud, Verhaeren and Charles Van Lerberghe. The first issue of *La Revue indépendente* appeared in November of 1886 and it was au courant in all aspects of art and literature, crammed with serializations of the latest books, art reviews, short stories, and studies of artists and writers. The first volume contained a chapter of Huysmans's *En Rade*, Mallarmé's "Notes sur le Théâtre," Théodor De Wyzewa on "Le comte de Villiers de L'Isle-Adam," Paul Bourget's "Le Fantôme" and a comedy by Leon Tolstoy, "The First Distiller, or how the little devil earned his slice of bread."[103] Articles on Gillray and Daumier were found in the pages of *La Revue indépendente*, as well as profiles of darker personalities like the Marquis de Sade and Sâr Péladan. The latter's books were reviewed regularly in Belgium; in 1888 *La Revue belge* discussed *Le Vice suprême* along with a review of Les XX. Edgar Baes, who was to inscribe an 1898 book to Ensor and who was later to publish a study of the image of Christ in art,[104] often wrote articles on art and in March of 1889 his articles on Neoimpressionism and Japonism appeared in *La Revue belge*. In the *Revue Wagnerienne*, published between 1885 and 1888, lithographs by Redon and Fantin-Latour appeared,

and contributions were also made by the writers Mallarmé, Verlaine, and Villiers de L'Isle-Adam. *La Revue blanche* began in Brussels in 1889 but moved to Paris in 1891, although it continued to report on the activities of Les XX.[105]

A copy of *La Revue blanche* from 1895 is among the books from Ensor's collection, but other journals would have been consulted as well. Besides Belgian periodicals, Ensor would have been interested in French periodicals such as the *Mercure de France*, which contained reviews of Belgian painting, for example the 1894 volume that discussed an exhibition of Brussels painters in Paris. Ensor's debt to foreign journals like the *Gazette des Beaux-Arts* and *The Studio* has been documented,[106] and in a reminiscence of Ensor's atelier, the Ostend painter Jean-Jacques Gaillard described a large table piled with "old documents, articles and works cut from journals: *La Flandre littéraire, Sélection, Die Kunst* and *Europa*."[107]

In January of 1887, the year Ensor was to begin his work on "The Entry of Christ into Brussels" and the year he painted the nightmarish "Tribulations of St. Anthony," *L'Art moderne* carried a three-page article entitled "Le Fantastique Réel."[108] It was the lead article, featured on its front page, and, although the author was not identified, it could have been written by Edmond Picard, since he was one of the

---

[103] Tolstoy's work was popular in Belgium and at one point Ensor drew the Russian writer. Signed but updated, it was a profile made with a light touch and free, wavy lines, perhaps taken from an illustration Ensor had come across in a periodical or book. Tannenbaum (*James Ensor*, p. 78) thinks the drawing was made from a photograph. Its style suggests a date of the late 1890s, or after the turn of the century; perhaps it was inspired by Tolstoy's *Qu'est-ce que l'art?* which was originally published in 1896. In Tolstoy's text it was suggested that modern writers became corrupt and that an overly sophisticated art was bad art. See Roland N. Stromberg, ed., *Realism, Naturalism, and Symbolism: Modes of Thought and Expression in Europe 1848-1914* (New York: Walker, 1968), p. 208.

[104] Edgar Baes, *La Physiognomie du Christ dans l'art* (Brussels: Abel Faivre, 1912). The book in Ensor's collection is *Cantique de spectres* (Brussels, 1898).

[105] Philippe Jullian, *The Symbolists* (2d ed., Oxford and New York: Phaidon/Dutton, 1977), p. 33. For a study of that periodical, consult A. B. Jackson, *La Revue blanche (1889-1903): origine, influence, bibliographie* (Paris: M. J. Minaud, 1960).

[106] See Lydia Schoonbaert, "Gazette des Beaux-Arts," 205-221.

[107] Quoted in Georges Fabry, *Jean-Jacques Gaillard, le voyageur de la lumière fantasque* (Ostend: Erel, n.d.), p. 105.

[108] *L'Art moderne*, no. 4 (January 23, 1887), p. 25.

main contributors to the periodical and he was particularly interested in such subjects. The writer observed that the fantastic was constantly evolving everywhere, all around one, and that it was a black region to explore, like unknown continents, an underdeveloped area for art and literature.[109]

Poe, Barbey D'Aurevilly, and Balzac were mentioned, as well as Shakespeare's Hamlet, Banquo and Lady Macbeth, but the message concerned the real world and the infusion of the fantastic upon the ordinary. In an account that recalls what Ensor had already achieved in his 1886 drawing of "My Sad and Splendid Portrait," and which may have been an impetus for the 1888 drawing "Haunted Mantelpiece," the etching "Haunted Furniture," and Ensor's additions to the 1885 painting of "Haunted Furniture," the author describes what he perceives as "Le Fantastique Réel":

... Here is the table, here is the writing-desk. ... Nothing is simpler. ... There had been a sighing of the wind in the corridor. There had been a cracking of the woodwork. I am worried, I am moved. A piano string breaks and vibrates in its closed case. From a dormant rose in a vase, its petals fall. ... Do I enter into the invisible world? No, it is reality. But seen reality, felt in its enigmatic accidents. ... Everything is vibrating with strangeness. The supernatural appeared underneath this peaceful life. Is everything simple? But to discern that, it takes an aspect of a special spirit and to realize it is a special art: ... Fantastic Reality.[110]

The writer advised that mystery was the most profound way to excite human emotions, and he suggested that "clusters of obscurity" should remain within a creation: "May there always be a secret. Let a riddle live ... and to express it in its grimacing darkness, that is the art of fantasy."[111]

It was also the year 1887 that a small book appeared, *Les Fumistes wallons*, which was quite remarkable in its assimilation of an incredible variety of images and motifs that would have interested Ensor. It was written by Albert Mockel, under the pseudonym of "L'Hemma" and its frontispiece was a lithograph by Félician Rops of a bare-breasted woman wearing a hat and looking into a mirror. A "fumiste" is a practical joker, and the book's title links its interest with the Belgians who associated themselves with *La Wallonie* and its young editors; thus it was the history of the beginning of a literary movement.[112] In its pages were references to Belgian journals, Redon's lithographs, the writings of Villiers de l'Isle-Adam and Catulle Mendes, bizarre furniture, a skeleton "auroral," the blind bourgeoisie, an auto-da-fé of red mannequins, "a sinister and cadaveresque countenance," Antoine Wiertz, and the Belgian historical painter, Louis Gallait. All of these concerns were woven into a story dedicated as a "story of some madmen by the maddest of them."

The description of an apartment creates the same sense of mood and mystery found in "Le Fantastique Réel":

Toward evening ... From the bay windows whose ample coarseness was veiled by the harmony of lowered blinds ...

[109] "Près de vous, tout près, constamment, le fantastique évolue. Des régions noires à explorer comme l'inconnu des continents non parcourus. Toute une friche pour l'art, pour littérature" (Ibid.).

[110] "... voici la table, voici l'écritoire. ... Rien n'est plus simple. ... Il y a eu un soupir du vent dans le corridor. Il y a eu un craquement de la boiserie. Je suis inquiet, je suis ému. Une corde de piano casse et vibre dans sa caisse fermée. D'une rose dormant dans une vase, des pétales s'effeuillent. ... Est-ce que je pénètre dans le monde invisible? Non, c'est le réel. Mais le réel vu, senti en ses accidents énigmatiques. ... Tout est vibrant d'és-

trangeté. Le surnaturel transparait sous cette vie paisible. Tout est simple? Non, rien vraiment n'est simple. Mais pour discerner cela, il fait une allure d'esprit spéciale, et le réaliser est un art spécial: ... Le Fantastique Réel" (Ibid.).

[111] Qu'il y ait toujours un secret. Qu'une énigme demeure ... et l'exprimer en ses ténèbres grimaçantes, c'est l'art du fantastique (Ibid.).

[112] *Les Fumistes wallons (histoire de quelques fous)* (Liège: H. Vaillant-Carmanne, 1887). For a discussion of the book's importance to the literary movement La Wallonie, see Mathews, *La Wallonie*, pp. 32-42.

filtered a hesitant light . . . but the lithographs—by Odilon Redon—in mat and white frames, caught several passing slivers of light, and this unctuous paleness gave to the atmosphere a half-light in which phosphorescences were floating.[113]

In a later description, a wall clock comes alive in the atmosphere of gloom:

The darkness took possession of the apartment for a time, all noise was killed and only the ticking of the hanging wall clock nailed to the wall, near a corner, the ticking clock with long hands of fantastic ivory, only the fantastic pendulum appeared to live in the darkness of the wings of lead.[114]

The mood changes and much is made of a night scene in the streets; the moon is seen as a luminous carnival mask and the surging crowds are described in detail:

People went down to the fair, from which the boom-boom hovering over the center of the city was an echo of rumbling cacophony. An enormous surge of idlers was strolling confusedly on the boulevards . . . thousands of lights penetrating the darkness of their blinking eyes, separated in a bizarre

splendor the sparkling crudeness of the gilding and the soiled banners. A deep din swelled in the air, interrupted incessantly by the bumping noises of the orchestras whose rhythmic racket was haltingly seconded by harsh shouts of the clowns: a doubtful harmony. Here and there was lighted obstinately the cruelty of several electric beacons varnishing with a pallid light the faces of the blind bourgeois and streaking the air with long, slender, powdery rays. And in among the storm of the tom-tom and the lights peacefully moved the wave of strollers whose placid faces take on a sinister and cadaverous air under the bluish flash of the electric lamps.[115]

The crowd is seen as a swarming, idle mob; shops along the way are described by their signs, and the protagonists enter a red hut where they watch a parade of grotesques:

. . . beneath their eyes all the sickness and morally hideous sights of the old world. Unfair lawyers, infamous bakers, priests, rabbis, and cooks, a great lady hiding a tumor in the fullness of her skirt, butchers, pastry-cooks, journalists, and hypocrites, all went to the footlights under the jeering that indignation brought to the public, all passed, penitent and burning without pity, whereas, from the height of its bloody tribunal the clown bellowed in order to curse them with great bursts of resounding imprecations. . . .[116]

---

[113] "Vers le soir. Des croisées dont l'ample crudité se voilait par l'harmonie des stores baissé . . . filtrait un jour indécis . . . mais des lithographies—par Odilon Redon—aux cadres blancs et mats, accrochaient au passage quelques brins de lumière, et cette onctueuse pâleur donnait à l'atmosphère une demi-clarté ou des phosphorescences planaient" (Les Fumistes wallons, p. 15).

[114] "Le sombre prit pour un temps possession de l'appartement, tout bruit se tut, et seul de tic-taquent cartel cloué à la muraille, près d'un angle, le tic-taquent cartel aux longues aiguilles d'ivoire fantastique, seule la fantastique pendule parut vivre dans les ténèbres aux ailes de plomb" (Ibid., p. 22).

[115] "On descendit à la foire, dont les boum-boums faisaient planer sur le centre de la ville un écho de cacophonie ronflante. Une houle énorme de

flaneurs roulait confusément sur les boulevards . . . les milliers de lumières trouant les ténèbres de leurs yeux clignotants, détachaient en un resplendissement bizarre l'éclatante crudité des dorures et des toiles barbouillées. Une rumeur profonde se gonflait dans l'air, déchirée incessamment par les fracas heurtés des orchestres dont les tapages rythmés scandaient boiteusement les aïgres criailleries des pitres: une harmonie douteuse. De distance en distance s'alluminait obstinément la cruauté de quelques phares électriques vernissant d'une clarté blafarde les visages des bourgeois aveuglés et zébrant l'air de longues élancées de rayons poudreux. Et parmi la tempête des tam-tams et des lumières, se mouvait paisiblement le flot des promeneurs, dont les faces placides prenaient, sous l'éclair bleuté des lampes électriques, un aspect sinistre et cadavérique" (Ibid., pp. 42-43).

[116] ". . . sous leurs yeux toutes les maladies et les hideurs morales du

Ensor's view of a vulgarized humanity will become similarly evident in his "Entry of Christ into Brussels" (Fig. 57), in which even clowns are included among the parade reviewers.

At the beginning of his tale, whether consciously or otherwise, Hemma established a link between himself and the Flemish tradition of De Coster and others by informing the reader that above all the story was meant to be humorous. He called it a "petit bout de marionette," a puppet who gamboled and kicked up his heels and said and did foolish things. And he reminded us that we all have our own spirited marionette inside ourselves.

Hemma became serious, however, when he wrote of "Le mouvement Wallon" and he listed those writers to whom contemporary Belgian literature was indebted: Verlaine, Mallarmé, Barbey D'Aurevilly, among others. He also wrote of the plastic arts, and it would have been gratifying for Ensor to read his own name along with Rops, Redon, and Khnopff.[117]

Like Hemma, Maurice Maeterlinck had been drawn to the world of puppets, in Belgium a popular form of entertainment for the masses, and in 1894 he wrote three plays for marionettes. Maeterlinck saw an analogy between man and the marionette in which both were manipulated by outer forces that controlled their lives. Fernand Khnopff's art has been seen as a visual counterpart to Maeterlinck's prose,[118] but when Maeterlinck chose puppets as the most appropriate way to portray the archetypal figure with which he was concerned, he was closer in spirit to Ensor, whose depictions of grotesques, costumed and masked with strange, lifeless grimaces, sometimes looked and gestured like marionettes. Maeterlinck's use of light and darkness and sight and blindness, as well as doors, windows, and lamplight, was intensely symbolic, simple but profound in implication. Personifications of death abounded in his works, but they were abstractions: "the death they symbolize is within, . . . the emblems are but masks thought puts on."[119] Maeterlinck's 1889 "The Intruder," where death was awaited with foreboding, has already been mentioned as recalling Ensor's earlier "Scandalized Masks."

We have seen that in a number of art works inspired by his personal life, Ensor investigated the implications of a reality that existed beneath the surface of banal experience. That he began these explorations in the early 1880s places him in the forefront of a developing Symbolist aesthetic.

Another theme was the deterioration and decay of mankind, both through a corrupt, uncaring society and through the physical and psychological stress of disease, old age, jealousy, cruelty, deceit, and perversion. With these preoccupations Ensor could be classified as a "decadent," and although that word has been overused as an easy way to define and dismiss the moral exhaustion of fin-de-siècle creativity, in 1886 it was the main concern of the journal *Le Décadence*, edited by the poet Anatole Bajou. A twentieth-century description of the "perennial decadent" would seem to fit Ensor's personality:

---

vieux monde. Avocats déloyaux, boulangers infâmes, prêtres, rabbins et cuisinières, grande dame cachant un gommeux dans l'ampleur de sa crinoline, bouchers, pâtissiers, journalistes et tartufes, tout passa aux feux de la rampe sous les huées que l'indignation arrachait au public, tout passa, contrit et brûlé sans pitié, tandis que, du haut de son tribunal sanglant, le pitre gonflait la voix pour les maudire à grands éclats d'imprécations to-

nitruantes . . ." (Ibid., p. 52).

[117] Ibid., p. 18.

[118] "Khnopff paints what Maeterlinck writes. He is a painter of inner life . . ." Hermann Bahr in *Secession*, quoted in Peter Vergo, *Art in Vienna 1898-1918* (London: Phaidon, 1975), p. 30.

[119] Taylor, *Maurice Maeterlinck*, p. 66.

. . . the artist, writer, or thinker who senses that he lives in a declining age, and who suffers neurotically from one or more of the three kinds of anxiety defined by Paul Tillich in *The Courage to Be*: ontic, moral and spiritual . . . i.e., he expects the collapse of his civilization. . . . The decadent is a mighty worrier. He may revel in the decadence of his age, or draw back from it in horror. Often he will do both, like the moth tortured by the flame.[120]

Despite these preoccupations, Ensor's art reaches beyond the strict confines of establishment decadence. And when the whole of his creative oeuvre is considered—with its remarkable assimilation of a wide range of sources, its multiplicity of themes, and its varied artistic experimentation—then his work transcends all boundaries.

[120] W. Warren Wagar, "Decadence: A Note on Definitions," *Essays on Decadence, Pro domo* publication of the "Seminar on Decadence" (Binghamton: State University of New York, 1975), p. 2.

V

TRIBULATIONS, TEMPTATIONS, AND TRANSFORMATIONS: ENSOR'S DEBT TO RELIGION AND HISTORY

In 1887 Ensor painted "The Tribulations of St. Anthony" (Pl. 7). It is a remarkably bold and innovative vision for its time, and Ensor's emotional expressionism—his free rein of the unconscious on canvas—was never more evident. Difficult to decipher because of its complex surface of garish color and heavily scumbled paint, the picture depicts St. Anthony surrounded on the land, and in the sea and the sky, with grotesque images of nightmarish intensity.

The real St. Anthony was a third-century Egyptian hermit whose life story, told by St. Athanasius, was considered the first classic of Christian biography. Anthony struggled against demons, retreated from admirers, and eventually made contact with his disciples. By the time of his death many had sought him out for his wise counsel: ". . . St. Antony . . .

represented the arch-ancorite, the very type of the solitary. His temptations make up a long and brilliant iconographical and popular tradition. . . .[1]

The legend of St. Anthony had become a popular story in the mid-nineteenth century,[2] and by the the 1880s Ensor's painting could have been inspired by a number of tributes to that saint. In 1883 Khnopff painted "The Temptation of St. Anthony according to Flaubert"[3] and in the same year L'Artiste ran a story about marionettes in which it was related that the story of St. Anthony was a classic in the marionette repertoire.[4] Félicien Rops's print of "La Tentation de St. Antoine" was discussed by Camille Lemonnier in an 1884 issue of La Revue indépendente;[5] in 1885 Gustave Flaubert's book on Anthony was reviewed at Les XX,[6] and in 1887 l'Art

---

[1] See the introduction by Mrosovsky in Flaubert, *The Temptation of St. Anthony*, p. 4.

[2] For the revival of interest in the theme of St. Anthony after 1840, see Theodore Reff, "Cézanne, Flaubert, St. Anthony and the Queen of Sheba," *Art Bulletin* 44 (1962): 113-125 and Jean Seznec, *Nouvelles Études sur la tentation de Saint Antoine* (London: The Warburg Institute, University of London, 1949).

[3] Brussels, Gillion-Crowet Collection, oil on paper, 33½" x 33½"; reproduced in *Belgian Art: 1880-1914*, p. 29.

[4] Paul Bonnefou, "Un Chapitre de l'histoire des marionnettes," *L'Artiste* 31 (1883): 391.

[5] "Une Tentation de St. Antoine de Félicien Rops," *La Revue indépendente*, no. 1 (1884), pp. 125-131.

[6] Francine-Claire Legrand, "Les Lettres de James Ensor à Octave Maus,"

CHAPTER V

FIG. 93. Jacques Callot. *The Temptation of St. Anthony*, 1635.

moderne featured a review of Les XX at Antwerp that included a discussion of Rops's St. Anthony print.[7]

A careful study of Ensor's painting reveals that the canvas is a complex statement, and one that has not yet been given the full attention it deserves. It is a monumental vision that considers the arguments between religious and scientific constituencies in the 1880s over metaphysics—arguments

still with us today in terms of education and the evolution versus creation debate. In addition, pointed autobiographical detail make the suffering saint a symbol for Ensor himself.

Whereas Khnopff and Rops chose to deal with Anthony's sexual temptations, Ensor built upon the long visual tradition that began with Bosch and Brueghel and continued through Callot's late etching, his second "Temptation of St.

Bulletin des Musées Royaux des Beaux-Arts de Belgique 15 (1966): 31.

[7] *L'Art moderne*, no. 12 (March 20, 1887), p. 90. Odilon Redon produced

his first series of illustrations for Flaubert's book in 1888 and a second edition in 1889.

FIG. 94. Gustave Doré. *Baron Munchausen aboard the Dutch ship in a sea of wine about to be swallowed by a monster*, 1865.

Anthony" (Fig. 93).[8] In those works it was the panoramic view of the multiple aspects of temptation and hallucination that were stressed, rather than any one aspect of psychological or physical torture. Monsters, grotesques, and evil demons abound and fill the sky as well as the ground. The flying figures in Charles Meryon's 1860s print, "The Ad-

miralty, Paris," which included large dolphins or porpoises, can also be considered part of the tradition for Ensor's sky figures,[9] as can the flying insects and fish in Gustave Doré's print of "Baron Munchausen aboard the Dutch ship in a sea of wine about to be swallowed by a monster" from *The Adventures of Baron Munchausen*, published in 1865 (Fig.

[8] Tannenbaum discussed Callot's connection to Ensor's painting (*James Ensor*, p. 71). Callot produced the etching under the stress of incurable cancer: *Jacques Callot 1592-1635* (Brown University and Rhode Island School of Design, 1970), fig. 55.

[9] For a discussion of the symbolism of Meryon's flying figures and their political and homeopathic connotations, see James Leo Yarnall, "Meryon's Mystical Transformations," *Art Bulletin* 61 (June 1979), esp. p. 292.

94). In all of these works, sinister and malevolent images are present in the sky, and suffering is explicit or implied. Ensor stressed these aspects in his painting by choosing the word "tribulations" for his title, rather than the more common "temptation," which is more suggestive of sexual enticements and sensuality.

In Ensor's painting the saint's world is divided into three diagonal sections: an area of land on the left, which also runs across the foreground of the picture; a middle range of sky and clouds of fiery paint echo the shape of the landmass on the left. These areas are separated by abrupt color changes that coalesce in the lower right through a smear of pink-red that flows across the water and connects the land on each side.

The air, water, and earth abound with incredible life, recalling John Milton's description in *Paradise Lost*: ". . . the tepid caves, and fens, and shores, Their brood as numerous hatch. . . ."[10] David Farmer has described it as: ". . . a world whose viscous atmosphere is filled with loathsome little creatures and a furious scribbling of hell fire. . . . Incandescent reds vibrate next to chalky surfaces, and sour yellow accents meet small but strident areas of green and pink. . . ."[11] Flaubert, who had written that his monsters were influenced in part by two of Ensor's favorite authors, Hoffmann and Poe,[12] had given his St. Anthony a nightmarish image hauntingly similar to Ensor's grotesques:

Then there file past them idols of all nations and all ages, in wood, in metal, in granite, in feathers, in skins stitched

together. The oldest of them, older than the Flood, are almost hidden by seaweed hanging down like manes. A few, too long for their bases, creak at the joints and break their backs as they walk. . . . They become horrifying—with tall plumes, globular eyes, arms terminating in claws, and the jaw of sharks.[13]

The creatures that populate Ensor's sky and sea are, however, diverse in character. Gert Schiff has characterized them as half from tradition and half from Ensor's personal symbolism.[14] Discussing the areas to the right of St. Anthony, Schiff identified several figures as having come from Bosch's Lisbon "Temptation of St. Anthony"[15] and others from Brueghel's "Big Fish eating Little Fish" and "The Fall of the Rebel Angels." He suggested that the tall figure at the lower right, who holds a giant syringe, was a reference to Ensor's dislike of doctors, a theme that Ensor would later expand in the painting of the "Bad Doctors" from 1892 and the etching of the same subject from 1895.

Schiff linked the balloon in the sky to Edgar Allen Poe's story of "The Unparalleled Adventure of One Hans Pfaal." The suffering of various animals who were taken along as guinea pigs on Pfaal's trip to the moon was noted, and Schiff pointed to the flaccid creature being removed from the balloon in Ensor's painting; according to Schiff the demon who pierces the balloon with a whip-like object is a reference to Ensor's lifelong fight against vivisection.

Within the context of Ensor's symbolism that balloon may have held an additional significance. Ballooning was a pop-

---

[10] Book VII, lines 417-418 in John Milton, *Milton's Paradise Lost*, introduction by Robert Vaughan (New York: Cassell, 1866).

[11] Farmer, *Ensor*, p. 26.

[12] Seznec, *Nouvelles Études*, p. 59.

[13] Quoted under a section entitled "Dead Gods" in Philippe Jullian, *Dreamers of Decadence* (New York: Praeger, 1975), p. 232.

[14] "New Light on Ensor," in "Unveiling the Mysteries: the Symbolist Period in Belgium; A Symposium on the Social and Historical Context of the Avant-Garde, 1880-1914," The Brooklyn Museum, May 3, 1980.

[15] Schiff observed that, "the very fact that Ensor claimed he hadn't even heard of Bosch when he was painting this picture is strong indication that he was influenced by him" (Ibid.).

FIG. 95. Charles Meryon. *Le Pont-au-change*, 1854.

ular sport; by 1866 there were already over 600 members in Nadar's Sociétés Aéronauts, among them Offenbach, Georges Sand, Dumas, and the Belgian painter Alfred Stevens.[16] The aerial balloon made numerous appearances in prints by Cruikshank, Grandville, Daumier, and others. Aerial balloons were also important politically: during the Prussian War French aerial reconnaissance was made by balloon, and balloons carried the world's first airmail letters over enemy lines. One print in particular makes an interesting comparison with Ensor's use of the balloon, the second through the sixth states of Meryon's 1850s etching, "The Exchange Bridge, Paris," part of his series in "Etchings of Paris" (Fig. 95). There, a balloon labeled "speranza" appears in the sky above the bridge in front of the Palace of Justice. In the water below a drowning man founders, stretching his arms out toward a boat. The incorporation of the drowning scene with a view

[16] Nigel Gosling, *Nadar* (New York: Alfred A. Knopf, 1976), p. 16.

of the Palace of Justice has been seen as "an ironic reference to the workings of Justice itself."[17] One could add that the balloon's lettering is a reference to "esperanza," "hope," and therefore makes an additional link with the Palace of Justice and the drowning man. In the eighth state of the print Meryon replaced the balloon with "an ominous flock of huge birds," a telling statement of his own disappointment with the government's concept of justice.[18]

In Ensor's painting the balloon appears in a prominent location above the head of St. Anthony, but also above the water. The outlines of colonnaded buildings, as well as suggestions of burning buildings, can be made out at the right, on the edge of the water. In the water there is a prehistoric bird that stands on a raft with a pole in its claw. To its left a giant lifts a boat out of the water and seems ready to throw it, along with its occupants. The link with Meryon's print may simply be a fortuitous coincidence, but Meryon's buildings, the boats and people in the water, and the aerial balloon, which is later replaced by giant birds, parallel Ensor's composition, his strong interest in symbolic connotations, and his painting's mood of enigmatic despair.

St. Anthony is shown in profile, but his features are difficult to see because the skin is mottled and pockmarked. Ensor's late copy (Fig. 96) of the painting, although inferior in quality to the first, helps to clarify some of the more obscure details. The saint turns toward the figures at his right: an assortment of grotesques that includes a long-nosed monster with large ears at the left edge of the painting, a tall male in profile who wears a uniform and hat and who drinks from a bowl with a long, bent, red straw, a horned creature who smokes a pipe, and the caricature of

a sturdy, muscled female nude directly next to Anthony.

In this cluster of fantastic forms one figure is remarkably different: it is not a caricature or a grotesque, but a woman who stands in three-quarter pose, nude, and with a red halo that outlines her head and neck and sets her apart from her bilious surroundings. Directly in front of her there is a table or tray with several bottles and glasses; below the tray a lyre is being played by a green monster. This woman has a prototype in Pieter Huys's sixteenth-century "Temptation of St. Anthony," in which a bare-breasted woman tempts the old saint with her body and a plate filled with food, which she holds under her breasts, in much the same position as the tray in Ensor's painting (Fig. 97). In fact, Ensor's composition is divided in a manner similar to Huys's painting, a diagonal arrangement of three areas. The upper right cloudy sky appears to be a direct reference to the same dark area in Huys's work.

In Huys's panel the nude wears a dark headdress that covers part of her hair, and it may have inspired Ensor to highlight the area around the head of his nude. The identity of Ensor's woman is a mystery; she doesn't resemble Mariette Rousseau and Ensor had not yet met Augusta Boogaerts. It is notable that the woman stands next to a lyre; Félicien Rops had, in a print produced the same year as Ensor's painting, shown a nude woman with a halo holding onto a lyre, which was played by other disembodied hands ("La Lyre," Fig. 98). Rops's female sits in a chair with large circular top, and it is interesting that Ensor's lyre has one distinctive round end. For Ensor the woman may have been a symbolic reference to the feminine principle in general, and he therefore depicted her with homage to Huys and Rops, the lyre

---

[17] Yarnall, "Meryon's Mystical Transformations": 289.

[18] Ibid. For a discussion of that symbolism, see p. 291. Meryon had also written and etched a poem, "Hope," to accompany his etching. It begins, "O divine hope! light balloon!" (Delteil, *Catalogue Raisonné*, fig. 35).

FIG. 96. Ensor. *The Temptation of St. Anthony*, 1927.

121

FIG. 97. Pieter Huys. *The Temptation of St. Anthony*, 1547.

122

and the red halo suggesting saintliness and sexuality. The bottles and glasses support this interpretation by implying drink.[19]

Ensor was ill at this time, as his letter on Christmas Eve of that year reminds us. The tall figure with the giant syringe in the lower right of the St. Anthony painting may be a reference to his illness, as well as to his disdain for doctors. Several additional personal associations should be pointed out: 1887 was, it will be recalled, the year that Ensor's father died. It was, in addition, a year of rejection and disappointment in terms of his art; but it was also the time in which he added a flowered hat to his self-portrait as a comment on his sexual maturity. In the "Tribulations of St. Anthony" Legrand has seen Ensor as transported and bewitched and revealing extraordinary events from within himself.[20]

Flaubert had described the torment and drive of an artist in a letter written in the 1850s. It was a telling description of his own struggle, but it could apply as well to that of Ensor as St. Anthony, and to that of all artists and saints whose solitary visions are strange and repugnant to society:

. . . Go on! Rend yourself, whip yourself, roll yourself in ashes, make matter vile, spit on your body, tear out your heart! You'll be alone, . . . none of what makes other people's joy will go to make yours, what are pinpricks to them will be laceration to you, and you'll flounder on, lost in the storm, with this little light on the horizon. . . .[21]

Like Ensor's contemporary, Paul Cézanne, whose anxiety became visualized for many observers as the main source of

FIG. 98. Félicien Rops. *La Lyre*, 1887.

[19] The bottles and glasses might also be a reference to Ensor's mother and her various illnesses; they would later be used in the final tribute at her deathbed, the 1915 painting in which they appear on a tray on a table between the viewer and the body (Fig. 15).
[20] Legrand, *Ensor, cet inconnu*, p. 88.
[21] Quoted in Flaubert, *The Temptation of St. Anthony*, pp. 24-25.

energy and inspiration in his art, Ensor's anxiety pervades "The Tribulations of St. Anthony." With this painting, which deals with the ultimate introspective theme of metaphysical being, Ensor became the archetypal modern artist. Although Flaubert is the main source for Ensor's canvas, Ensor's anxiety is similar to that of the Balzac character Frenhofer, the tortured artist who yearned to express the inexpressible and to make concrete the abstract in *Le Chef-d'oeuvre inconnu*.[22] Paul Valéry has been quoted within the context of a discussion on Frenhofer, and his observations apply to Ensor:

What would we do without the help of what does not exist? . . . our very unoccupied minds would pine away if myths, fables, misunderstandings, abstractions, beliefs and monsters, hypotheses and the so-called problems of metaphysics did not people the darkness and the depths of our natures with abstract creations and images.[23]

Balzac was attracted to concepts of a definable void, an abyss that had a source in the tenets of Swedenborg, whose philosophy was so amenable to Poe and Baudelaire and Ensor as well.[24] Balzac had Frenhofer exclaim: "To the abode of the departed I would go to seek thee, O celestial beauty! Like Orpheus, I would go down into the hell of art, to bring back life from there."[25] Ensor's incredible canvas suggests a similar search, an approach in which the artist has allowed himself no restrictions in an attempt to represent raw, elemental matter. This substance oozes from the canvas surface and catches its inhabitants in the slime of primordial muck. In

Flaubert's 1849 version of *The Temptation of St. Anthony*, the saint's companion, a pig, recounts a dream about a large pond of greasy water:

A whole world's rotting filth was spread around me to satisfy my appetite, I caught sight of clots of blood through the fumes, blue intestines and every kind of animal excrement, the vomit or orgies, and like slicks of oil the greenish pus that runs from wounds; it all thickened around me, so that I was walking with my four trotters almost sinking in this sticky slime, and on my back there fell a continuous drizzle of hot rain, sweet and sickly. . . . All this gurgled inside my body, all this lapped against my ears, I was gasping, I was howling, I was eating and swallowing it all. Ugh! Ugh! . . .[26]

It is an internalized hell of revolting hallucination that is similar in spirit to Ensor's panoramic vision. The surface of Ensor's painting, with its dark browns, blood-reds, and bile-greens, as well as the application of the pigments themselves, has been seen as closer to smeared excrement than to carefully applied paint:

. . . within the context of the Temptation of St. Anthony excremental images were often depicted. Prior to Ensor, however, these usually formed only a small episode in the larger fabric of the St. Anthony story. Iconographically, even Ensor's painting shows only one instance of the actual depiction of excretion. Nonetheless . . . Ensor has made these ideas central by his method of applying pigments and by his dung-brown, blood-red oriented palette.[27]

This sense of the excremental, however, carries a far more

---

[22] For the most recent discussion of the Balzac story and its influence on Cézanne, see Ashton, *A Fable of Modern Art*, chaps. 1 and 2.

[23] Ibid., p. 29.

[24] Drawings found in Ensor's collection, with notes from Swedenborg in Ensor's handwriting, were made by Ensor's young friend, the painter Jean-Jacques Gaillard (now in the collection of Madame Van der Perre, Brussels, who was kind enough to show them to me).

[25] Quoted in Ashton, *A Fable of Modern Art*, p. 26.

[26] Flaubert, *The Temptation of St. Anthony*, p. 14. The first version of Flaubert's book was the longest, and by the 1856 version, the image of the pig, a companion who had become part of the saint's iconographical entourage in the Middle Ages, had been deleted.

[27] See Marshall Neal Myers "James Ensor's 'The Tribulations of St. Anthony': Permutations of the Excremental Vision," *Arts Magazine* 54, no. 4

important significance than its obvious reference to the scatological and its continuation of the popular northern preoccupation with low-life themes and earthy peasant humor.[28] It refers, rather, to St. Anthony's urge to become "sheer matter," and it is in this context, as developed in Flaubert's last, 1874 version of his story, that Ensor's painting can best be understood.

Anthony's search is both secular and religious. In Flaubert's last version there is an open Bible: ". . . the very locus of temptation. It engenders the whole visionary sweep and shows that 'evil is not incarnate in characters, but incorporated in words.' "[29] In Ensor's painting St. Anthony holds a large, open book on the brown mass that acts as a table, but rather than read it, he distinctly looks away toward the figures at his right.

In Flaubert's philosophy the skeleton of Death is a major element, as it will be in Ensor's later works, such as the 1889 print "My Portrait Skeletonized." In *The Temptation of St. Anthony*, Flaubert's skeleton speaks a fatalistic message and is suggestive of the poignant drawing Ensor made on his Christmas Eve letter to Maus in 1887, in which Ensor was led from his sick bed by a winged skeleton (Fig. 37): "Now or later, what does it matter! You are mine like the suns, the nations, the towns, the kings, the snow on the peaks, the meadow grasses. I outsoar than [sic] the sparrowhawk, I outrun the gazelle, I touch hope itself, I have conquered the son of God!"[30]

Flaubert was the son of a doctor, and like Spinoza he believed in an infinite variety of forms. A good friend who was a biologist kept him informed of scientific progress and of the theories concerning evolution and the nature of matter that were abundant in the 1870s:

. . . the state of scientific and philosophic play was such that there was no clear demarcation between organic and inorganic matter. One current hypothesis was that of primitive "protoplasmic" forms of life which might arise from non-organic matter. Another was that of a primary organic substance from which all species had evolved. The conflicting hypothesis about the origins of life and the nature of matter were very much bound up with philosophically vexed questions: people were anxious to find solutions that would amount neither to downright materialism nor to blinkered idealism.[31]

Ensor's friendship with Mariette Rousseau, the botanist who had introduced him to the revelations found under a microscope, had fed Ensor's interests in such concerns.

When Flaubert's Devil carries Anthony off on a trip through the heavens, he is eventually led to scrutinize an incredible range of life that includes the smallest particles of living matter, a combination of "fantasy and science, monsters and molecules, that ushers Anthony to the brink of quasi-amoebic bliss."[32] A griffin digs up the ground, a thousand voices answer him and various hybrid monsters spring out: ". . . alligator's heads on roe-deers feet, owls with snakes's tails, . . . frogs as furry as bears, quadruple foetuses linked by the navel and waltzing like tops, winged stomachs hovering like gnats. . . ."[33]

Despite the horrors of these discoveries, Anthony's last words are a joyous celebration of what he has seen as the birth of life itself, the beginnings of movement: ". . . I'd like

---

(December 1979): 88.

[28] Myers' article reproduces and discusses numerous examples of northern scatalogical imagery, including works by Bosch, ̓ n Wellens de Cock,

Leohnard Beck, and Peter Flotner.

[29] Flaubert, *The Temptation of St. Anthony*, p. 27.

[30] Ibid., p. 218.   [31] Ibid., p. 49.   [32] Ibid., p. 17.   [33] Ibid., p. 229.

to have wings, a carapace, a rind . . . to be inside everything . . . flow to water . . . to curl myself up into every shape, to penetrate each atom, to get down to the depth of matter—*to be matter!"[34]*

Anthony's despair and agony, his tribulations as well as jubilation, his conflict with the Bible and science, and his desire to comprehend the true meaning of existence itself by becoming one with matter and therefore with God, are all reflected in Ensor's amazing canvas. It pays homage to masters of the past who have attempted to depict Anthony's hell, and it breaks totally new ground by attempting to express the concepts of metaphysics through the palpable expression of matter in its multifarious forms. Thus the ooze and slime of matter's beginnings are suggested, as well as the ultimate outcome, matter's end in excrement: through the evolutionary development of the fish who crawls out of the sea and appears on the land, as well as through the hybrid creatures who populate the sea and the air; through classical civilization, as seen in the skeletons of colonnaded buildings and the destruction of cities in a cataclysmic fire;[35] and through Ensor's own personal torments and pleasures, which appear to the right of St. Anthony and hold his attention.

For Ensor, as for Flaubert, the legend of St. Anthony was relevant on an intensely personal level through an introspective journey of hope and despair. But through the quest for knowledge of the self, universal questions of broader significance, which held a particular appeal for nineteenth-century intellectuals, could be considered: questions about religion, about the ultimate meaning of existence and about the evolution of the species. Furthermore, these considerations could be investigated with contemporary society in mind. Mrosovsky has observed that in Flaubert's St. Anthony "... the tiny-minded half-animate creatures like the Sciapodes expose the cautious bliss of the despised bourgeoisie—signifying 'obscurantism itself' as Flaubert noted."[36] Ensor's "Tribulations of St. Anthony" contains similar images suggestive of diseased society, for example, the balloon image in the sky and the burning of classical buildings, as well as the depiction of half-human grotesques at St. Anthony's right.

This concern with the bourgeoisie became a crucial element in much of Ensor's production from 1887. When these observations on Belgian life were intermeshed with a treatment of religious themes, as they often were, they became some of the most successful images, both artistically and sociopolitically. For Ensor religious history was a complex intermingling of fantasy with fact and past with present. Although he was not religious, through a complex arrangement of historical and contemporary time his religious works illustrated the pain and suffering inflicted upon both the innocent and the creative. Further, Ensor's vivid and frightening depictions of a mob illustrate his fascination with the concept of the crowd and the psychodynamics of its power.

A drawing from 1887 on the same St. Anthony theme, but entitled "The Temptation of St. Anthony," continues the use of social comment within the context of religious imagery (Fig. 99). It is a remarkable piece, a tour de force both for its imaginative creatures and for its execution: a densely packed drawing composed of seventy-two individual sheets of paper combined to make a rectangle over six feet tall. The kneeling saint occupies the center foreground of the drawing, and his figure dwarfs the surrounding hordes by his size and

---

[34] Ibid., p. 232. Emphasis added.
[35] Schiff has identified dinosaurs at the entrance to the burning buildings,

perhaps a reference to a doomed species.
[36] Flaubert, *The Temptation of St. Anthony*, p. 48.

massive dark robe. Above his head a female nude appears, and above that is the head of Christ, disembodied in an aureole of light surrounded by dark clouds.

In 1888 Ensor had planned on exhibiting the work with Les XX. In a page of the catalog that reproduced the artist's writing and drawing and listed the works of the artist, Ensor included a quotation from Alban Stolz's book *Vie des Saints* under his entry "La Tentation de Sainte-Antoine":

One day when he had been tempted more than usual, it seemed to him that our Lord appeared to him radiating with light. He says to him with a sigh: Good Jesus, where have you been? Why haven't you come sooner to support me? And he replied to him. When you were fighting I was near you; because know that I will always help you. But the devil, without tiring, offered him other traps. He sowed in his heart lewd thoughts; he suggested to him shameful desires; during his sleep he stirred up in his imagination lubricious dreams.[37]

That text could well have been used as inspiration, but Flaubert's *Temptation of St. Anthony* was also a source, specifically with reference to the nude and to the head of Christ above the saint. In Flaubert's book Anthony's last lines, "to be matter!" are followed by a final description:

Day at last dawns; and like the raised curtains of a tabernacle, golden clouds furling into large scrolls uncover the sky. There in the middle, inside the very disc of the sun, radiates the face of Jesus Christ. Anthony makes the sign of the cross and returns to his prayers.[38]

In Flaubert's text the torso of the nude is seen within the context of a discussion with Death:

[37] Legrand, "*Lettres à Octave Maus*": 32; reproduced in Haesaerts, *James Ensor*, p. 342.
[38] Flaubert, *The Temptation of St. Anthony*, p. 232.

FIG. 99. Ensor. *The Temptation of St. Anthony*, 1887.

It is a death's head with a crown of roses. It rises above a woman's torso, pearly white. Beneath this, a shroud starred with dots of gold acts as a sort of tail- and the whole body undulates, as might a gigantic worm lifting upright.[39]

The nude woman is transferred by Ensor to a prominent position directly below the head of Christ. The descriptive term "pearly white" like "mother of pearl" will appear in Ensor's writings when he discusses Venus and images of female beauty.[40] It is also notable that at St. Anthony's right several worm-like tail shapes appear, one of which connects to a skeleton, while at the other end a strange gnome with an infant's body feeds the worm's extremity to another skeletal creature. In this same area of the drawing Diana of Ephesus appears, closely related to Flaubert's description:

. . . below are three rows of breasts; and from her stomach to her feet she is caught in a narrow sheath, its whole length leaping with bulls, stags, griffins and bees. She can be seen by the white glimmer of a silver disc, as round as the full moon, set behind her head.[41]

The intermingling of forms is so complex in this drawing that it is often impossible to determine the exact circumstance depicted. Further, some of the areas are filled with barely perceptible lines, so light and delicate that their complete forms are lost. Some areas will reappear in individual works of Ensor, such as the composition of the sheet just above and directly to the right of St. Anthony's head, where Queen Parysatis and her attendant, both nude, are shown

slaying the body of a eunuch, a theme that will become the subject of an 1899 etching.[42]

At the bottom left of the drawing the bourgeoisie are explicitly mocked as shopkeepers in crude, unflattering terms. They wear black top hats with white bands imprinted with various slogans, "beans provençale" and "good fricasseed sausages." One black-faced man in a top hat holds a feathered carcass in one hand while the other carries an upright pot into which a large insect appears to be defecating. With Ensor's "Entry of Christ into Brussels" the sexual and scatological imagery evidenced in this drawing will disappear, whereas the mockery of the bourgeoisie, seen here in the lower left, will become more highly developed.

In another work based upon Anthony's torments, the 1888 etching "Fight of the Demons," Ensor dealt with violent sexual imagery (Fig. 100).[43] Martin Schongauer's fifteenth-century engraving of "The Temptation of St. Anthony" could have been its prototype (Fig. 101). Schongauer's flat, circular composition with Anthony being mauled by monsters in the middle of the air was used by Ensor as inspiration for an aerial scene of explicit fornication and amputation. In the middle of Ensor's work a robed figure holding a long sword recalls Schongauer's St. Anthony. He has a long mustache and beard and under his robe several clawed feet repeat the motif of the clawed foot of a monster that appears directly under Schongauer's St. Anthony. The head of Ensor's figure is surrounded by an aureole of light in which the heads of other beings can be seen, but most notable is Ensor's double

[39] Ibid., p. 220.
[40] E.g., when referring to his "Consoling Virgin," "I kissed her little feet of snow and mother-of-pearl" (Haesaerts, *James Ensor*, p. 228). Also see Ensor, *Mes Écrits*, p. 98, and Chapter VI of this study.
[41] Flaubert, *The Temptation of St. Anthony*, p. 176.
[42] Taevernier lists the titles Ensor used for the etching: "Queen Parysatis

Flaying a Eunuch," "Little Persian Tortures," or "Tortured Criminals under Ivan the Terrible" (*James Ensor*, p. 289 and pl. 116).
[43] According to Taevernier that title was Ensor's whereas Taevernier lists it as "Devils thrashing Angels and Archangels" (*James Ensor*, p. 73). A colored version entitled "Combat des demons" is reproduced in Janssens, *James Ensor*, p. 43.

Fig. 100. Ensor. *The Fight of the Demons*, 1888.

FIG. 101. Martin Schongauer. *The Temptation of St. Anthony*, c. 1470-1475.

vision in the face of the figure: it can be read at once as both profile and full face. Who is fighting whom and who is winning are uncertain, but the aerial combat suggests Émile Zola's description of a similar scene in *Le Rêve*, volume sixteen of the popular Rougon-Macquart series published the same year as Ensor's print:

Then opposite the saints, behold the evil spirits! They often fly about us like insects, and fill the air without number. The air is also full of demons, as the rays of the sun are full of atoms. . . . It is even like powder! The saints are always victorious, and yet they are constantly obliged to renew the battle. The more the demons are driven away, the more they return.[44]

Various types of female figures are involved in the fighting and in most cases they seem to be losing the battle. In the upper left two long-haired women are being sawed by the long snout of a large fish; in the lower left a female holds a long delicate cross and floats upside down while her exposed vulva is pierced by the end of the central figure's large sword. Other females are stabbed and lie murdered, and at the far right, at the middle of the page, a woman with fat buttocks is being violated anally by the sword of a hybrid creature whose own private parts are in jeopardy. With its emphasis on sexual acts, Ensor's print can be compared with a description found in a story published in 1888 by the Belgian writer Georges Eekhoud. Eekhoud's protagonist in "The New Carthage" had made friends with a group of river pirates, and he described a nocturnal scene he witnessed in a dark attic, where outlaws of both sexes slept:

This promiscuity determined almost unconscious and somnambulistic copulations, amorous mistakes . . . where did

[44] Émile Zola, *The Dream*, translated by Eliza E. Chase (London: Chatto and Windus, 1907), p. 29.

130

FIG. 102. Ensor. *Stars at the Cemetery*, 1888.

reality commence and nightmare end? The noctambulists turned each other upside down, fighting with arms and legs, picked themselves up in positions like those of the Last Judgment or the Fall of the Angels.[45]

Ensor's print is remarkable for 1888; it follows upon the bold experiments with color and surface from the 1887 "Tribulations of St. Anthony" with breakthroughs in print-making: the use of space and form affirms the two-dimensional surface and patterns it with movement, paving the

way for the twentieth-century abstractions of artists like Kandinsky and Klee.

In the same year Ensor produced another etching of sky imagery, "Stars at the Cemetery" (Fig. 102), which is the antithesis of his scene of fighting demons. Ensor entitled it "The Cemetery" and in a letter he confirmed that this plate was the result of an experiment with sulphuring and that he had only taken a few proofs.[46] Although no other states are known, Taevernier has questioned whether Ensor may

[45] Georges Eekhoud, *The New Carthage*, translated and introduced by Lloyd R. Morris (New York: Duffield, 1917). In 1888 Ensor painted his own

"Fall of the Rebel Angels" (Antwerp: Musées Royaux des Beaux-Arts).
[46] Taevernier, *James Ensor*, p. 147.

have overengraved the crosses in the foreground after he had taken some proofs. It is a reasonable question, given the flatness of the image with the bottom area of the cemetery obfuscated. In this condition the blackness of the night, broken by the shining light of stars that seem to pervade the surface from top to bottom, speaks for a celebration of cosmic energy and a spiritual reverence for nature that is akin to Van Gogh's. The etching stands alone as a remarkable image quite unlike anything ever made on a copper plate at that time.

Between 1885 and 1888 Ensor produced a number of important drawings and paintings that explored religious themes. Opinions vary on Ensor's own religious philosophy, and during the years of his greatest religious output he never revealed his exact beliefs. An early clue, which may be somewhat misleading, comes from around 1883: "The figure of Christ makes its appearance in Ensor's work. We learn through a project scribbled on a page in a sketch book that he was reading the Bible and finding it a comfort during his moments of depression."[47] In a charcoal drawing from 1884 Ensor makes a gesture with his hand, a finger pointing back toward the artist, which has been seen as a reference to St. John the Baptist. In this "narcissistic posture of the self-appointed"[48] he thus becomes part of the chain leading to Christ Himself. Yet, according to Tannenbaum, Ensor identified not with the Christ associated with tradition: ". . .

but [with] an excruciatingly tortured and personal vision in which the artist projects himself into the agony of the crucified. . . . It is not with Christ as divine being but merely as the archetype of persecuted truth that the identification is made."[49] Thus in the drawing "Calvary," dated 1886, the cross on which Christ hangs carries a large sign with Ensor's name. At the right of the cross a figure representing Longinus pierces Christ's side with a lance carrying the name "Fétis," a hostile critic of Ensor's art.[50]

In an interview from 1949, in the month of his death, Ensor was asked about his beliefs. He was ill at the time and at his advanced age of eighty-nine he may have answered the questions truthfully. He claimed that he saw no evolution, rather ". . . only a considerable irresolution."[51] When asked whether he believed in life after death he answered: "No, I don't believe in life after death. . . . The individual human being has no special meaning as species"[52] and Ensor pointed to the depiction of a woman and asked, "God! Why not?"[53] From his art it appears that religion occupied his interest as a compulsion that controlled people's lives, caused wars, and offered comfort and solace, and that its incredible powers had to be taken into account: "Christ is a very great figure, a figure to whom much attention has been given. You have to consider his significance obligatory."[54]

Ensor's fascination with Christ echoed the interest of nineteenth-century thinkers who attempted to come to terms

---

[47] *Retrospective James Ensor*, introduction by Walter Vanbeselaere (Antwerp: Musées Royaux des Beaux-Arts, 1951), p. 12.

[48] Leslie D. Morrisey, "James Ensor's Self-Portraits," *Arts Magazine* 54 (December 1979): 92.

[49] Tannenbaum, *James Ensor*, p. 61.

[50] Julius Kaplan has suggested that Ensor knew the legend of Longinus's conversion to Christianity, therefore implying that Fétis would come to believe in Ensor's art ("The Religious Subjects": 199).

[51] ". . . seulement une forte indecision." Quoted in J. P. Hodin, "James

Ensor: On the Ultimate Questions of Life," in *The Dilemma of Being Modern* (London: Routledge and Kegan Paul, 1956), p. 37.

[52] "Non. Je ne crois pas à un autre vie après la mort. . . . L'individu n'a aucune signification spéciale" (Ibid., p. 38). Marilyn Gaddis Rose believes Ensor is punning here.

[53] Ibid.

[54] "Christ est une figure très grande. On s'est beaucoup occupé de cette figure-là. Le Christ, c'est une signification obligatoire" (Ibid.).

with religion in a contemporary world that popularized positivistic belief. Following Ernest Renan's *La Vie de Jésus*, originally published in 1863, D. F. Strauss wrote a new *Life of Jesus*, updating his 1835 book of the same subject. Strauss credited Renan's arguments for accepting Jesus as a remarkable human being capable of making mistakes,[55] and Strauss's conclusion was the same as Renan's, that Jesus was a great religious genius, but not unique in that he might be surpassed by others who would live after him. The influence of Strauss's book on the theological world of the nineteenth century was profound and it opened up a critical investigation of the Bible in a manner not before possible. In 1872 Strauss published *The Old Faith and the New* in which he relied on scientific information from Darwin, Buchner, and others. His conclusion related man to the infinite universe and the cosmos, not to any personalized and transcendent God.[56]

It is notable that Émile Littré translated Strauss's *Life of Jesus* into French, for Littré, who was a celebrated positivist philosopher and lexicographer, appears in a prominent position and in extra-large proportion as a parade director in Ensor's 1885 drawing "The Alive and Radiant: the Entry of Christ into Jerusalem," sometimes identified as "Hail, Jesus, King of the Jews" (Fig. 103).[57] Littré had not been included in the small version, a preliminary sketch for the larger drawing. Perhaps his presence in the latter was an afterthought, for the portrait of Littré had been made as a separate drawing

FIG. 103. Ensor. *Hail Jesus, King of the Jews (The Alive and Radiant: The Entry of Christ into Jerusalem)*, 1885.

[55] Richard S. Cromwell, *David Friedrich Strauss and His Place in Modern Thought*, foreword by Wilhelm Pauck (Fairlawn: R. E. Burdick, 1974), pp. 141-142.

[56] Ibid., p. 156.

[57] Eugène Demolder first identified Littré's presence in *James Ensor* (Brussels: Paul Lacomblez, 1892), p. 18. Littré looks out at the spectator and holds a baton in his hand in the lower right of the drawing.

pasted on the paper, making an early collage. Julius Kaplan questioned Littré's presence but concluded that as he was a well-known positivist he would be opposed to religion and therefore his prominent position would accentuate the insincerity of the crowd.[58] A more credible possibility was suggested by Auguste Taevernier who had mentioned Littré in connection with Strauss's book. He reasoned that Ensor must have consulted Strauss's translated work, which may have inspired him to realize a project of six drawings concerning Christ, of which "The Entry of Christ into Jerusalem" was the second.[59] Littré, who had been called "un saint laïque," a nondenominational saint,[60] had died in 1881 and *L'Art moderne* had that year included a review of his book *Conservation, revolution, positivisme*, "three tendencies of the modern spirit."[61] Thus Littré's image could have been included as a tribute to the dead philosopher, an intellectual with whom Ensor could identify and one who had worked to demystify religion.

Littré's portrait is one of several in the series of drawings based on Christ's life. In the third drawing, also produced in 1885 and entitled "The Flood: Jesus Shown to the People," Ensor included portraits of his friends Willy Finch and Octave Maus and his own self-portrait as well.[62] Later, in the

1888 painting of "The Entry of Christ into Brussels," portraits would again appear among the crowd. Ensor's drawing of "The Entry of Christ into Jerusalem" would also serve as a model for other aspects of that later "Entry of Christ": for the figure of Christ on a donkey, barely visible in the center of both compositions; for the densely packed crowd surging forward and oblivious to His presence, and for slogans on banners and signs with references to contemporary life.[63]

Two of Ensor's religious drawings were of extraordinary size; both "The Temptation of St. Anthony" and "The Entry of Christ into Jerusalem" were over six feet tall. With these monumental drawings Ensor elevated the status of a pencil and charcoal sketch to that of an oil painting. These were major statements, central to Ensor's development, and they served to challenge the hierarchy that had always implied that drawing was less valuable than painting.

Ensor was to achieve a similar coup with his gigantic oil painting of "The Entry of Christ into Brussels" (Fig. 57), a canvas over fourteen feet in width, which elevated caricature into a realm of art once reserved for pious, wall-size frescoes. The painting was a nineteenth-century billboard and a cinemascopic vision of major proportion described by Tannenbaum as:

[58] Julius Kaplan, "The Religious Subjects": 184.

[59] Taevernier, *Le Drame Ensorien*, pp. 27-28. The title for the six, noted in Taevernier's own title, was "Christ's Haloes or the Sensitivities of Light." They were listed by Ensor in the following manner:

1. The Merry: Adoration of the Shepherds; 2. The Alive and Radiant: The Entry of Christ into Jerusalem; 3. The Flood: Jesus shown to the People; 4. The Sad and Broken: Satan and the Fantastic Legions; 5. The Tranquil and Serene: The Descent from the Cross; 6. The Intense: Resurrection. Also see Gisèle Ollinger-Zinque, "Les auréoles du Christ ou les sensibilités de la lumière," *Bulletin des Musées Royaux des Beaux-Arts de Belgique* 17 (1968): 191-202. Legrand has called this series a projection of Ensor's personality into that of Christ (*Ensor, cet inconnu*, p. 76). She also quotes from an unpublished text in which Ensor observed, ". . . Artistes, amis purs et

hautains réagissez et vertement et condamez à l'example du Christ . . ." (*Ensor, cet inconnu*, p. 106, bn. 10, "Haro, Haro, Haro, sus aux censeurs," Brussels, Archives de l'Art contemporain, inv. 10274).

[60] *La Grande Encyclopedie, Inventaire raisonné des sciences, des lettres et des arts*, vol. XXII (Paris: Librairie Larousse, 1886-1902), p. 347.

[61] *L'Art moderne*, no. 15 (June 12, 1881), p. 113ff. In the preceding issue Ensor's own art had been praised.

[62] For a discussion of this remarkable drawing, which has been linked to Rembrandt's etchings of Christ, see Taevernier, *Le Drame Ensorien*, pp. 37-51.

[63] E.g., "Salute, Jesus King of the Jews," "Coleman's Mustard," "Belgian Impressionists." Kaplan discusses these slogans in "The Religious Subjects": 184.

. . . endlessly fascinating in its details. Each head shocks the observer anew with the strength and directness and originality of its characterization. Beyond the immediate impact of the canvas, it is this power that causes the eye to move across it in slow discovery as though it were a written page in which each word must be understood. . . .[64]

Ensor's painting can also be seen to have been inspired by the desire to upstage, through both size and subject matter, Georges Seurat, whose programmatic investigation of Parisian landscape and society, "Sunday Afternoon on the Island of La Grand Jatte," was heralded by Les XX as a modern masterpiece when it appeared at their 1887 exhibition. Ensor's painting is 169½" in width, making it larger than Seurat's 120" canvas and considerably larger than any of Ensor's other pictures. More crucial than size, however, was subject matter: Ensor's painting, which depicts brutalized, contemporary Belgian society, stands in direct contrast to the French artist's vision of calm, classless utopia. Seurat's painting was embraced by many of the young Belgian artists associated with Les XX, many of whom transformed into Belgian Neopointillists. Les XX's leader, Octave Maus, had gone so far as to call Seurat "this Messiah of a new art" when he wrote about his painting in L'Art moderne,[65] an appellation that may have furthered Ensor's determination to deal with Christ's image in an oil painting of giant scale.

Ensor's full title for the painting, "The Entry of Christ into Brussels Mardi Gras of 1888,"[66] gave it an undeniable and

specific point in "present" but "continuing" time, just as Seurat had with his choice of a Sunday afternoon on the island of La Grande Jatte. Ensor would have agreed with Laforgue, whose Moralités was concerned with the fact that the past, through history, myth, and legend, exists everywhere and for all of us: that we are in it and it is in us.[67] The carnival dates back to pre-Christian origins in pagan fertility rites, and Ensor's carnival, with its reference to a Mardi Gras, makes a historical link with the Middle Ages, when Shrove Tuesday was first celebrated. Vanbeselaere saw a specific association between Ensor's painting and the Belgian tradition of the Procession of the Holy Blood:

I suppose that he was present at the spectacular procession of the Holy Blood at Bruges. There one finds Christ seated on an ass at the time of his triumphal entry into Jerusalem, the fanfares, the extraordinary figure of the drum major brandishing his cane, at the same time as the worshipers kneel on the vast balcony, which occupies half of the foreground.[68]

This procession dates back to the fourteenth century, and it has been described as a pageant with contradictory elements: popular imagery vying with attempts at historical accuracy. Floats immobilize actors in tableaux while groups of horseback riders and others on foot sing or call to one another. Scenes from the Old and New Testaments are reproduced, and at the end of the procession a golden casket from the Crusaders is carried, which is thought to contain a drop of

---

[64] Tannenbaum, James Ensor, pp. 74-75. For a lengthy study of the painting, consult McGough, "Ensor's Entry of Christ."

[65] The article was written anonymously and analyzed the 1886 Impressionist exhibition in Paris. Jane Block mentions the quotation and discusses the steps taken to prepare the Belgian public for its encounter with "La Grande Jatte" in "Les XX: Forum of the Avant-Garde," p. 27. She also deals with the reaction to Belgian artists who changed their style under the impact

of Seurat's works (pp. 27-28).

[66] "L'Entrée du Christ à Bruxelles le Mardi gras de 1888" Walter Vanbeselaere, L'Entrée du Christ à Bruxelles (Brussels: Weisenbuch, 1958), p. 15, and Legrand, Ensor, cet inconnu, p. 76.

[67] See Warren Ramsey, Jules Laforgue and the Ironic Inheritance (New York: Oxford University Press, 1953), p. 62.

[68] Vanbeselaere, L'Entrée du Christ, p. 15.

the Holy Blood brought back from Palestine by Thierry d'Alsace in 1150.[69]

There are other processions in Belgium with similar striking details. The "Magdalene March" from the region between the Sambre and Meuse rivers differs somewhat from other ceremonies in that the religious procession contains military units, composed of voluntary companies wearing rented uniforms. In their antiquated assortment of costumes they have been described as a veritable masquerade:

This mixture of religious and lay elements, sometimes even in caricature, is not merely accepted, but actually demanded by the people of the region; the many attempts on the part of the clergy to separate the two elements have given rise to conflicts in which the religious authorities usually meet defeat.[70]

And the procession at Veurne (Furnes) on the last Sunday in July should also be mentioned. It coincides with a fair, and the market place is filled with booths and stands: "Here, amidst banners and pennants, the parade swings into action."[71]

Ensor's painting recalls a whole genre of processionals, from the first religious medieval parades to the politically inspired "Joyous Entries" of the Renaissance. In *La Vie Quotidienne en Belgique*, Georges H. Dumont has observed that Belgians adore cavalcades, which remind them of the time of the "Joyeuses Entrées" and the "Ommengangs."[72]

During the Renaissance, members of royalty throughout Europe were given a special welcome when they entered a town. This meeting between the city and the monarchy was a "fête bourgeoisie" paid for by the townspeople, who hoped for royal favors in return:

In the Catholic Low Countries, however, this random and vaguely cordial relationship had been sharpened by several centuries of ritual definition into an instrument for establishing the public law governing the relationship between cities and kings, especially on the occasion of a change of reign affecting the privilege of the Flemish cities.[73]

The concept of a triumphal entry can be seen to date back to Roman times, when citizens welcomed back their victorious armies, but it was the succession of a new ruler that later became the celebrated event. Jean Sans Peur made his "Joyous Entry" into Ghent in 1405 amidst a parade that stressed the cult of the hero through references to pagan antiquity.[74] Often it was with a mixture of symbolic associations that the ruler was welcomed: "The Middle Ages had cultivated allegory and multiplied the levels of interpretation. Holidays still drawing on their medieval origins had placed biblical history on a parallel with local or national history."[75] The Flemish model for a joyous entry was copied in other countries and when Philip II made his entry into Lisbon in 1619 the "Belgian" format had been assimilated through numerous books and engravings that explained the proceedings.[76]

Legrand has observed that Ensor's painting has its iconographic origin in historical triumphal entries and has noted that Hans Makart's 1878 painting commemorating the sev-

[69] Charles Leirens, *Belgian Folklore. No. 7: Art, Life, and Science in Belgium* (New York: Belgian Government Information Center, 1946), pp. 27-28.

[70] Ibid., p. 43.   [71] Ibid., pp. 44-45.

[72] Georges H. Dumont, *La Vie quotidienne en Belgique sous le regne de Léopold II (1855-1909)* (Paris: Hachette, 1974), p. 191.

[73] G. Kubler in *Les Fêtes de la Renaissance*, edited by Jean Jacquot and Elie Konigson, 3 vols. (Paris: Centre National de la Recherche Scientifique, 1975), p. 171.

[74] Marcel Lageirse in *Les Fêtes de la Renaissance*, p. 297.

[75] Jean Jacquot in *Les Fêtes de la Renaissance*, p. 12.

[76] Kubler in *Les Fêtes de la Renaissance*, p. 199.

enteenth-century "Entry of Charles V at Antwerp" had already been linked with Ensor's painting.[77] Significant for Ensor's "Entry" is the joining of a political event with that of the carnival. André Chastel has noted that from the time of the Renaissance there were two sorts of festivals: the celebration of an event memorable for the country and the monarchy, and the carnival. Further, he noted that the importance of the latter for the development of festivals from the sixteenth century on has not been properly considered:

There was a decisive transformation of traditional Mardi Gras floats and processions upon the introduction of mythological floats and allegorical tableaux vivants. . . . Comedy in the ancient manner appeared around 1510 in conjunction with the carnival festivities and furnished a piquant finale. . . . The tradition celebrated on the Eve of Lent still furnished a framework and, no doubt, more than one vital element of the new type of festivity.[78]

Ensor's use of the Mardi Gras combined with the joyous entry theme effectively blended two festivals central to Belgian life. The historical, the religious, and the political are intertwined in a statement that combine local, national, and international significance through the return of Christ and His triumphal entry. Thus in 1888 Christ becomes the last monarch to attempt such an event, documented in a final painting in the series of joyous entries that began during the early Renaissance. Christ appears in the middle of the composition behind the marching band. A small figure with a huge halo resembling a golden sombrero, he stretches out a tenative arm in a gesture of benediction as he rides His donkey (Fig. 104). His pupils are barely visible at the bottom edge of his eyes and the whites are distinctive, suggesting

Fig. 104. Detail of Christ in *The Entry of Christ into Brussels*, 1888.

that he is shocked by the crowd. A huge scarlet banner with the words "Vive La Sociale" extends over the area in which he appears, and, together with the suggestion of architecture on the left and a long vertical tricolor flag on the right, a symbolic triumphal arch may be intended. A platform at the far right holds the welcoming party consisting of two clowns, a Chinese man, and a bourgeois official wearing a Homburg and a sash across his emaciated chest.[79] Near the platform

[77] Legrand, *Ensor, cet inconnu*, p. 76 and p. 106, n. 11, where she cites *Zeugnisse der Angst in moderne Kunst* (Darmstadt, 1963), pp. 63-64.

[78] André Chastel in *Les Fêtes de la Renaissance*, p. 419.

[79] Ashton points to Callot and the *commedia dell'arte* figures ("Ensor's

scaffolding masked figures hold a sign that reads "Vive Jésus Roi de Bruxelles."

It has often been observed that Christ would be crucified again were He to return to the contemporary world,[80] yet in Ensor's painting He is ignored amidst the celebration of an event that His death inspired. This "Mardi Gras," the day before Lent, is a festival of physical abandon commemorated with gusto before a long period of penance and deprivation. It is a time for music, drinking, gluttony, and sexuality. Ironically, in Ensor's painting Christ chooses to ride into Brussels at a time when Belgians are most irreligious. For Ensor, Christ has erred by being too early, and in doing so He has shown Himself to be human.

An observation was made earlier (see Chapter III) about the similarities between Ensor's "Entry of Christ into Brussels" and Rop's early prints for *Uylenspiegel*, the 1858 lithographs "Printemps" and "Garde Civique" (Figs. 55 and 56). In the lithographs a high vantage point shows the crowd spilling out from narrow streets in an earthy celebration that includes musicians, marching militia, a drum major, and banners and flags. A crucial difference, however, lies in Ensor's rejection of the light sense of humor that infuses Rops's prints with charming spontaneity and his emphasis instead on the coarseness and mockery of the crowd.

There were other influences on Ensor's "Entry into Brussels," and they came from disparate sources. The composition as a whole, with its masses of tightly packed bodies, large banner, and smaller flags and signs, bears a resemblance to a print by George Cruikshank and Henry Mayhew, "From

1851, or The Adventures of Mr. and Mrs. Sandboys" (Fig. 105). The English in the print do their own celebrating while attempting to view the "Great Exhibition" and the large banner that spans two buildings carries a political message that also blesses the masses. Verhaeren had contended that Ensor's Flemish-English heritage had affected his art and had observed that Ensor's interests were closer to Gillray and Rowlandson than to Turner.[81] Ensor had paid a tribute to English influence in 1935, when in applauding Rops, he had stated: "And you great English humorists taking on everything and especially you, our own Rops, cutting and generous. . . ."[82]

In the right background of Ensor's painting, at the left of the reviewing platform, tiny ant-like figures form columns that criss-cross. They are reminiscent of similar miniscule swarming hordes of people in Antoine Wiertz's celebration for Louise-Marie, the 1859 study of "The Apotheosis of the Queen" discussed in Chapter III (Fig. 45). Baudelaire had characterized the Belgian population in great detail in *Pauvre Belgique*.[83] He described them further in a preface to Léon Cladel's *Martyrs ridicules* as "the whole wretched society, with its vile habits, its risky morality, its incurable illusions. . . ."[84] Ensor's observations are similar, but they are not new opinions of Belgian society: Brueghel had expressed similar thoughts in religious paintings in which Christ was lost in the madding crowd, a tiny figure surrounded and ignored by the evil masses.

Paradoxically, Belgium had been a country of refuge for many renegade intellectuals: Marx, Hugo, Baudelaire, and,

---

Re-Entries": 138). McGough also notes that they are actors giving a free performance as advertisement for the *commedia dell'arte* ("The Entry of Christ into Brussels in 1889," p. 163).

[80] For example in Dostoyevsky's treatment of the Legend of The Grand Inquisitor, which Gert Schiff has discussed in connnection with Ensor's

"Entry of Christ into Brussels" ("Ensor the Exorcist," pp. 725-726).

[81] Verhaeren, *James Ensor*, p. 4.

[82] Ensor, *Mes Écrits*, p. 191.

[83] *Oeuvres complètes* (Paris: Gallimard, 1961), pp. 1317-1457.

[84] Cladel, *Martyrs ridicules*, p. 5.

FIG. 105. George Cruikshank and Henry Mayhew. *London in 1851.*

139

in 1880, Jules Valles, who was to be an important influence on the socialist Belgian press.[85] Yet in the mid-1840s Antoine Wiertz had begun a "Triumph of Christ," a huge, sincere Catholic statement completed in 1848—ironically the very year that Karl Marx published his *Communist Manifesto*.[86] As in other European countries, the juxtaposition of religious conservatism with political and social cries for reform produced a nineteenth-century Belgian society in flux, one that was torn between religious heritage, bourgeois materialism, and the increasing dehumanization brought by industrialization. Ensor's painting would comment upon these conflicting interests: he created an image of a city at festival time in which all social restraints were gone, and in which the crowd was therefore exposed to the inexplicable forces that govern its life. Thus the white-faced skeleton in the lower left corner simultaneously defies and deifies Death itself.

Ensor's Brussels can be seen as the protagonist in a human drama that, because of its specific religious-carnival associations, sets it distinctly apart from other cities, as distinctly apart as, for example, Dickens's London, Joyce's Dublin, or the Paris of Balzac, Hugo, and Zola. Ensor's friend, the Belgian writer Georges Eekhoud, described a carnival scene in a book published in 1888:

The people themselves were swept by a giddiness, took a double holiday, sought in a fleeting drunkenness and brutishness a refuge from the sinister reality, celebrated like a ragged Decameron this exceptional carnival. . . . During the length of the carnival Laurent made it a point of honor never to see his bed, nor quit his tattered Pierrot domino. . . . Loafing in the streets that had been turned over to maskers, he was wherever the sport was at its giddiest, the crowd most effervescent. The din of horns and rattles reverberated from street to street, and pig-bladders blown up and brandished like clubs beat down with an ill thud upon the backs of wayfarers.[87]

In Ensor's 1885 drawing "The Entry of Christ into Jerusalem" the numerous banners and signs reproduced popular political slogans of the day. By including "Les XX" and "Les Impressionistes Belges" alongside these slogans, Ensor was explicitly associating the artistic struggle with the political one.[88] Furthermore, the "Colman's Mustard" that appeared on a sign may have been Ensor's reference to materialism and the banality of popular advertising. Emile Verhaeren had included a similar suggestion, perhaps under the influence of Ensor's drawing, in an 1888 letter: "So go back to your Colman's Mustard and soap, in your Manchesters and Liverpools covered with coal smoke and bird droppings."[89] Despite these associations, which spoke for Ensor's contemporaneity, one critic of the day imagined he saw a political statement of proletarian abuse, which simply does not correspond with the faces Ensor created: ". . . deformed by physical labor, convulsed by the fatigue of the procession, distorted by rancor, vengeance and craving. . . ."[90]

In Ensor's "Entry of Christ into Brussels" the written po-

---

[85] See Dumont, *La Vie quotidienne*, chap. 12.

[86] Robert Rosenblum noted this fact in "Ensor in Context," lecture at the Solomon R. Guggenhein Museum, March 1, 1977.

[87] Eekhoud, *The New Carthage*, pp. 329, 331.

[88] Jane Block, "Les XX," p. 32. She also points to Ensor's slogan, "Liberté, Égalité, Fraternité" as an important Freemason motto: "The Vingtistes were acutely aware of Freemason ideals. Félicien Rops was a Freemason, as was

Edmond Picard's father. Freemasons favored compulsory education, betterment of the laboring class, and in 1834 founded the Free University of Brussels" (p. 40, n. 67).

[89] Verhaeren, *Letters à Marthe Verhaeren*, p. 164.

[90] A. J. Wauters in *La Gazette*, quoted by Jane Block, "Les XX," p. 33 and p. 40, n. 68.

Fig. 106. Detail of lower left in *The Entry of Christ into Brussels*, 1888.

litical message is less evident and not specific enough to be expository. There are only three signs with legible lettering: "Vive Jésus Roi de Bruxelles," "Vive La Sociale," a slogan that could be translated as "long live the Social State" and "Fanfares Doctrinaire Toujours Réussi," a sign carried by the marching band and commenting on both their pedantic playing, and the taste of the crowd. Since the painting was large enough to include many more signs and banners with lettering, Ensor must have deliberately chosen to keep words at a minimum and to let the crowd carry the message.

Paul Fierens related an opinion that Ensor had meant the painting as a manifesto in favor of universal suffrage: "It's been claimed that Ensor conceived this canvas as a manifesto promoting universal suffrage. . . . What it is, is the manifesto of a painter who is more universal than we usually recognize."[91] Although there had been a demonstration for universal suffrage in Brussels in 1886, there is no visual evidence in the painting that Ensor meant to promote such a message. There is one specific political image that can be found in the painting, however, and its symbolism makes a more

[91] Fierens, *L'Art en Belgique*, p. 486.

141

FIG. 107. Hieronymous Bosch. Detail of
The Hay-Wain, 1485-1490.

subtle and complex message than a written sign. In a prominent location in the lower left of the canvas two kissing figures are singled out by an area above them that is multicolored, but which contains no distracting faces (Fig. 106).

Bosch had used a similar image in "The Hay-Wain," in which two kissing figures were isolated by a large bush at the top of the hay wagon (Fig. 107). Bosch's painting was a symbol of vanity, illustrating the Flemish proverb, "The world is a haystack and each man plucks from it what he can," and the message in the triptych was that licentiousness leads to Hell.[92] Other early sixteenth-century illustrations convey a similar message. In the title page for an edition of *Le Grand Testament Villon*, for example, a woman kisses a fool who wears a tall dunce cap with a top that curves forward, similar to the hat worn by Ensor's kissing woman.[93]

In these examples the kiss carries a negative connotation; it refers to sin and foolishness.[94] Within the context of Ensor's carnival crowd, the kiss has an obvious reference to sexual promiscuity. But there is a further level of symbolism that needs consideration. The kissing woman is a symbolic representation of Marianne, a "femme du peuple." Marianne was a popular figure originating with the Jacobins during the French Revolution of 1789, and she was usually shown wearing a Phrygian cap, a distinctive hat also worn by the symbolic figure of Liberty and similar to the one in Ensor's painting.[95] This hat is shown on two male figures who embrace and kiss before they hang in a counterrevolutionary illustration that carried the sardonic inscription, "Time Binds Together the Bonds of Brothers and Friends."[96]

Ensor would continue to use the image of kissing figures

[92] See Charles De Tolnay, *Hieronymus Bosch* (New York: William Morrow, 1966), p. 24.

[93] For *Le Grand Testament Villon* see Edward Lucie-Smith, ed., *The Walking Dream: Fantasy and the Surreal in Graphic Art 1450-1900* (New York: Alfred A. Knopf, 1975), p. 18.

[94] A discussion of the numerous implications of the kiss is found in Nicolas James Perella, *The Kiss Sacred and Profane* (Berkeley: University of California Press, 1969).

[95] For example, see Philippe Sagnac and Jean Robiquet, *La Revolution de*

1789, vol. II (Paris: Éditions Nationales, 1934), p. 90. Francine-Claire Legrand and Frank Edebau clarified this identification for me; I mistakenly described this figure as male in "Ensor in his Milieu": 59.

[96] Reproduced in Armand Dayot, *La Révolution française . . . d'après des peintures, sculptures, gravures . . .* (Paris: Ernest Flammarion, 1896), p. 467. Grandville had shown Marianne as a vicious Punch and Judy caricature with long, ratty hair, who attacked with a vengeance; Gillray used her hat and unkempt hair to depict French soldiers in a cartoon that mocked French bravery, "French Volunteers Marching to the Conquest of Great Britain."

in later works, in the 1891 "Baptism of Masks" and in a political painting of 1892 "The Gendarmes" (Fig. 108), which was inspired by a fishermen's strike in Ostend, during which some of the strikers were killed by police.[97] In "The Gendarmes" the police are shown as unnecessarily brutal: one soldier threatens the auguished crowd while another cleans blood off his weapon, and a third holds coins in his palm, a reference to Judas and the money one receives for betrayal. The kissing figures in the upper right of the painting suggest the kiss of Judas, the ultimate act of betrayal.

Marianne's kiss to the surprised bourgeois citizen in the "Entry of Christ into Brussels" can be seen to carry a complex combination of associations: it is a kiss of lust representative of the carnival; a kiss of liberty and charity imposed by a symbol of the common people; but also a kiss of betrayal, a warning about duplicity and the precariousness of political alliances and the naiveté and stupidity of the bourgeoisie.

It is not surprising to find Ensor commenting upon the brutality of the police, the evils of sanctioned government, or the gullibility of the bourgeoisie; during this period most of Ensor's friends, especially those associated with Les XX, had socialist leanings. In fact, Rops's son-in-law, Eugène Demolder, published the first serious study of Ensor's art in an 1891 issue of *La Société nouvelle*, a socialist review.[98] In 1888 and 1889 three works in addition to the print of "The Gendarmes" and "The Entry of Christ into Brussels" were

FIG. 108. Ensor. *The Gendarmes*, 1892.

concerned with politics: a colored-pencil drawing of "The Strike in Ostend, 1888," which included several banners filled with messages exhorting the crowd to be patient, and the 1889 print "Doctrinal Nourishment," in which King Leopold and his retinue sit on the rim of a wall and defecate

---

As late as 1916 the Belgian cartoonist Louis Raemaekers depicted her as an obsessed instigator, pounding a drum as she led her soldiers with the cry, "Liberté! Liberté, Chérie!"

[97] See Tannenbaum, *James Ensor*, pp. 79-80. A print of the same subject with six separate states had been etched in 1888, but the kissing figures did not appear until the 1892 painting, where they were shown in the upper right corner, next to a man who looked down upon the scene and smiled. For a discussion of the six states of the print, see Taevernier, *James Ensor*,

pp. 141-145. Elesh has found a seventh state of this print *The Complete Graphic Work*, vol. 11, p. 150. Tannenbaum has pointed out that Ensor's composition for "The Gendarmes" had been inspired by Louis Gallait's famous 1851 historical picture, "The Last Honors Rendered to the Counts d'Egmont and Hornes," a depiction of two Belgian heroes who lost their heads while fighting to save Belgium from Philip II (James Ensor, p. 80). For a discussion of the strikes, see Mathews, *La Wallonie*, pp. 9ff.

[98] Tannenbaum, *James Ensor*, p. 78.

Fɪɢ. 109. Detail of lower right in *The Entry of Christ into Brussels*, 1888.

into the eager faces of the populace below. The implication in the last example is that the crowd is as wretched in its gullibility as the government's leaders are in their self-satisfaction. In 1890 Ensor was to pay tribute to the memory of Hector Denis, the anarchist-socialist who had been the organizer of labor unions in Belgium, and who had died in the same year, with a portrait of Denis that carried an inscription on the print, "À Hector Denis, James Ensor."

Despite his political commentaries, Ensor was not an ac-

tive socialist, nor did he profess specific answers to society's problems. In 1898, when he etched "The Entry of Christ into Brussels," some of the signs in the foreground linked the name of Jesus with a popular socialist leader of the 1880s, "Vive Anseele et Jésus," thus associating the impoverished religion of one group with the impotent politics of another.

Tannenbaum observed that Ensor was "too distrustful of the resources of mankind in any possible direction"[99] to become involved in a political fight. Furthermore, as an older, celebrated artist he capitulated; Taevernier related that when Ensor became a baron he withdrew as many of the five states of "Doctrinal Nourishment" as he could find and that he also ruined the plate, making those prints the rarest of Ensor's oeuvre.[100]

It was with the complex combination of good and evil in all levels of society that Ensor was concerned. Thus the fisherman was seen both as a steadfast but simple toiler, as in the 1883 "Rower," and as a besotted alcoholic in "The Drunkards" of the same year. The clergy, judges, and the medical profession were attacked, but so were the common people who continued the tradition of the masquerade. "The Entry of Christ into Brussels" was Ensor's own "Uylenspiegel," a mirror in which all levels of society appeared. Ensor can be seen there in profile, dressed as a clown with a tall, scarlet dunce cap, directly above the kissing couple. On the other side of the canvas, under the scaffolding, the familiar mask with blue glasses from the 1883 painting of "Scandalized Masks" reappears (Fig. 109). She has long been identified as Ensor's grandmother,[101] and Jean Stevo has given the mask a name of its own, "La Vieille."[102]

[99] Ibid., p. 80.

[100] Taevernier, *James Ensor*, p. 199. ". . . Delteil was not able to find any print of this etching and . . . he did not reproduce it in his catalogue. Croquez mentions it, but also without reproducing it. He writes, 'No prints are

known to be on the market. . . .' "

[101] E.g., by Schwob, *James Ensor*, p. 136.

[102] Stevo, *James Ensor*, p. 20.

To the left of "The Old One" are two female masks; both of them wear white collars and caps and they appear much more attractive than the grotesques that surround them. Perhaps they are meant to represent Ensor's sister Mitche and their mother. The mask worn by Ensor's father in "Scandalized Masks" is not present and its absence reminds us that the elder Ensor died in 1887. Ensor left no written record identifying these participants at Christ's Mardi Gras; he chose instead to describe the charade:

One should just see those masks under our wide opal sky. And when they appear what a smearing of clashing colours, how miserable they look, bent, stooping, wretched in the rain. What a lamentable rout of terrified figures, at the same time both cheeky and timid, sullen and chirpy, their voices screeched in falsetto or rancous like a trumpet call. . . This repulsive but lively bunch of humanity, dressed in their old garments, sparkling with gold-dust, which seems as if it were snatched from the moon.[103]

Here the vast crowd is completely without monumentality; it is a sea of masked sardines squeezed together in a dissonant orchestration of jarring color: livid green, ochre, blue, and red. Yet as Jean Lorrain perceived of Ensor, "What marvellous insight he has into the invisible and into the atmosphere created by our vices . . . our vices which turn our faces into masks."[104]

Difficult though it may be to find any redeeming qualities within Ensor's crowds, their raison d'être originates in the eternal appeal of the masks' protective powers. As Picasso had observed with reference to African masks:

. . . Men had made those masks and other objects for a sacred purpose, as a kind of meditation between themselves and the unknown hostile forces that surrounded them, in order to overcome their fear and horror by giving it a form and an image. At that moment I realized what painting was all about. . . .[105]

Ensor's early paintings of people are quiet statements, depictions of solitary, monumental figures like "The Rower," "The Woman Eating Oysters" or his sister Mitche as "Somber Lady" or "Woman in Distress." Two people at most occupy a room in these paintings and often they suggest a quiet psychological drama, as in the "Scandalized Masks" or "Children Dressing." With Ensor's "Entry of Christ into Brussels" the drama of the individual yields to the drama of the crowd and to Ensor's investigations into history and religion, politics, tradition, tribulations and temptations. Ensor had described a "wide opal sky" and a "smearing of clashing colors"—the serenity of nature contrasting with the reality of bestial humanity. Under a cloudless blue sky Seurat had populated his landscape with images of silent humanity frozen with themselves as within a dream. In "Entry of Christ into Brussels," Ensor's protagonists abandon themselves to revelry, their psyches hidden, their despair masked in noisy escapism.

---

[103] Ensor, *Lettres à André de Ridder*, p. 57; translated in Legrand, *Symbolism in Belgium*, p. 122.

[104] Quoted in Philippe Jullian, *Dreamers of Decadence*, p. 244.

[105] Quoted in Françoise Gilot and Carlton Lake, *Life with Picasso*, in Sorrell, *The Mask in the Arts*, p. 167.

VI

ENSOR'S LAST YEARS OF CREATIVITY AND
THE DECLINE OF HIS ART

If an artist dies young, as Georges Seurat did at thirty-two, his reputation as a creative individual with a potentially brilliant future remains secure. If Ensor had died young he would have been regarded as an innovative genius whose large number and variety of masterpieces from the 1880s suggested an incredible artistic future. Instead Ensor lived to be eighty-nine. He continued painting until his death, but after 1900 his creativity declined notably, and he produced numerous mediocre paintings and stale copies of his great works from the early years. For some critics, the importance of his artistic legacy was diminished by his total oeuvre; for others his reputation remains secure, but the decline is a perplexing conundrum.

In a psychoanalytic investigation of Ensor's art, Dr. H. T. Piron used Ensor's memories of his youth to investigate this decline.[1] He also considered the intense anxiety with which

Ensor lived, both as a result of his family situation and from the virulent and sustained attacks on his art. Ensor's loss of creativity was seen by Piron to have been bound up with his failure to become a father and his inability to earn a living, the two together resulting in a loss of virility and a castration complex.[2]

Piron's explanations, however, leave a great deal unsaid, and they do not enable the reader to understand the artist. It is possible to gain additional insight into Ensor's loss of creativity through an understanding of his own self-assessment, as shown, for example, in the visual and written messages in his paintings from the 1890s and early 1900s, in a poster from 1931, and in a poem and a revealing letter from the 1920s. Ensor's relationships with women, especially with Augusta Boogaerts, and his feelings about women in general, play a significant role in these autobiographical documents.

---

[1] For example, Ensor's reminiscence of a large sea bird that flew in an open window and frightened him as he lay in his crib, thus linking him, through a shared experience, with Leonardo da Vinci (H. T. Piron, *James Ensor, een psychoanalytische studie* [Antwerp: De Nederlandsche Boekhandel, 1968], pp. 20-42).

[2] Ibid., pp. 126-128.

Ensor's tie with Augusta Boogaerts lasted until his death in 1949. There are only a few portraits of her, however, and these depictions range from a pleasant drawing that showed her to be an attractive woman with a slight smile turning up the corners of her mouth,[3] to outright caricature, in which Ensor mocked her unmercifully. It has already been mentioned that Augusta, whom Ensor nicknamed "La Sirene," may have been the intended female in the "Call of the Siren" (Fig. 58), painted in 1893. In this comic illustration, Ensor showed himself as a pathetic coward fearful of entering the ocean, a metaphor for his fear of the woman who awaited him there with arms outstretched in aggressive impatience. His last lines of the acerbic 1925 poem "On Woman" may also be a reference to Augusta, "constant mask and endless smile," since Haesaerts has described her, "with enigmatic smile forever on her lips."[4] In 1905, however, Ensor painted a small "Double Portrait" in which he dealt with her in kinder terms (Fig. 110). She is shown fully dressed, with her gloves on, a fur stole in her lap, and a large flowered hat on her head. The hint of a smile is evident as she looks toward a window at the left edge of the painting. In her right hand she holds a flower; flowers also lie at her feet, seemingly having fallen from a vase on the table. Thus the figure of Augusta, then thirty-five and unmarried, is shown holding a symbol of her own sexual maturity in 1905.[5] There is a sense of light intrigue here, of clandestine moments stolen by unmarried lovers. Despite the painting's charm, however, the portrait hints at a psychic and physical distance that exists and will remain between the lovers: their heads and bodies are turned in opposite directions and Ensor has further

[3] Reproduced in Haesaerts, *James Ensor*, p. 210.
[4] Ibid., p. 211.
[5] Lesko, "Ensor in His Milieu": 62.

FIG. 110. Ensor. *Double Portrait*, 1905.

FIG. 111. Ensor. *The Ray*. Copy of the 1892 painting (date unknown).

distanced himself from Augusta by portraying his image as across the room, reflected in the glass of a mirrored wardrobe.

They never married, although they could have, especially after the death of Ensor's mother in 1915 and of his aunt the following year. Instead Augusta took on the duties of an unofficial business manager. She not only supervised Ensor's production and kept an inventory, but she also grouped ob-

jects into still-life compositions for him to paint.[6] Haesaerts's monograph included a note Ensor left for Augusta and her reply, a repartee that illustrated her tenacity, as well as her sense of humor. To the admonition, "Do not take anything; I have counted everything," she replied, "Do not count anything; I have taken everything."[7]

Farmer and others have commented on the fact that once

[6] Haesaerts, *James Ensor*, p. 220. [7] Ibid.

Ensor gained a measure of success the quality and number of works he produced was significantly diminished.[8] In Ensor's sketchbook, which reproduced all his paintings, the initials "A. B." appear along with dimensions and dates under many of the late still-lifes.[9] It seems apparent that Augusta Boogaerts had some impact on these works, and since many of them show the same rigid triangular composition, they may have been arranged by her hand. These paintings are among Ensor's most banal pictures and one wonders why he would allow someone else to dictate the composition of a painting?

He might have allowed such direction if he believed that his creative powers had left him and that he could no longer work effectively. The numerous copies of his masterpieces, such as the copy (Fig. 111) of the 1892 "Ray" (Pl. 8), are so poorly done that they add credence to that possibility. Nevertheless, Ensor retained his wry sense of humor, and a 1935 self-portrait included a touching inscription on the canvas. It recalls in spirit the poignant 1888 etching of "My portrait in 1960": "This portrait, like its author, is about ready to cave in."[10]

Sometimes his attempts at humor could be strained, as in his 1920 painting, "Droll Smokers" (Fig. 112). A mediocre picture at best, it comments upon Augusta's bold personality and Ensor's visual reply. She is shown with a cigarette in a raised hand, while the painter Willem Paerels plays the role of butler and carries a cigar-smoking skull on a plate; withered lilies have been placed in a large vase in the lower left and another skull smokes a pipe as it rests on the floor in

FIG. 112. Ensor. *Droll Smokers*, 1920.

[8] Farmer, *Ensor*, p. 32. By 1900 Ensor had begun to acquire a positive reputation; in 1903 he was made Chevalier of the Order of Leopold, and in 1905 he exhibited twenty pictures at Antwerp, where he gained the patronage of François Franck, a Belgian minister of state who began buying steadily.

[9] Collection of the Chicago Art Institute. E.g., "préparé par A. B." "A. B. mis deux conches." I am grateful to the staff of the Guggenheim Museum for allowing me to examine the entire sketchbook during the Ensor exhibition in 1977.

[10] Reproduced in Ollinger-Zinque, *Ensor by Himself*, no. 101, p. 144.

the background. On the back wall Ensor included two of his own compositions as pictures within a picture: the oil painting "Portrait of Old Woman with Masks," and his etching of himself as "The Pisser." Graffiti stick figures also appear on the back wall; they are recognizable as having come from the actual print of "The Pisser." However, the inscription from Ensor's etching, "Ensor est un fou," has been removed.

The title "Droll Smokers" suggests an amusing topic and at first glance it appears to be a straightforward comic representation. Its subject matter recalls seventeenth-century northern genre paintings, such as Theodore Rombouts's "The Smokers." But it also warns about the evils of smoking and, further, about the implications inherent in women smoking. Jacob Balde's seventeenth-century antismoking pamphlet "Die Truckene Truckenheit" ("The Dry Drunkenness") comes to mind; in it puffs of smoke arise from the eye sockets of a smoking skeleton and a man with pipe in hand vomits on the table. Alfred Rethel continued that theme with his smoking skeletons in the mid-nineteenth century, and Grandville commented upon smoking and female liberation in a print from the 1844 *Un Autre Monde*.[11]

In the nineteenth century women who enjoyed a cigarette in public were identified as "lorettes," prostitutes or women of easy virtue.[12] Apparently it wasn't until the twentieth century, perhaps after World War II, that a smoking woman was not thought to be loose. The French photographer Lartigue observed that women had just begun to smoke on the streets in 1927: "To see them with lighted cigarettes in their mouths was no longer an unusual sight, but it was not commonplace either."[13]

In "Droll Smokers" it is notable that Ensor has chosen to include two of his past works as heavy-handed criticisms: the old woman, associated with flower symbolism and sexual availability, is a reference to ludicrous female foolishness; and Ensor's presence and his act comment upon the situation in 1920. It is the year of women's suffrage in the United States, but that event will not occur in Belgium until 1946. Augusta Boogaerts is shown gesturing with a cigarette as she grins out at the viewer; the dried flowers, smoking skeletons, and pictures on the wall are enhanced by the painting's garish coloring, all of which add to Ensor's indictment of Augusta, her smoking, and women's liberation in general.

By 1925 Ensor's attitude toward women appears to have been one of full-blown misogyny. A poem he composed that year was filled with vicious scatalogical imagery and mocking animal symbolism:

Deceiving sex, respector neither of law nor of religion,
  heartless and devoid of honor
Sink of hypocrisy
Hotbed of lies and dissimulation
Mud-pit of malice
Cavern of greed and the deadly sins
Pandora Box

---

[11] "Les femmes adoptent le costume et les habitudes des hommes" showed one woman smoking a pipe and another with a large cigar in her mouth, while the man between them, dressed in tights, stood with one hand in a fur muff. In a drawing from *Petites Misères* Grandville depicted a woman who sprawled across a table and held a cigarette in one hand as she made a sweeping gesture with an upraised empty wine bottle. Rops's *Uylenspiegel* commented on the subject in 1856 in a design by Gerlier that showed a woman smoking while she leaned on a rail and was surrounded by men ("Les Casinos," *Uylenspiegel*, no. 11 [April 13, 1856]).

[12] Beatrice Farwell, "Courbet's 'Baigneuses' and the Rhetorical Feminine Image," in *Woman as Sex Object*, edited by Thomas B. Hess and Linda Nochlin (New York: Newsweek, 1972), p. 75.

[13] Jacques-Henri Lartigue, *Les Femmes aux cigarettes* (New York: Viking, 1980).

Miry pool crawling with bad beasts
Liquid manure, stick and oozing with vermin
Sneaky and hostile morass
Horrible cesspool teeming with leeches
Beast with claws and suckers and teeth for tearing live
   flesh
Blowing she-satyr, blowing hot and cold
Inspirer of the worst villainies
Treacherous in friendship
Gamy hen, proud and stupid
Featherbrained goose
Unscrupulous climber looking for accomplices
Weather vane creaking with every ill wind
Triple hole of felony, unfathomable betrayal, and devouring
   selfishness
Vast walking lie, belly forward, bottom tastefully larded
The scourge of heaven and of earth
Constant mask and endless smile.[14]

It has been suggested (in Chapter IV) that as Ensor's artistic powers declined he replaced his expressive, potent visual imagery with words. His poem "On Women" illustrates that observation. Like the "Droll Smokers" it echoes much of the distaste and fear that surrounded the increasingly liberated woman of the 1920s. But, although Ensor's poem was calculated to shock, its written message was actually a retardataire recollection of nineteenth-century misogynist literature. From Delacroix's fantasy of treating woman as "the flower beneath the foot,"[15] to the image of the succubus in Balzac, Huysmans, and Barbey d'Aurevilly, the nineteenth-century woman was often described as a vain, vicious monster, a daughter of Eve who incorporated all the evils of the world. The popularity of this motif has already been discussed in Chapter III, and any number of examples might

be quoted, but one of Baudelaire's descriptions is particularly apt because it pays homage to Balzac's skeleton in "Jesus Christ in Flanders" while it incorporates that imagery with vampire symbolism. Parts of Ensor's poem are similar in tone and phrase:

When she had sucked the marrow from every bone,
I turned to her languid as a stone
To give her one last kiss . . . and saw her thus:
A slimy rotten wineskin, full of pus!
. . .
. . . the cold ruins of a skeleton
Shivered, creaking like a weather vane
Or like a sign hung out on an iron arm
Swinging through long winter nights in the storm.[16]

Legrand has observed that for the Symbolists Death itself is portrayed by Woman, "for fear of death and eroticism make good bed companions."[17] There had been vicious depictions of women from the early years of Ensor's artistic production. In the crudely painted 1880 "Judith and Holofernes" Judith holds the decapitated head aloft, while with the other hand she grasps a blood-soaked knife above the groin of the recumbent figure. Several of Ensor's etchings, discussed in earlier chapters, have women whipping or flaying their male victims, and in Ensor's sketch book there is an illustration of a little-known painting of a witch being burned at the stake with the word "sorceur" on the placard above her head.

Ensor's poem is a caricature of negative female imagery, and it is notable that when Ensor chose to show a femme fatale, she was not the nineteenth-century decadent woman

---

[14] Haesaerts, *James Ensor*, p. 360.

[15] Quoted in Jullian, *Dreamers of Decadence*, p. 109.

[16] Translated by Jackson Mathews in Charles Baudelaire, *The Flowers of*

Evil, edited by Marthiel and Jackson Mathews (rev. ed., New York: New Directions Books, 1963), p. 161.

[17] Legrand, *Symbolism in Belgium*, p. 51.

who combined satanic or repressed sexuality with the mask of innocence, as, for example, in the works of Munch, Stuck, or Rops, but a caricature of that type. Both "Portrait of Old Woman with Masks" and "Intrigue" (Fig. 13) depicted women as vain and foolish in their attempts to be sexually alluring. And Ensor's siren in the "Call of the Siren" is an eager grotesque who lacks the magnetic sexuality needed to lure her victim to her side.

Ensor's personal experiences may have influenced the cruel generalities of his poem, as well as his visual caricatures of females. He had lived with domineering female relatives who slept away a large part of their lives and who complained of illnesses, demanding constant attention when they were awake. He had seen his sister's moodiness and her flights from the family, as well as her failed marriage. There was the possibility of an unrequited love for Mariette Rousseau, an older married woman, and, finally, there was the constant attention of Augusta Boogaerts, a woman seen as below his class, yet one who never gave up her intention of remaining with him. These associations, negative at least in part, and combined with the influence of misogynist literature, may have caused Ensor to damn all women.

Yet, when Ensor was referring to a creative feminine principle he could write appreciatively, and protectively:

I love the Sirens and that blond Venus and her seashells rising on the luminous shore.[18]

. . .

Protest! The virginity of the dunes is threatened. . . . Cry over the polluted breast-shaped hill, the rounded rumps, the nests of yellow woods. . . . Why ransack, ravage . . . spoil, deflower . . . befoul, bestink adorable sites worthy of respect?[19]

When asked what kind of death Ensor would prefer, it was reported that he described it as "that of a flea crushed on a virgin's white breast."[20] A reminiscence by Jean Stevo, which quotes Ensor, serves to illustrate this lighter tone with regard to women and suggests by its content highly personalized memories of an inability to communicate:

Woman, he says, this bizarre one, oh! This bizarre animal. One thinks to grasp it, understand it . . . pfuitt! One holds the hand: nothing more. Vanished. Flown away. Flower, butterfly, star? Shooting star. Strange fawns, fugitive, diverse, versatile, changeable. Women . . . oh, la, la![21]

René Lyr's descripton of Ensor's feeling for women ends with the observation, "Ensor loved only his mother. . . ." Whether or not this is the case, his other perceptions are convincing:

. . . Ensor . . . shows all the signs of the male. But his powers are of the mind. The license of his imagery, the libidinous moods in his drawings, all these female bodies wreathed in flowers . . . betray the terror of a sin which he never commits. It is the temptation of a virgin, the night-mare of St. Anthony.[22]

The temptation and the nightmare were irreconcilable and Ensor's are declined, at least in part, as a direct result of his suffering.

Ensor had begun to comment specifically about his personal problems in 1892 when he was just thirty-two. In fact, we shall see that two key paintings from that year were

---

[18] Ensor, *Lettres à Andre de Ridder*, p. 61.
[19] Quoted in Haesaerts, *James Ensor*, p. 361. For the complete version, see Ensor, *Mes Écrits*, pp. 102-103. No date is given for the essay.
[20] Quoted in Sorel, *The Mask in the Arts*, p. 162.

[21] Stevo, *James Ensor*, p. 37.
[22] Letter to his son, Claude Lyr, Ostend, July 17, 1945. Quoted in Ollinger-Zinque, *Ensor by Himself*, p. 41.

crucial statements and contained pointed comments about his situation. In reconstructing Ensor's life it becomes evident that at that time he felt a strong need for consolation. He must have been pleased with Eugène Demolder's monograph that appeared that year, and there were light-hearted moments, photographed on the dunes at Ostend, when Ensor and his friend Ernest Rousseau, Jr. staged a mock fight with skeleton bones. But 1892 was also the year that his sister eloped. She had a baby and returned with her child in the same year to live in the Ensor home. We have seen that Ensor spoke of Mitche's predicament in the bitingly sarcastic painting "Intrigue."

In January Ensor had been ill, "I have been in bed for eleven days suffering from pneumonia."[23] In another letter, believed to be from the same year, he wrote of his mother's illness, as well as his own: "I had terrible emotions. My mother was and is still very gravely ill. The doctors weren't able to diagnose before yesterday. Now she is better. I was sick with pneumonia, I am cured."[24]

He felt it necessary to make a trip to London in November, a very rare excursion for Ensor. From the postscript of a letter Ensor wrote to Octave Maus it becomes evident that he went hoping to find a buyer for his art: "I wrote to M. Pranger in London asking him to send me the invitation list. . . . I want to exhibit in London, I have family there and hope to sell there."[25] There is no evidence of any tangible results from Ensor's attempt. By 1893 he may have become desperate for money, because he tried to sell the entire contents of his studio at a package price of 8,500 francs.[26] The fact that Les XX voted to disband in that year could only have aggravated his sense of failure and caused him great anguish. As we

FIG. 113. Photograph of Ensor in his studio, c. 1893.

have seen, he was the only objector and he complained bitterly that he wasn't informed of the discussions that considered the proposal to abolish.

In 1893 Ensor had a photograph taken of himself in his

[23] Letter of January 11, 1892 in Legrand, "Lettres à Octave Maus": 37.
[24] Ibid.
[25] Ibid.: 40.
[26] Stevo, "Ensor l'Ostendais," in *L'Art Belge*, p. 14.

studio, seated at his easel and surrounded by his paintings (Fig. 113). Perhaps it was meant to be a memento, commissioned in response to the forthcoming sale for which he hoped. As mentioned earlier, the photograph inspired a painting, "Skeleton Painter in His Studio" (Fig. 41), in which, in a clever and touching self-assessment, Ensor depicted himself with a skull for a head, a skeleton of his former self who had found no buyers and who was still at work at his easel.[27]

It was in the previous year that Ensor had produced two major paintings, "The Consoling Virgin" (Fig. 61) and "The Ray" (Pl. 8). Visually they appear to stand in direct opposition to one another, but they can be seen as two sides of a single coin, each complementing the other. The "Consoling Virgin" is a small picture that illustrates an epiphany: the Virgin appears to Ensor after he has painted her portrait with the infant Jesus. It is an oil painting on a wooden panel, and with its pale colors and flat outline a number of Renaissance "Annunciations" come to mind. Here, however, in a reversal of roles, Mary holds the lily and the artist kneels in homage, separated from the supernatural vision by a distinct color division in the floor. Ensor had spoken of the Virgin in possessive terms filled with glowing wonder: "I recorded her graceful features on a panel of good quality. . . . I kissed her little feet of snow and mother-of-pearl. On the hard substance of the old panel the diaphanous image can still be

made out; I guard it jealously; it is mine, and I love it."[28]

Flowers lie on the floor and surround the Virgin. They appear again around her neck and in the folds of her gown. At the top of the picture vines grow outside the wall, and a rainbow can be seen in the blue sky above her head. Flowers are associated with Venus through their link back to Flora,[29] and Ensor had associated the goddess of love with his own birth. He had described meeting her as a sensual experience: "At my birth Venus came toward me, smiling, and we looked long into each other's eyes. She smelt pleasantly of salt water."[30] Ensor's title identifies the role of his Virgin: as a chaste Virgin-Venus she has appeared to offer comfort and consolation.

It is notable that in a book of poetry Emile Verhaeren published in 1891, he included a poem called "She of the Garden," in which he wrote of his "Guardian Angel" and of the "sun flowers [that] rose behind her like a crown. . . . Sure, she was one who, being dead, yet brought me, Miraculous, a strength that comforteth, and the Viaticum of her survival Guiding me from the further side of Death."[31]

In the early fifteenth-century *Epistle of Othea to Hector*, the Tibertine Sibyl confronts a kneeling Augustus as she points to the Virgin and Child. There the gloss tells us to disdain not the counsel of a wise woman.[32] In Ensor's painting the Virgin can also be seen as the personification of female wisdom: holding the lily for Ensor, she is like Ver-

[27] Farmer, *Ensor*, gives ca. 1900 for the date of the photograph (p. 25); Ollinger-Zinque, *Ensor by Himself*, gives 1893 (p. 151). Ensor's appearance coincides with the earlier date, and "Skeleton Painter in His Studio," usually dated ca. 1896, was based on the photograph. However, I believe that the painting's quality and its brilliant color speak for a slightly earlier date, closer to the 1893 photograph.

[28] Haesaerts, *James Ensor*, p. 228. The description comes from a 1925 speech. See *Mes Écrits*, p. 98:

[29] See Julius Held's article, "Flora, Goddess and Courtesan," *De Artibus*

Opuscula, X: Essays in Honor of Erwin Panofsky, edited by Millard Meiss (New York: New York University, 1960), pp. 201-218.

[30] Quoted in Frank Patrick Edebau, "James Ensor and Ostend," in Farmer, *Ensor*, p. 9.

[31] Emile Verhaeren, *Poems of Emile Verhaeren*, translated by Alma Stretell (New York: John Lane, 1915), pp. 79-80.

[32] Consult James Daniel Gordon, *The Epistle of Othea to Hector* (Philadelphia: n.p., 1942), no. 100, "Augustus and the Sibyl" (Ensor could have known the manuscript, Brussels 9392).

FIG. 114. Ensor. *The Miraculous Draught of the Fishes*, n.d.

haeren's guardian angel, as well as a Holy Mother, and a muse for his art as well. Ensor's symbol for his art, the red or sour herring (hareng saur)—a verbal pun on "l'art Ensor"—lies on the floor in the painting's foreground. Piron has observed that the picture on the easel—a picture within a picture—is like a play within a play; the Virgin is identically dressed in both, and for Piron the kneeling Ensor becomes the baby at the mother's breast.[33] Piron has also pointed to the paintbrush that emerges from under a palette-shield and effectively replaces the phallus, suggesting that Ensor's sexuality was associated in some way with his art.[34]

Ensor's "Ray" makes a similar analogy, but the painting

[33] Piron, *James Ensor*, p. 27. It's interesting to note that when the Virgin stands before Ensor she lacks the ample bosom of the nursing Mary in the painting on the easel.

[34] Ibid., and Legrand, *Ensor, cet inconnu*, p. 78. The palette and phallic imagery had been included in the 1890 "Ensor and Leman Discussing Painting," which has been discussed in Chapter II.

is bolder in its assertion (Pl. 8). Visually it stands in direct opposition to the "Consoling Virgin": it is a canvas of thick, palpable paint, brilliant color, and common subject matter. The large ray sprawls on a table top; its eyes and mouth are clearly delineated and it looks very much alive. To the left a wicker basket is filled with fish, and a smaller variety of fish lies piled on the table. Next to them a large conch shell has been placed upon the edge of a white cloth. The painting is beautifully colored: in the area above the ray, pastel blues, pinks, yellows, and ochre form the back wall; golden straw encircles one side of the basket; the conch shell reveals a sensual deep red and pink interior, and the body of the ray contains within its opalescent skin all the colors of the canvas.

Werner Haftmann rightly calls this painting a masterpiece but notes that "the perfection of this Impressionist feast of colours would fill us with joy: but suddenly the skate stares out at us with its demonic mask and then soft shadows of decay fall on the iridescent colours."[35] Frank Edebau has also seen an anthropomorphized fish: "The skate's head has almost human features. . . ."[36] Edebau pointed to Ensor's 1882 painting of the same subject (Fig. 4) and observed a difference in the realism of the earlier work. An additional observation should be made: not only was the 1882 ray painted in a different style, but the earlier ray did not look toward the viewer; instead its stiff tail was pointed into the middle of the opening of a large basket that had been tipped on its side. Thus the beautiful, but aggressively masculine ray of 1882 was replaced by a ray who revealed its soft lumpy underparts and flaccid tail. Furthermore, it had been propped up to look out at and to engage the viewer in a direct confrontation.

Ensor had seen the sea and the creatures within it in universal terms that combined a life force with sexuality and creativity:

Medicinal sea, worshiped Mother, I should like to offer one fresh, simple bouquet celebrating your hundred faces, your surfaces, your facets, your dimples, your rubescent underparts, your diamond-studded crests, your sapphire overlay, your blessings, your delights, your deep charms.[37]

He also spoke of the sea as his lover and of "sublimated kisses": "Night and morning I give her long embraces. Ah! my beloved sea's good kisses, sublimated kisses, perfumed with foam, tangy, bracing."[38]

There is strong evidence that for Ensor the ray, like the sea in which it lived, held several associations that were interlinked. Edebau has given a wide-ranging description of the ray, sometimes called the "poisson-masque": "It's a melange of crucifixion, cadaver, mask, clown face, and at the same time, the smile of chaos and succulent flesh."[39]

Ensor had linked the ray with Christ in a drawing entitled "The Miraculous Draught of the Fishes" (Fig. 114). There a large ray, the broad mouth of which appeared to be smiling, sprawled at Christ's feet. In a drawing dated after 1900 and entitled "St. Anthony Tormented," a stingray can be seen in the lower left, and St. Anthony's right hand holds the top of its head.[40] Ensor's self-identification with Christ and St. Anthony has been discussed in earlier chapters, but a further association should be considered: in 1931 Ensor included his self-portrait with that of a ray in a poster advertising the

---

[35] *Painting in the Twentieth Century*, p. 63.

[36] Text for a catalog translated into Japanese. Mr. Edebau kindly lent me the English translation (no pagination) in October of 1977.

[37] Quoted in Haesaerts, *James Ensor*, p. 105.   [38] Ibid.

[39] Film dialogue prepared by Edebau and M. Merckx, seen in October 1977 at Ostend's Musée des Beaux-Arts.

[40] Reproduced in Paul Fierens, *James Ensor* (Paris: Hyperion, 1943), p. 137.

Ostend carnival (Fig. 115). Surrounded by familiar faces from his family of masks, Ensor's face and shoulders loom above the head of a smiling ray. In fact, Ensor's chin touches the prominent bump on the top of the ray's head. On one poster Ensor included a pointed inscription to a friend, Blanche Hertoge, whom he identified as "la muse medusée du studio d'Ostende."[41] In associating this "muse" with Medusa, he recalled the frightening aspects of the female gorgon, a designation that is also used to identify another creature of the sea, the jelly fish, which in its tentacled, free-swimming sexual stage is called a "medusa."

Although the poster is visually lighthearted and amusing, and it reproduces a caricature of the lively seventy-one year old artist, the paintings from 1892 are serious. The "Consoling Virgin" and "The Ray" can be seen as autobiographical statements; diametrically different visually, they are nevertheless variations on a single theme: Ensor's recognition of his failing powers. Both deal with images of Venus and the sea, and both speak about creativity and the loss of virility. The "Consoling Virgin" speaks through style, subject, and color to dream and fantasize about comfort through the visionary; the impotent fish in "The Ray" suggests a direct physical analogy with Ensor's own condition.

In a 1928 letter to André de Ridder Ensor wrote of the personal importance that these two paintings held. He saw the pictures as a happy marriage, different in subject and

[41] The poster with the inscription is no. 974, collection of Dr. J. Maniewski. Also see Taevernier, *James Ensor*, pl. 142. The number and extent of Ensor's friendships with women remain a tantalizing mystery. Besides Mariette Rousseau, Augusta Boogaerts, and Emma Lambotte, his friend and patron, there are other names that appear in cryptic inscriptions in Ensor's sketchbook: Blanche Hertoge is one, and the names Margo Knoeckert, Elsa Stejus (?), and Carla appear in poems and under sketches of the Virgin and Venus. Jean Stevo mentioned that Hertoge opened a gallery in Ostend called "The Studio" ("Ensor l'Ostendais," p. 14).

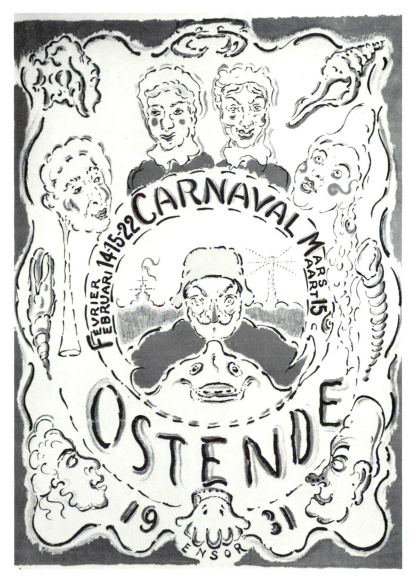

FIG. 115. Ensor. *Poster for the Carnival at Ostend*, 1931.

style, but the meeting of two extremes. Furthermore, he implied their significance by prefacing his description with the apology that he must not speak of them: "I must not speak of 'The Ray,' 1892, of the Musée de Bruxelles, nor of the 'Consoling Virgin,' 1892, works of very opposite subjects and style, but where the vision is suited [corresponds] musically. Happy marriage where extremes touch [meet] each other."[42]

For Ensor, his own sexuality was inextricably linked to his creative ability as an artist. In 1892 and 1893 his life and his art had reached a point of crisis. This is evident through his paintings of the "Consoling Virgin," "The Ray," and the "Call of the Siren." He was fearful, he needed consolation, and he identified with his depiction of the ray: a once noble creature now limp and dying, propped up and displayed for the curious.

It is a tribute to Ensor that, although his remarkable genius flourished for little more than twenty-five years, his brilliant art from the 1880s and 1890s continues to elude complete explanation. E.T.A. Hoffmann has observed that:

. . . to this hour nothing is so distasteful to me as when, in a story or novel, the stage on which the imaginary world has been in action is swept so clean by the historic broom that not the smallest grain or particle of dust is left on it;

when you go home so completely sated and satisfied that you have not the faintest desire left to have another peep behind the curtain.[43]

The introduction to this study observed that although Ensor literature is vast, there remained a large number of perplexing questions still to be answered. Some of these questions have been dealt with here, but the desire to look behind the curtain is still strong. Paintings such as "The Astonishment of the Mask Wouse" (Fig. 87) illustrate this point. The word "Wouse" itself remains a mystery and the painting continues to puzzle viewers. Baudelaire's "Danse macabre" contains a few lines that parallel the pathos of Ensor's picture:

With tunes of fiddles, with flames of candles,
Do you hope to chase the mocking nightmare[44]

And Baudelaire recalls also the Belgian carnival and the frenetic gaiety so well illustrated in Ensor's art:

And do you ask a flood of orgies to cool
the hell that's lighted in your heart?[45]

Yet in the end the meaning is still not clear; the masks and skeletons lie on the floor in a jumbled heap, waiting, while a single candle with a puny flame illuminates their patient presence.

---

[42] Ensor, *Lettres à André de Ridder*, p. 62.
[43] E.T.A. Hoffmann, *The Best Tales of Hoffmann*, introduced and edited by E. F. Bleiler (New York: Dover, 1967), p. 102.
[44] Au chant des violons, aux flammes des bougies,

Espères-tu chasser ton cauchemar moqueur (Baudelaire, *Oeuvres complètes*, p. 93).
[45] Et viens-tu demander au torrent des orgies
De rafraîchir l'enfer allumé dans ton coeur? (Ibid.).

SELECTED BIBLIOGRAPHY

Archives de l'art belge, en dépôt temporaire aux Archives Générales du Royaume, Brussels.

Archives de l'art contemporain en Beligique, Brussels: Musées Royaux des Beaux-Arts de Belgique.

Arnold, Sydney. *L'école de peinture d'Ostende: Le groupe d'Ensor (1925-1930)*. Introduction by Denis Saurat. London: A. V. Huckle & Son, 1946.

L'Art Belge, Ensor number special (December 1965).

L'Art flamand d'Ensor à Permeke. Paris: Musée de l'Orangerie, 1970.

L'Art moderne. 34 vols., 1881-1914.

L'Artiste (Revue de Paris; Histoire de l'art contemporain), 150 vols., 1831-1901.

Les Arts plastiques: James Ensor. Brussels: Connaissance, 1950.

Ashton, Dore. *A Fable of Modern Art*. London: Thames and Hudson, 1980.

————. "James Ensor's Re-Entries." *Arts Magazine* 51 (March 1977): 136-138.

Autour de 1900: L'Art belge (1884-1918). Introduction by Francine-Claire Legrand. London: Arts Council, 1965.

Avermaete Roger. *James Ensor*. Brussels: Cercle d'Art, 1947.

Babut Du Marès, J[ean]-P[ierre]. *Félicien Rops*. Ostend: Erel, 1971.

Bade, Patrick. *Femme Fatale: Images of Evil and Fascinating Women*. New York: Mayflower Books, 1979.

Baedeker, Karl *Belgium and Holland*. Leipzig: Karl Baedeker, 1897.

Baldick, Robert. *The Life of J.-K. Huysmans*. Oxford: Clarendon, 1955.

Balzac, Honoré de. "Jesus-Christ en Flandre." *La Comédie humaine: études philosophiques*. Vol. IX. Paris: Librairie Gallimard, 1950. Pp. 250-266.

Baudelaire, Charles. *The Flowers of Evil*. Edited by Marthiel and Jackson Mathews. Rev. ed. New York: New Directions, 1963.

————. *Oeuvres complètes*. Paris: Gallimard, 1961.

Belgian Art 1880-1914. New York: The Brooklyn Museum, 1980.

Béranger, P. J. *Oeuvres complètes de P. J. Béranger*. 2 vols. Paris: Perrotin, 1857.

Berthoud, S. Henry. *Légendes et traditions surnaturelles des Flandres*. New ed. Brussels: Libraire F. De Nobele, 1862.

Block, Haskell. *Mallarmé and the Symbolist Drama*. Detroit: Wayne State University Press, 1963.

Block, Jane. "Les Vingt and Belgian Avant-Gardism, 1868-1894." Ph.D. dissertation, University of Wisconsin at Milwaukee, 1980.

————. "Les XX: Forum of the Avant-Garde." *Belgian Art 1880-1914*. New York: The Brooklyn Museum, 1980.

Bourke, John Gregory. *Scatalogic Rites of All Nations*. Washington, D.C.: W. H. Lowdermilke, 1891. Reprinted New York: Johnson Reprint, 1968.

Brison, Charles. *Pornocrates: An Introduction to the Life & Work of Félicien Rops*. London: Charles Skilton, 1969.

Brombert, Victor. *The Romantic Prison: The French Tradition*. Princeton: Princeton University Press, 1978.

Buyck, Jean F. "Antwerp, Als Ik Kan, and the Problem of Provincialism." *Belgian Art, 1880-1914*. New York: The Brooklyn Museum, 1980.

Castelot, Jollivet. *Croquis scientifiques et philosophiques.* Paris: Durville, 1912.

Chapeaurouge, Donat de. "Die Kathedrale als modernes Bildthema." *Jahrbuch der Hamburger Kunstsammlungen* 18 (1973): 155-172.

Cladel, Léon. *Les Martyrs Ridicules: Roman Parisien.* Preface by Charles Baudelaire. Brussels: Henry Kistemaeckers, 1880.

Clark, Kenneth. *The Nude: A Study in Ideal Form.* Garden City: Doubleday, 1956.

Colleye, H. *Antoine Wiertz.* Brussels: La Renaissance du Livre, 1957.

Cornette, A. H. *L'Oeuvre de James Ensor.* Paris: Musé National du Jeu de Paume, 1932.

————. "James Ensor." *La Revue de l'art ancien et moderne* 62 (1932): 17-32.

Cromwell, Richard S. *David Friedrich Strauss and His Place in Modern Thought.* Foreword by Wilhelm Pauck. Fairlawn, Conn.: R. E. Burdick, 1974.

Croquez, Robert. *Ensor et le Rotary.* Preface by Franz Hellens. Ostend: Erel, 1973.

————. *Ensor en son temps.* Ostend: Erel, 1970.

Cuypers, Firmin. *Aspects propos de James Ensor.* Bruges: A. G. Stainforth, 1946.

————. *James Ensor: L'Homme et l'oeuvre.* Paris: Écrivains Réunis, 1925.

Damase, Jacques. *James Ensor; L'oeuvre gravé.* Geneva: Motte, 1967.

Dayot, Armand. *La Révolution française . . . d'après des peintures, sculptures, gravures. . . .* Paris: Ernest Flammarion, 1896.

De Coster, Charles. *Contes brabacons.* Paris: Michel Lévy frères, 1861.

————. *Flemish Legends.* Translated from the French by Harold Taylor. New York: Frederick A. Stokes, n.d.

————. *The Glorious Adventures of Tyl Ulenspiegel.* Translated by Allan Ross Macdougall. New York: Pantheon Books, 1943.

de France, Hubert. *James Ensor, essai de bibliographie commentée—James Ensor: proeve van gencommentariëerde bibiliografie.* Bibliographia Belgica. Vol. 53. Brussels: Bibliographia Belgica, 1960.

De l'allegorie au symbole. Introduction by Francine-Claire Legrand. Brussels: Musées Royaux des Beaux-Arts de Belgique, 1968.

Delevoy, Robert L. *Symbolists and Symbolism.* Translated by Barbara Bray, Elizabeth Wrightson, and Bernard C. Swift. New York: Rizzoli International, 1978.

Delteil, Loys. *Catalogue Raisonné of the Etchings of Charles Meryon.* New York: W. P. Truesdell, 1924.

————. *Le Peintre graveur illustré (XIX et XX siècles).* Vol. XIX. Paris, 1925.

De Maeyer, Marcel. "De genese van masker—, travestie en skeletmotieven in het oeuvre van James Ensor." *Bulletin des Musées Royaux des Beaux-Arts de Belgique* 10 (1963): 69-88.

————. "De mysticke dood van een godgeleer de van James Ensor." *Jaarboek van het Koninklijk Museum voor schone Kunsten Antwerpen* (1962-1963): 131-158.

————. "Derrière le masque: L'Introduction du masque, du travesti et du squelette comme motifs dans l'oeuvre de James Ensor." *L'Art Belge* (December 1965): 17-30.

————. "Ensor au chapeau fleuri." *L'Art Belge* (December 1965): 41-45.

————. "Note biographique et critique." *L'Art Belge* (December 1965): 60-65.

Demolder, Eugène. *James Ensor.* Brussels: Paul LaComblez, 1892.

————. *Félicien Rops: Étude patronymique.* Paris: Pincepourde, 1894.

————. *Impressions d'art.* Brussels: Madame Veuve Monnone, 1889.

de Ridder, André. *James Ensor.* Paris: Rieder, 1930.

de Smet, Frédéric. "James Ensor." *Gand Artistique: Art et esthétique,* no. 12 (December 1925).

Desmeth, Paul. *James Ensor.* Brussels: L. J. Kryn, 1926.

————. *Paysages Bruxellois suivis d'une étude sur James Ensor.* Brussels: Vromant, 1937.

Des Ombiaux, Maurice. *Le Général Leman.* Paris: Blond & Gay, 1916.

De Tolnay, Charles. *Hieronymus Bosch.* New York: William Morrow, 1966.

Dommartin, Henry. *Les Eaux-Fortes de James Ensor.* Brussels: Rene van Sulper, 1930.

Doré's Illustrations for Rabelais: A Selection of 252 Illustrations by Gustave Doré. Selected and Introduced by Stanley Appelbaum. New York: Dover, 1978.

Dumont, Georges H. *La Vie quotidienne en Belgique sous le regne de Léopold II (1855-1909)*. Paris: Hachette, 1974.

The Earthly Chimera and the Femme Fatale: Fear of Woman in Nineteenth-Century Art. Introduction by Reinhold Heller. Chicago: The University of Chicago, David and Alfred Smart Gallery, 1981.

Edebau, Frank Patrick. *La Maison de James Ensor*. Brussels: Connaissance, 1957.

Eekhoud, Georges. *The New Carthage*. Translated and introduced by Lloyd R. Morris. New York: Duffield, 1917.

Elesh, James N. *James Ensor, The Complete Graphic Work*. Vol. 141 of *The Illustrated Bartsch*. Edited by Walter L. Strauss. New York: Abaris Books, 1982.

Ensor, James. *Lettres à André de Ridder*. Antwerp: Librairie des Arts, 1960.

——. *Lettres à Franz Hellens - Eugène Demolder*. Liège: Dynamo, 1969.

——. *Mes Écrits*. Preface by Franz Hellens. 5th ed. Liège: Éditions Nationales, 1974.

Ensor dans les collections privées. Brussels: Galerie Isy Brachot, 1965.

Ensor: ein Maler aus dem Späten 19. Jahrhundert. Stuttgart: Staatsgalerie, 1972.

Ensor in de Gentse Verzamelingen ingericht door het museum voor schone Kunsten van Ghent. Ghent, 1969.

Ensor-Magritte. Brussels: Palais des Beaux-Arts, 1975.

Exteens, Maurice. *L'Oeuvre gravé et lithographié de Félicien Rops*. 4 vols. Paris: Pellet, 1928.

Fabry, Georges. *Jean-Jacques Gaillard: le voyageur de la lumière fantasque*. Ostend: Erel, n.d.

Fantasmagie (issue on James Ensor), no. 3 (October 1960).

"La Fantastique Réel." *L'Art moderne*, no. 4 (January 23, 1887): 25-27.

Farmer, John David. *Ensor*. New York: George Braziller, 1976.

Farwell, Beatrice. "Courbet's 'Baigneuses' and the Rhetorical Feminine Image." *Woman as Sex Object*. Edited by Thomas B. Hess and Linda Nochlin. New York: Newsweek, 1972.

Fassmann, Kurt. "James Ensor: The Reality of Masks." *Die Kunst und das shone Heim* 10 (October 1969): 471-474.

Félicien Rops. Charleroi: Palais des Beaux-Arts, 1960.

——. Ixelles: Exposition musée communal d'Ixelles, 1969.

Fels, Florent. *James Ensor*. Brussels: Weisenbuch, 1958.

Fiedler, Leslie. *Freaks, Myths and Images of the Secret Self*. New York: Simon and Schuster, 1978.

Fierens, Paul. *James Ensor*. Paris: Hyperion, 1943.

——. *L'Art en Belgique*. Brussels: La Renaissance du Livre, n.d.

——. *Les dessins d'Ensor*. Brussels: Apollo, 1944.

Filozof, Veronique. *Der Totentanz: La Danse macabre*. Basel: Pharos-Verlag, 1976.

Finke, Ulriche, ed. "Degas and the Literature of His Time." *French Nineteenth-Century Painting and Literature*. New York: Harper and Row, 1972.

Flaubert, Gustave. *The Temptation of St. Anthony*. Translated with an introduction and notes by Kitty Mrosovsky. Ithaca: Cornell University Press, 1981.

Fraenger, Wilhelm. "Die Kathedrale." *Die graphischen Kunste* 49, no. 4 (1926): 81-98.

Friedrich, David. *Strauss and his Theology*. Cambridge: Cambridge University Press, 1973.

Garcin, Laure. *J. J. Grandville, révolutionnaire et précurseur de l'art du mouvement*. Paris: Eric Losfield, 1970.

Gerlo, Alois. *Charles De Coster en Vlaanderen*. Antwerp: Uitgevery S. M. Ontwikkeling, 1959.

Gindertael, Roger van. *Ensor*. Boston: New York Graphic Society, 1975.

Gordon, James Daniel. *The Epistle of Othea to Hector*. Philadelphia: n.p., 1942.

La Grande Encyclopédie, Inventaire raisonné des sciences, des lettres et des arts. Vol. XXII. Paris: Libraire Larousse, 1886-1902.

Grandville, Jean-Ignace-Isidore-Gérard. *Grandville: Das gesamte Werk*. 2 vols. Munich: Roger and Bernhard, 1969.

——. *Les Métamorphoses de jour par Grandville*. Paris: Bulla, 1829.

——. *Petites Misères de la vie humaine*. Paris: Fournier, 1843.

The Graphic Work of George Cruikshank. Edited by Richard A. Vogler. New York: Dover, 1979.

The Graphic Works of Odilon Redon. Introduction by Alfred Werner. New York: Dover, 1969.

Haesaerts, Paul. *James Ensor.* Translated by Norbert Guterman. New York: Harry N. Abrams, 1959.

———. *James Ensor.* Brussels: Les Ateliers d'Art Graphique Meddens, 1973.

———. "Quand James Ensor peignait *L'Entrée du Christ à Bruxelles.*" *Oeil* 131 (November 1965): 26-35, 82.

———. "Stridences et bigarrures des écrits d'Ensor," *L'Art Belge* (December 1965): 32-40.

Haftmann, Werner. *Painting in the Twentieth Century.* Vol. I. Translated by Ralph Manheim. 6th ed. New York: Praeger, 1969.

Halls, W. D. *Maurice Maeterlinck: A Study of His Life and Thought.* Oxford: Clarendon, 1960.

Hamelius, Paul. *Introduction à la littérature française et flémalle de Belgique.* Brussels: J. Lebèque, 1921.

Hartley, Anthony, ed., *Mallarmé.* Introduction by Anthony Hartley. Baltimore: Penguin Books, 1965.

Heidelberg, Betty Lou. "Narrative Art in the *Contes cruels* of Villiers de l'Isle-Adam." Ph.D. dissertation, University of Minnesota, 1972.

Held, Julius. "Flora, Goddess and Courtesan." *De Artibus Opuscula, X: Essays in Honor of Erwin Panofsky.* Edited by Millard Meiss, New York: New York University, 1960.

Heller, Reinhold. *The Earthly Chimera and the Femme Fatale: Fear of Woman in Nineteenth-Century Art.* Chicago: The University of Chicago, David and Alfred Smart Gallery, 1981.

Hemma, L. [Albert Mockel.] *Les Fumistes wallons (histoire de quelques fous).* Liège: H. Vaillant-Carmanne, 1887.

Herbert, Robert and Eugenia. *The Artist and Social Reform: France and Belgium 1885-1898.* New Haven: Yale University Press, 1961.

Hermans, Georges. "Un 'Cahier Ensor' d'Emma Lambotte." *Bulletin des Musées Royaux des Beaux-Arts de Belgique* 20, nos. 1-4 (1971): 85-121.

Hess, Thomas B. "Ensor, the Masked Marvel." *New York,* February 21, 1977, p. 90.

Hetzel, Pierre Jules. *Scènes de la vie privée et publique des animaux.* Paris: J. Hetzel et Paulin, 1842.

Hirsh, Sharon Latchaw. "Arnold Böcklin: Death Talks to the Painter," *Arts Magazine* 55 (February 1981): 84-89.

Hodin, J. P. "James Ensor: On the Ultimate Questions of Life." In *The Dilemma of Being Modern.* London: Routledge and Kegan Paul, 1956.

———. "Ensor—Avant and Après." *The Painter and Sculptor* 2 (Spring 1959): 15-21.

Hoffman, E.T.A. *The Best Tales of Hoffmann.* Introduced and edited by E. F. Bleiler. New York: Dover, 1967.

Hoffmann, Edith. "Notes on the Iconography of Félicien Rops," *Burlington Magazine* 123 (January-June 1981): 206-218.

Hofstatter, Hans H. *Symbolismus und die Kunst der Jahrhundertwende.* 4th ed. Cologne: DuMont, 1978.

Hommage à James Ensor. Brussels: Galerie Genges Giroux, 1945.

Huysmans, J[oris-K[arl]. *Against Nature.* Translated by Robert Baldick. Baltimore: Penguin Books, 1959. Reprint 1966.

———. *Against the Grain.* Introduction by Havelock Ellis. New York: Three Sirens Press, 1931.

———. *La Cathédrale.* Paris: Librairie Plon, n.d.

———. *Certains. Oeuvres complètes de J.-K. Huysmans.* Vol. X. Paris: G. Cres, 1929.

Jackson, A. B. *La Revue blanche (1889-1903): Origine, influence, bibliographie.* Paris: M. J. Minard, 1960.

Jacques Callot 1592-1635. Brown University and Rhode Island School of Design, 1970.

Jacquot, Jean, and Konigson, Elie, eds. *Les Fêtes de la Renaissance.* 3 vols. Paris: Centre National de la Recherche Scientifique, 1975.

James Ensor. Preface by Francois Fosca. Brussels: Palais des Beaux-Arts, 1929.

James Ensor Festschrift zur ersten deustchen Ensor-Anstellung. Hanover: Kestner-Gesellschaft, 1927.

James Ensor: Omelettes bourrées. Preface by Franz Hellens. Liège: Dynamo, 1962.

"James Ensor, peintre de masques." *Les Sommets de la peinture.* Brussels: Elsevier, 1959.

Janssens, Jacques. *James Ensor.* Paris: Librairie Flammarion, 1978.

Juin, Hubert, ed. *Histoires étranges et récits insolites.* Paris: Livre Club du Libraire, 1965.

Jullian, Philippe. *Dreamers of Decadence.* New York: Praeger, 1975.
———. *The Symbolists.* 2d ed., Oxford and New York: Phaidon/ Dutton, 1977.
Kaplan, Julius. "The Religious Subjects of James Ensor, 1877-1900." *Revue belge d'archéologie et d'histoire de l'art*, nos. 3-4 (1966): 175-206.
Kiefer, Theodore. *J. Ensor.* Aurel: Bongers, Recklinghausen, 1976.
Knapp, Bettina. *Maurice Maeterlinck.* Boston: Twayne, 1975.
Kozaky, P. Stephan. *Geschichte der Totentanze.* 3 vols., Budapest: Magyar Tortenti Muzeum, 1936.
Kramer, Hilton. "James Ensor's Rebellion Against Fate." *New York Times*, November 21, 1976, p. 27.
Kronhausen, Phyllis and Eberhard. *The Complete Book of Erotic Art.* Vol. 1. New York: Bell, 1978.
Kubler, G. "Archiducal Flanders and the Joyeuse Entrée of Philip III at Lisbon in 1619." *Jaarboek van het Koninklijk Museum voor Schone Kunsten.* Antwerp, 1970: 157ff.
Lanoye, Robert. *L'Épopée ostendaise.* 2d ed. Ostend: Erel, 1971.
Lartigue, Jacques-Henri. *Les Femmes aux cigarettes.* New York: Viking, 1980.
Lebeer, Louis. *James Ensor aquafortiste.* Antwerp: De Sikkel, 1952.
———. *Prints of James Ensor.* New York: DaCapo, 1971.
Lederer, Wolfgang. *The Fear of Women.* New York: Harcourt Brace Jovanovich, 1968.
Legrand, Francine-Claire. *Ensor, cet inconnu.* Brussels: La Renaissance du Livre, 1971.
———. *Le Groupe des XX et son temps.* Otterlo; Rijksmuseum Kroller-Muller, 1962.
———. "Les Lettres de James Ensor à Octave Maus." *Bulletin des Musées Royaux des Beaux-Arts de Belgique* 15 (1966): 17-54.
———. *Symbolism in Belgium.* Translated by Alistair Kennedy. Brussels: Laconti, 1972.
Leirens, Charles. *Belgian Folklore.* No. 7: *Art, Life, and Science in Belgium.* New York: Belgian Government Information Center, 1946.
Lejeune, Rita. *La Wallonie, le pays et les hommes.* Edited by Jacques Stennon. Brussels: La Renaissance du Livre, 1977.
Lemonnier, Camille. *Félicien Rops.* Paris: H. Floury, 1908.

———. "Une Tentation de St. Antoine de Félicien Rops." *La Revue indépendente* 1 (1884): 125-131.
Le Roy, Gregoire. *James Ensor.* Brussels and Paris: G. Van Oest, 1922.
Lesko, Diane. "Cézanne's 'Bather' and a Found Self-Portrait." *Artforum* 15 (December 1976): 55-56.
———. "Ensor in His Milieu." *Artforum* 15 (May 1977): 56-62.
———. "James Ensor's Transformations of Tradition: A Study of His Life and Art During the Creative Years 1877-1899." Ph.D. dissertation, State University of New York at Binghamton, 1982.
Lucie-Smith, Edward, ed. *The Waking Dream: Fantasy & the Surreal in Graphic Art 1450-1900.* New York: Alfred A. Knopf, 1975.
McGough, Stephen. "James Ensor's 'The Entry of Christ Into Brussels in 1889.' " Ph.D. dissertation, Stanford University, 1981.
Mallarmé, Stephane. *Mallarmé.* Introduced and edited by Anthony Hartley. Baltimore: Penguin Books, 1965.
———. *Stephane Mallarmé: Oeuvres complètes.* Paris: Bibliothèque de la Pléiade, 1945.
Maret, François. *Les Peintres luministes.* Brussels: Cercle d'art, 1944.
Marie, Aristide. *Le Peintre Poète Louis Boulenger.* Paris: H. Floury, 1925.
Marinus, Albert. *Le Folklore Belge.* 3 vols. Brussels: Les Editions Historiques, n.d.
Mathews, Andrew Jackson. *La Wallonie, 1886-1892: The Symbolist Movement in Belgium.* Morningside Heights: King's Crown Press, 1947.
Maus, Madeleine Octave. *Trente Années de lutte pour l'art belge, 1884-1914.* Brussels: Librairie L'Oiseau bleu, 1926.
Mellerio, André. *Odilon Redon: peintre, dessinateur et graveur.* Paris: H. Floury, 1923.
Meurant, René, and Vanderlinden, Renaat. *Folklore en Belgique.* Brussels: Paul Legrain, 1974.
Michaud, Guy. *Mallarmé.* Translated by Marie Collins and Bertha Humez. New York: New York University Press, 1965.
Milner, John. *Symbolists and Decadents.* New York: E. P. Dutton, 1971.

Milton, John. *The Complete Poems of John Milton.* Notes by Thomas Newton. New York: Bonanza Books, 1936.

―――. *Milton's Paradise Lost.* Introduction by Robert Vaughan. New York: Cassell, 1866.

Moakley, Gertrude. *The Tarot Cards, Painted by Bonifacio Bembo for the Visconti-Sforza Family.* New York: The New York Public Library, 1966.

Mockel, Alfred. *Antoine Wiertz.* Brussels: n.p., 1946.

Morrisey, Leslie D. "James Ensor's Self-Portraits." *Arts Magazine* 54 (December 1979): 90-95.

Muls, Jozef. *Een Eeuw Portret in Belgie.* Diest: Pro Arte, 1944.

Myers, Marshall Neal. "James Ensor's 'The Tribulations of St. Anthony': Permutations of the Excremental Vision." *Arts Magazine* 54, no. 4 (December 1979): 84-89.

"Nos Flamands." *L'Art moderne* 22 (July 6, 1884): 217-219.

Oliver, E. J. *Balzac the European.* London and New York: Sheed and Ward, 1959.

Ollinger-Zinque, Gisèle. *Ensor by Himself.* Translated by Alistair Kennedy. Brussels: Laconti, 1977.

―――. "Les auréoles du Christ ou les sensibilités de la lumière." *Bulletin des Musées Royaux des Beaux-Arts de Belgique* 17 (1968): 191-202.

Passeron, Roger. "James Ensor Graveur." *L'Oeil*, no. 275 (1978): 25-31.

"Peinture mate par M. Wiertz." *Uylenspiegel: Journal des débats artistiques et littéraires*, no. 22 (July 3, 1859):1.

Péladan, Josephin. *La Décadence esthétique.* Vol. I: *L'Art ochlocratique: salons de 1882 et de 1883 avec une lettre de Jules Barbey D'Aurevilly.* Paris: Camille Dalou, 1888.

―――. *Les Maîtres contemporains: Félicien Rops.* 1st. ed. Brussels: Callewert père, 1885 (originally printed in *La Jeune Belgique* [May 1883]).

Perella, Nicolas James. *The Kiss Sacred and Profane.* Berkeley: University of California Press, 1969.

Pierard, Louis. *Félicien Rops.* Antwerp: De Sikkel, 1949.

Pincus-Witten, Robert. *Occult Symbolism in France: Josephin Péladan and the Salons de la Rose-Croix.* New York: Garland, 1976.

Piron, Dr. H[ermon] T[héo]. *James Ensor, een psychoanalytische studie.* Antwerp: De Nederlandsche Boekhandel, 1968.

Pittore, E. "La Sorcière de M. Wiertz." *Uylenspiegel: Journal des débats artistiques et littéraires*, no. 36 (October 4, 1857): 2-3.

La Plume, special Ensor edition (Paris, 1898); also issued separately (Paris, 1899).

―――, special Rops edition (June 15, 1896).

Poe, Edgar Allan. *The Complete Tales and Poems of Edgar Allan Poe.* New York: Random House, 1975.

―――. *Great Short Works of Edgar Allan Poe.* Introduced and edited by G. R. Thompson. New York: Harper and Row, 1970.

Praz, Mario. *The Romantic Agony.* Translated by Angus Davidson. 2d ed. London: Oxford University Press, 1951.

Rabelais, François. *The Works of Mr. Francis Rabelais.* Illustrated by W. Heath Robinson. London: Richard Clay and Sons, 1931.

―――. *The Histories of Gargantua and Pantagruel.* Translation and introduction by J. M. Cohen. Baltimore: Penguin Books, 1976.

Raitt, A. W. *The Life of Villiers de L'Isle-Adam.* Oxford: Clarendon, 1981.

Ramiro, Erasthené. *Catalogue descriptif et analytique de l'oeuvre gravé de Félicien Rops.* 2d ed. Brussels: E. Deman, 1893.

Ramsey, Warren. *Jules Laforgue and the Ironic Inheritance.* New York: Oxford University Press, 1953.

―――, ed. *Jules Laforgue: Essays on a Poet's Life and Work.* Preface by Harry T. Moore. Carbondale: South Illinois Press, 1969.

Réau, Louis. *Iconographie de l'art chrétien.* Vol. 1. Paris: Presses Universitaires de France, 1955.

Reff, Theodore. "Cézanne, Flaubert, St. Anthony and the Queen of Sheba." *Art Bulletin* 44 (1962): 113-125.

Renan, Ernest. *La Vie de Jésus. Oeuvres complètes d'Ernest Renan.* Vol. IV. Paris: Calmann-Lévy, 1947.

Retrospective James Ensor. Introduction by Walter Vanbeselaere. Antwerp: Musée Royaux des Beaux-Arts, 1951.

Revins, Lee. *The Graphic Work of Félicien Rops.* New York: Land's End Press, 1968.

La Revue belge; Journal littéraire et artistique. 5 vols. 1888-1893.

La Revue indépendante de littérature et d'art. Directed by Edouard Dujardin. Edited by Felix Fenéon. 1884-1889.

Rewald, John. *Post-Impressionism; From van Gogh to Gauguin.* 3rd ed., rev. New York: Museum of Modern Art, 1978.

Roberts-Jones, Philippe. *Beyond Time and Place; Non-Realist Painting in the Nineteenth Century.* Oxford: Oxford University Press, 1978.

———. "L'Image irréaliste chez Antoine Wiertz." *Bulletin de la classe des beaux-arts, Académie Royale de Belgique,* 59, nos. 2-4 (1977): 55-63.

Rose, Marilyn Gaddis. "Villiers de L'Isle-Adam and the Decorative Arts: A Decadent Departure from Symbolism." Third Annual Colloquium in Nineteenth-Century French Literature, Ohio State University, 1977.

Rosman, Corrie. "Ensor Demasqué?" *Nieuw Vlaams Tijdschrift* 11, no. 7 (1957): 678-704.

Sagnac, Philippe and Robiquet, Jean. *La Révolution de 1789.* Paris: Éditions Nationales, 1934.

Schiff, Gert. "Ensor the Exorcist." In *Art the Ape of Nature*: Studies in Honor of H. H. Janson. Edited by Moshe Baraschand and Lucy Freeman Sandler. New York: Harry N. Abrams, 1981.

Schlumberger, Evelyn. "Project for a Film on James Ensor." *Réalitiés,* December 1970, pp. 78-87.

Schoonbaert, Lydia. "Addendum beschrijvende catalogus 1948, Een verzameling tekeningen van Ensor (deel I)." *Jaarboek van het Koninklijk Museum voor Schone Kunsten.* Antwerp, 1968: 311-342.

———. "Addendum beschrijvende catalogus 1948, Een verzameling tekeningen van Ensor (deel II)." *Jaarboek van het Koninklijk Museum voor Schone Kunsten.* Antwerp, 1969: 265-284.

———. "Addendum beschrijvende catalogus 1948, Een verzameling tekeningen van Ensor (deel III)." *Jaarboek van het Koninklijk Museum voor Schone Kunsten.* Antwerp, 1970: 305-322.

———. "Addendum beschrijvende catalogus 1948, Een verzameling tekeningen van Ensor (deel IV)." *Jaarboek van het Koninklijk Museum voor Schone Kunsten.* Antwerp, 1972: 285-311.

———. "Gazette des Beaux-Arts en The Studio als inspiratienbronnen voor James Ensor." *Jaarboek van het Koninklijk Museum voor Schone Kunsten.* Antwerp, 1978: 205-221.

———. "Schilderend geraamte van James Ensor." *Jaarboek van het Koninklijk Museum voor Schone Kunsten.* Antwerp, 1973: 321-337.

Schwob, Lucien. *James Ensor.* Ostend: n.p., 1963.

Seznec, Jean. *Literature and the Visual Arts in Nineteenth-Century France.* London: University of Hull, 1962.

———. *Nouvelles Études sur la tentation de Saint Antoine.* London: The Warburg Institute, University of London, 1949.

———. "The Temptation of St. Anthony in Art." *Magazine of Art* 11 (1947): 86-93.

Smith, William Jay, ed. and trans. *Selected Writings of Jules Laforgue.* New York: Grove Press, 1956.

Sorrel, Walter. *The Other Face: The Mask in the Arts.* New York: Bobbs-Merrill, 1973.

Stevo, Jean. "Ensor l'Ostendais." *L'Art Belge* (December 1965): 9-17.

———. *James Ensor.* Brussels: Éditions Germinal, 1947.

Stith-Thompson. *Motif Index of Folk Literature. Frazer's Apollodorus.* Vol. 2. Bloomington: Indiana University Press, 1966.

Strauss, David Friedrich. *The Life of Jesus.* 2 vols. Translated from the 4th German ed. by Marian Evans. New York: Calvain Blanchard, 1860. Republished Michigan: Scholarly Press, 1970.

Stromberg, Roland N., ed. *Realism, Naturalism, and Symbolism: Modes of Thought and Expression in Europe 1848-1914.* New York: Walker, 1968.

Le Symbolisme en Europe. Paris: Musées Nationaux, 1976.

Taevernier, Auguste. *Le Drame Ensorien: Les Auréoles du Christ ou les sensibilités de la lumière.* Ghent: N. V. Erasmus Ledeberg, 1976.

———. *James Ensor, catalogue illustré de ses gravures, leur description critique et l'inventaire des plaques.* Ghent: N. V. Erasmus, 1973.

Tannenbaum, Libby. "James Ensor: Prophet of Modern Fantastic Art." *Magazine of Art* 36 (May 1943): 244-249.

———. *James Ensor.* New York: Simon and Schuster, 1951.

Taylor, Una. *Maurice Maeterlinck: A Critical Study.* Port Washington: Kennikat, 1968.

Teugels, Jean. *Variations sur James Ensor.* Ostend: l'Aquarium, 1931.

Thalmann, Marianne. *The Romantic Fairy Tale: Seeds of Surrealism.* Translated by Mary B. Corcoran. Ann Arbor: University of Michigan Press, 1964.

Uylenspiegel: Journal des débats artistiques et littéraires. 1856-1864

Vanbeselaere, Walter. "Ensor en Wouters," *Jaarboek van het Koninklijk Museum voor Schone Kunsten.* Anthwerp (1973): 167-188.

———. *L'Entrée du Christ à Bruxelles.* Brussels: Weisenbuch, 1958.

Van Lennep, Jacques. "Les Expositions burlesques à Bruxelles de 1870 à 1914: l'Art zwanze—une manifestation pré-dadaiste?" *Bulletin des Musées Royaux des Beaux-Arts de Belgique,* 19 (February 1970): 127-148.

Vergo, Peter. *Art in Vienna 1898-1918.* London: Phaidon, 1975.

Verhaeren, Emile. *À Marthe Verhaeren; deux cent dix-neuf lettres inédites 1889-1916.* Paris: Mercure de France, 1951.

———. *James Ensor.* Brussels: G. Van Oest, 1908.

———. *Poems of Emile Verhaeren.* Translated by Alma Strettell. New York: John Lane, 1915.

Villiers de l'Isle-Adam, Comte de. *Claire Lenoir.* New York: A. & C. Boni, 1925.

———. *Contes cruels: Nouveaux contes cruels.* Paris: Garnier frères, 1968.

———. *Tribulat Bonhomet.* Paris: Librairie Jose Corti, 1967.

Wagar, W. Warren. "Decadence: A Note on Definitions." *Essays on Decadence. Pro domo* publication of the "Seminar on Decadence." Binghamton: State University of New York, 1975.

Warmoes, Jean. "Les XX et la littérature." *Cahiers van de Velde,* no. 7 (Brussels, 1966): 19-42.

Whitford, Frank. "Ensor's Entry of Christ into Brussels." *Studio International* 183 (September 1971): 936.

Wiertz, Antoine. *Oeuvres littéraires.* Paris: Librairie Internationale, 1870.

Yarnall, James Leo. "Meryon's Mystical Transformations." *Art Bulletin* 61 (June 1979): 289-300.

Zola, Émile. *The Dream.* Translated by Eliza E. Chase. London: Chatto and Windus, 1907.

PHOTOGRAPHIC CREDITS

A.C.L. Brussels: Figs. 1, 3, 4, 5, 7, 10, 12, 13, 15, 16, 17, 19, 22, 23, 24, 26, 30, 31, 36, 37, 41, 43, 44, 45, 46, 50, 51, 52, 53, 55, 56, 57, 61, 64, 65, 69, 72, 74, 81, 87, 88, 89, 90, 96, 99, 103, 106, 108, 109, 110, 111, 112, 114.

Archives of Contemporary Art in Belgium, Brussels: Figs. 25, 40.

The Art Institute of Chicago: Figs. 9, 47, 95.

Bibliothèque Royale Albert Ier, Cabinet des Estampes, Brussels: Fig. 66.

De Schutter, Antwerp: Plate 4, Fig. 29.

James Elesh, Evanston, Illinois: Figs. 6, 27, 28, 34, 38, 39, 54, 62, 63, 76, 77, 80, 82, 83, 84, 85, 91, 100, 102, 115.

Sharon Hirsh, Carlisle, Pennsylvania: Fig. 35.

Kimbell Art Museum, Fort Worth, Texas: Pl. 6.

Koninklijk Museum voor Schone Kunsten, Antwerp: Pls. 1, 2, 8.

Metropolitan Museum of Art, New York: Fig. 33.

Musées Royaux des Beaux-Arts de Belgique: Pl. 3.

Museum of Modern Art, New York: Pl. 7.

Réunion des Musées Nationaux, Paris: Fig. 97.

Rijksmuseum Kröller-Müller, Otterlo, The Netherlands: Fig. 20.

Stedelijk Museum voor Schone Kunsten, Ostend: Plate 3, Figs. 2, 11, 18, 21, 70, 113.

Photographs with the credit A.C.L., Brussels, are copyrighted by the Institut Royal du Patrimoine Artistique.

Photographs not listed under credits are from the author's collection.

Index

NOTE: Titles of all works except Ensor's are followed by the name of the author or artist in parenthesis.

À Rebours (J.-K. Huysmans), 4, 11, 83, 86
À Hestor Denis, James Ensor, 144
Admiralty, Paris, The (Charles Meryon), 117
Adventures of Mr. and Mrs. Sandboys, The (G. Cruikshank, and H. Mayhew), 138
African masks, 145
Afternoon at Ostend, 14
Alive and Radiant: The Entry of Christ into Jerusalem, 133
Annunciation, The, Renaissance paintings of, 154
Apotheosis of the Queen, The (Antoine Wiertz), 60, 64, 138
Art moderne, L', 51, 56-57, 109, 115-116, 134
Art Nouveau, 93
art *zwanze*, 48n48, 49, 50
Artan, Louis, 6n2
Artist Decomposed, The, 42n34, 47
Artist in His Studio, The, 25
Artist's Father in Death, The, 32

Artist's Mother in Death, The, 17-18
Astonishment of the Mask Wouse, The, 104-105, 114, 158
Astruc, Zachary, 21
At the Corner of the Street (Félicien Rops), 81
Augustus and the Sibyl (anonymous), 154n32
Auto-Da-fé, 98

Bajou, Anatole, 113
Balde, Jacob, 150
balloon in *Tribulations of St. Anthony*, 118, 120, 126
ballooning as sport, 118, 119
Balzac, Honoré de, 84-86, 91-92, 124n22, 151
Baron Munchausen aboard the Dutch ship . . . (Gustave Doré), 117
Baths at Ostend, The, 13
Battle between Carnival and Lent, The, (Pieter Brueghel), 24n38

Battle of the Golden Spurs, The, 100
Baudelaire, Charles, 53, 57, 64n17, 124, 138, 151, 158
Belgium: and Flemish-French controversy, 53n72, 73; art of, in competition with Paris, 51-52; as refuge for Marx, Hugo, Baudelaire, 138
Belle Rosine, La (Antoine Wiertz), 47
Berthoud, S. Henry, 85, 101
Block, Jane, 9
Bonnard, Pierre, 25
Boogaerts, Augusta, 66n19, 72, 78, 120, 147-148, 150, 152
Bosch, Hieronymous, 108-109, 116, 118n15, 142
Boulenger, Hippolyte, 6n2, 58n87
Boulenger, Louis, 37-38
Braquemond, Félix de, 57
Breakwater, The, 50
Bresdin, Rudolphe, 39
Broken Pitcher, The (Jean-Baptiste Greuze), 26n49
Brueghel, Pieter, 24n38, 110n75, 116, 138

Cabin on the Beach, The, 3

Call of the Siren, The, 66, 68-69, 147, 152, 158

Callot, Jacques, *Temptation of St. Anthony*, 116

Capture of a Strange City, 63-64

Carnival King, 24n38

carnival tradition, 13, 135

Cathedral, The, 4, 86-90, 93

Cathedral at Ostend, and fire, 88-89; as metaphor for art, 90n36

Cemetery, The, 131

Cercle Artistique, Le, 8n7

Cézanne, Paul, 3, 8, 55n76, 56, 123-124n22

Chardin, Jean-Siméon, 9

Chef-d'oeuvre inconnu, Le (Honoré de Balzac), 124

Children Dressing, 24-28, 105, 145

Chronique, La, 56

Chrysalide, La, 8n7, 56-57

Cladel, Léon, *Les Martyrs ridicules*, 138

Classic Academy Model, 7

Claudel, Paul, 18

Combat des démons, 128n43

Communist Manifesto, The, 140

Conscience, Henri, 53n71

Consoling Virgin, The, 69-70, 128n40, 154, 156-158

Convalescent, The, 14-15

Convive de dernières fêtes, Le (Villiers de l'Isle-Adam), 93

Cortège of Devils, The, 100

Cranach, Lucas, 26n46

Cruel Joke on the Peasant, The, 100n75

Cruikshank, George, and Mayhew, Henry, *From 1851, or Adventures of Mr. and Mrs. Sandboys*, 138; *London in 1851*, 139

d'Aurevilly, Barbey, 21, 113

dance of death, 39n29

Dangerous Cooks, The, 81n60, 96

"Danse macabre" (Charles Baudelaire), 158

Daumier, Honoré, *Peace, an Idyl*, 39

Daveluy, Alex (Ensor's niece), 16

De Braeckeleer, Henri, 58n87

De Coster, Charles, 76, 85-86, 97-98, 101, 113

De Maeyer, Marcel, 41n34, 50n58, 78n55

de Mont, Pol, 8n6

Dead at Age Fifteen, Beautiful, Happy, and Adored (Louis Boulenger), 38

Death and a Doctor by a Gravestone, 36-37

Death in Armor (Titian), 47

Death Pursuing the People, 39-40

Déballage (Félicien Rops), 66

Décadence, Le, 113

Decadent Romans, 114

Degas, Edgar, 55n76

Demolder, Eugène, 31, 57, 84, 86, 143, 153

Demons Taunting Me, 54, 56

Denis, Hector, 144

Des Esseintes, 83

Devil's Mirror, The, 107

Devils Thrashing Angels and Archangels, 128n43

Diaboli virtus in lumbis (Félicien Rops), 80

Diana at the Bath, 28

Diana of Ephesus, 128

Doctrinal Nourishment, 143-144

Domain of Arnheim, The, 94-95

Doré, Gustave, 37, 39, 117

Dostoyevsky, Fyodor, 138n80

Double Portrait, 72-73, 147

Drinker, The (Le Buveur), 22

Droll Smokers, 149-151

Drunkards, The, 19-20, 24, 28, 144

Dry Drunkenness, The (Die Truckene Truckenheit) (Jacob Balde), 150

Dubar, André, 6n2

Dubois, Louis, 8n7, 58n87

Dunes of Ostend, 6-7

Écorché, L', 70-71

Eekhoud, Georges, 53n71, 84, 86, 109, 130, 140n87

Élan Littéraire, L', 109

Ensor, James Frédéric, 18n19, 19, 22-24, 32

Ensor, James Sidney, adopts etching, 43n39; as decadent, 113; as St. Anthony, 116; association with Christ, 132; birthplace, 11; birthplace and skeletons, 40n32; bourgeoisie, 128; "Classic Dozen," 58; collection of books, 63n7; correspondence, 29; criticism, 8n8, of Impressionism and Pointillism, 52, 53, of paintings, 8; description of masks, 145; early seascapes, 6; erotic drawings, 71-72n35; essays, 84; family of masks, 145; father, 18n19, 22-24, 32; fear of outside influences, 83; feelings about family, 28; female relatives, 11, 13, 17n18; first skeletons, 41; flower symbolism, 78, 80, 81; friendships, 28, with women, 157, with writers, 84; guardian angel, 155; identification with Christ, 50, with Emile Littré, 134; illnesses, 17, 43n38, 77-78, 123, 153; influence of Balzac, 86, 91, S. Henry Berthoud, 101, 102, Callot, 116, De Coster, 98-101, *Les Fumistes wallons* (Albert Mockel), 112-113, literary reviews, 109-111, Poe, 95-96,

Rops, 59, 80, 81, the Rousseaus, 30, 31, supernatural, 102, 105, 107-109, 111, Symbolist writers, 114, Villiers de l'Isle-Adam, 93, 94, Wagner, 11, Wiertz, 59, 63; introspection, 3; love of mother, 152, of Venus, 152, of words, 84; made baron, 75n41; Manniken-pis, 75n41; misogyny, 151-152; mother's illness, 153, death, 17-18; nationalism, 4, 51; photo at Rousseau home, 45; photo in death, 19; photo of Ensor in a crowd, 29; physical similarities to father, 19; Pierrot la mort, 28; poem, "On Woman," 147, 150-151; praise from *L'Art moderne*, 57; regard for Mariette, 32n16, 33, 36; rejection, 56; relatives, 11, 13-14, 18, 152; Rousseau as surrogate father, 32n11; saves all sketches, 29; scatology, 125; sense of humor, 44; sister Marie (called Mitche), 11, 14; socialism, 144; solitary condition, 4; spider symbol, 44, 78; teachers, 6n3; training, 6-8; travel, 4, 83, 153; Verhaeren on Flemish-English heritage, 138; Whistler's art, 50-51n61; winged skeleton, 42-43, 125; youth, 3

Ensor, Mitche, 14-17, 24, 26, 96, 102, 153
Ensor and Death, 42-43
Entry of Charles V at Antwerp, The (Hans Makart), 137
Entry of Christ into Brussels, The, 4, 44n39, 52, 56, 61, 66, 67, 85, 110, 113, 128, 134-135, 137, 140-141, 143-145
Entry of Christ into Jerusalem, The, 134, 140
Epistle of Othea to Hector, The, 154n32
Ernest Rousseau, 31-32
Essuie—Mains Réactifs Belges (Félicien Rops), 69

Essor, L', 110
Europa, 110
Exchange Bridge, Paris, The (Charles Meryon), 119

Fall of the Rebel Angels, 60, 62, 131
Family in the Orchard (Théo van Rysselberghe), 52n66
"Fantastique Real, La" (anonymous), 110-111
Fantômes, Les (Victor Hugo), 37
Flandre littéraire, La, 110
Fiedler, Leslie, 96
Fight of the Demons, The, 129
Finch, Willy, 83n3, 96, 134
Fisherman, The, 28
fisherman's strike, Ostend, 143
Flagellation, The, 71-72
Flaubert, Gustave, 57, 99n72, 113, 115, 123, 125, 127
Flemish Legends (Charles De Coster), 76
Flood, The: Jesus Shown to the People, 134
Flying Dutchman, 11n13
Four Nudes, 73
Franck, François, 149n8
Frédéric, Léon, 48-49
Freemasons, 140n88
Fumistes wallons, Les (Albert Mockel), 111

Gaillard, Jean-Jacques, 59n2, 110, 124n24
Gallait, Louis, 143n97
Garde Civique (Félicien Rops), 65n18, 66, 138
Garden of Love, The, 34-35n21
Gauguin, Paul, 3, 56
Gazette, La, 8n8
Gazette, des Beaux-Arts, 110

Gendarmes, The, 143n97
Gide, André, 109
Gillray, James, 101n78
Goncourt Brothers, 57, 70
Goya, Francisco, 14
Grandville, J. J., 55, 150
Greuze, Jean-Baptiste, 26n49

Haegheman, Maria-Catharina (Ensor's mother), 11, 13, 17-18, 26-27, 152-153
Hail, Jesus, King of the Jews, 133
Hannon, Théo, 30, 56, 83n3, 84
Haunted Furniture (etching), 108, 111
Haunted Furniture (painting), 102-103, 105n91
Haunted Mantelpiece, 106-107, 111
Hay-Wain (Hieronymous Bosch), 142
Hemma, L., 111, 113
Hertoge, Blanche, 157n41
Hoffman, E.T.A., 84-85, 96-97, 158
Hommage à Pan (Félicien Rops), 74
Hugo, Victor, 37, 90, 138
Huys, Pieter, 120, 122
Huysmans, J.-K., 4, 11, 21, 57, 83, 86

Impatience de la foule, L' (Villiers de l'Isle-Adam), 93
Impressionism, 52-53
Infernal Cortège, 99-100
Ingres, J.A.D., 27n49
Interior with Skeletons, 21, 47
Intrigue, 16, 152-153
Intruder, The, 23n36, 113

Jacquemart, Jules, 57
Jarry, Alfred, 97
Jesus Christ in Flanders (Honoré de Balzac), 85-86, 93, 151
Jeune Belgique, La, 24n36, 110

Jinx, The (Stéphane Mallarmé), 82
joyous entries, 136
Judith and Holofernes, 151

Khnopff, Fernand, 49n51, 55, 83, 113n118, 115-116
King Leopold, 143
kissing figures, 142
Knoeckert, Margo, 157n41
Kunst, Die, 110
Kurth, Hans, 39

Laforgue, Jules, 23, 135
Lantier, Claude, 55n76
Last Honors Rendered to the Counts d'Egmont and Hornes (Louis Gallait), 143n97
Leman, General, 35-36n22-23
Lemonnier, Camille, 28n53, 86
Lenoir, Claire, 93
Les Vingt (Les XX), 9n10, 24, 43, 50-53, 55-56n77, 57, 64, 78, 83, 93, 115-116, 127, 135, 143, 153
Lespès, Léo, 102
"LI SPERE," 47
Life of Jesus (D. F. Strauss), 133
Listening to Schumann (Fernand Khnopff), 55
Little Sorceress (Félicien Rops), 81
Littré, Émile, 133
Lorrain, Jean, 145
Lyre, La (Félicien Rops), 120

Maeterlinck, Maurice, 23n36, 84, 93, 113n118
Magdalene March, 136
Makart, Hans, 136-137
Mallarmé, Stéphane, 51n61, 57, 77-78, 82, 113

Man of Sorrows, 56
Manniken-pis, 75n41, 101
Marchand des Masques, Le (Zachary Astruc), 21
Marianne, as symbol, 142-143
Martyrs ridicules (Léon Cladel), 138
Marx, Karl, 138, 140
Masque of the Red Death, The (Edgar Allan Poe), 21
Masques Parisiens (Barbey d'Aurevilly), 21n23
Massacre of the Innocents, The, 100n75
Maus, Octave, 42, 50-51, 55-56, 84, 125, 134-135
Mayhew, Henry, 138
medieval tomb sculpture, 45n41
Mercure de France, 110
Merkel, Karl Gottfried, 39-40
Meryon, Charles, 39n31, 90, 117-119
Miraculous Drought of Fishes, The, 155-156
Mirbeau, Octave, 57
Mockel, Albert, 85, 111
Modernité (Félicien Rops), 81n60
Monet, Claude, 90
mouvement Wallon, Le, 113
Munch, Edvard, 3, 80, 152
Musée Wiertz, 60
My Portrait in 1960, 41, 44-45, 59, 149
My Portrait Skeletonized, 44, 90, 125
My Sad and Splendid Portrait, 105-107

Nadar, Felix Tournachon, 66, 68, 118
New Carthage, The (Georges Eekhoud), 130
Notre-Dame de Paris (Victor Hugo), 90
Nymph Embracing a Herm, 73-74

Oeuvre, L', 55, 85

Old Faith and the New, The (D. F. Strauss), 133
Old Gate of the Palace of Justice, Paris, The (Charles Meryon), 39n31
Old Woman Asleep, The, 14
On Woman, 147, 150-151

Paerels, Willem, 149
Pair in an Open Landau, 16
Parysatis, Queen, 128
Patriote, Le, 8n8
Pauvre Belgique, La (Charles Baudelaire), 53, 138
Pears, 8
Peculiar Insects, 33, 35, 78
Peinture Erotique, La (Félicien Rops), 70
Péladan, Joséphin, 24n36, 49n51, 57, 73
Pest-Death, The (Karl Gottfried Merkel), 39-40
Petites Misères de la vie humaine (J. J. Grandville), 55
Philip II in Hell, 98
photograph of Cathedral at Ostend, 89
photograph of Ensor, 20 rue Vautier, 45
photograph of Ensor in his studio, 153
photograph of an Ensor letter, 76
Picard, Edmond, 84, 107-108, 110
Picasso, Pablo, 145
Pierrot la mort, 28n53
Piron, H. T., 146
Pisser, The, 75, 100, 150
Plague Here, Plague There, Plague Everywhere, 96, 97
Poe, Edgar Allan, 21, 84, 94, 95n54, 109, 118, 124
Plume, La, 23
Pointillism, 52-53
Portrait of the Artist's Aunt, 13
Portrait of the Artist's Father, 18-19

Portrait of the Artist's Mother, 26-27
Portrait of the Artist's Sister, 14
Portrait of Mitche, 15-16
Portrait of an Old Woman Surrounded by Masks, 80n57, 150, 152
Poster for Carnival at Ostend, 157
Pride, detail from *The Seven Deadly Sins* (Hieronymous Bosch), 109
Princesse du Pays de Porcelain, La (J. M. Whistler), 50
Printemps (Félicien Rops), 65n18, 138
procession at Veurne (Furnes), 136
psychoanalytic study of Ensor, 146

Queen Parysatis Flaying a Eunuch, 71n30

Ray, The (1882), 9-11, 156; (1892), 149, 154-155, 157-158; copy of 1892 painting, 148
Reactive Belgian Hand Towels (Félicien Rops), 66
Reading, The (Théo van Rysselberghe), 52
Reclus Brothers, 31
Redon, Odilon, 21, 47, 78, 95, 107n95, 112-113
Rembrandt, 59n1, 78
Renan, Ernest, 133
Rethel, Alfred, 39, 150
Retté, Adolphe, 109
Rêve, Le (Émile Zola), 130
Revolt of Hell Against Heaven, The (Antoine Wiertz), 61
Revue Belge, La, 110
Revue blanche, La, 110
Revue indépendente, La, 51n61, 110
Revue Wagnerienne, La, 110
Rodin, Auguste, 91
Rombouts, Theodore, 150
Rops, Félicien, 5, 8n7, 21n23, 31, 35n18,

39, 48-49n51, 57, 59n1, 65-66, 68-70, 74-77, 80-81n60, 98, 102, 111, 113, 115-116, 120, 123, 138, 140n88, 143, 150n11, 152
Rosa, Salvator, 97
Rosebud, The (Antoine Wiertz), 78
Rouen Cathedral (Claude Monet), 90
Rousseau, Blanche, 30, 36
Rousseau, Ernest, Jr., 30n3, 31, 40, 153
Rousseau, Ernest, Sr., 31n9, 32n11
Rousseau, Mariette, 30n3, 31, 33, 35-36, 45, 60, 72, 78, 96, 120, 125, 152
Rout of the Mercenaries, The, 100
Rower, The, 11-12, 24, 28, 144, 145
Rubens, Peter Paul, 53n71, 78
Russian Music, 55, 83n3

Sad and Broken, The: Satan and His Fantastic Legions Tormenting the Crucified Christ, 41
St. Anthony, 115-116
St. Anthony Tormented, 156
St. Athanasius, 115
St. Barbara, 89n26
St. John the Baptist, 132
Satyr, 73
Scandalized Masks, 20-24n36, 94, 105, 113, 144, 145
Schongauer, Martin, 128, 130
Séléction, 110
Self-Portrait in a Flowered Hat, 78, 81-82
Self-Portrait Surrounded by Masks, 78-79
Seurat, Georges, 52, 135, 146
Seven Deadly Sins, The (Hieronymous Bosch), 109
She of the Garden (Émile Verhaeren), 154
Sick Tramp, The, 22, 49n52
Simonon, Charles, 47
Sirène, La, 147

Skeletons Fighting for the Body of a Hanged Man, 49
Skeletons Playing Billiards, 75
Skeletons Trying to Warm Themselves, 49n52, 91-92
Sleep of Reason (Francisco Goya), 14
Sleeping Woman, 13
Small Bizarre Figures, 78
Smokers, The (Theodore Rombouts), 150
Société nouvelle, La, 143
Somber Lady, 14, 24, 145
Source, La (J.A.D. Ingres), 27n49
Spinoza, Benedict de, 125
Squelette regardant des Chinoiseries, 50
Stars in the Cemetery, 131
Stéjus, Elsa, 157n41
Stevens, Alfred, 9, 53n74, 63, 119
Stevo, Jean, 19
Stolz, Alban, 127
Strauss, D. F., 133
Strike in Ostend, The, 143
Stuck, Franz, 152
Studio, The, 110
Studio Interior (Léon Frédéric), 48-49
Study for Christ Walking on the Sea, 50
Sunday Afternoon on the Island of La Grand Jatte (Georges Seurat), 52, 135
Susannah and the Elders, as prototype, 28
Swedenborg, Emmanuel, 124n24
Symbolism: and death, 151; and Ensor, 113-114; and literature, 23n36, 57, 93, 109; and painting, 93; as art movement, 25

Temptation of Christ, The, 43
Temptation of St. Anthony, 56n77, 71, 99n72, 115-116, 120-121, 126-128, 134
Temptation of St. Anthony (Jacques Callot), 116

Tentation de St. Antoine (Félicien Rops), 115

Titian, 47

Tolstoy, Leo, 110

Tribulations of St. Anthony, 4, 9, 110, 115, 118, 120-124, 126, 131

Triumph of Christ, The (Antoine Wiertz), 61, 140

Triumph of Death, as motif, 39

triumphal entry, as motif, 136

Truckene Trunkenkeit, Die (The Dry Druckenness) (Jacob Balde), 150

Turner, J.M.W., 25, 51

Twilight (Henry van de Velde), 52

Two Waders, 30

Unlucky, The (Stéphane Mallarmé), 82

Uylenspiegel, 57n86, 59, 65, 98, 100, 102, 108, 138, 144

Valéry, Paul, 109, 124

Valles, Jules, 140

van de Velde, Henry, 52

van de Woestyne, Karel, 84, 86

van der Goes, Hugo, 26n46

Van Dyck, Anthony, 53n71

Van Eyck, Jan, 53n73, 89n26

Van Gogh, Vincent, 3, 56, 132

Van Guyck, Michael, 6n2

van Rysselberghe, Théo, 52

Vie de Jesus, La, 133

Vengeance of Hop-Frog, The, 96

Verhaeren, Émile, 83-84, 109, 154

Verlaine, Paul, 18, 57

Verlat, Charles, 53n73

Villiers de l'Isle-Adam, Comte de, 57, 85, 92, 93

Viollet-Le-Duc, Eugène, 90

Vogels, Guillaume, 6n2, 8n7

Vuillard, Edouard, 25

Wagner, Richard, 11n13

Wallonie, La, 109, 111

Waterloo Medal, The (Félicien Rops), 76

Welt, Frau, 81

Whistler, James A. McNeill, 25, 50, 51

White Girl, The (James A. McNeill Whistler), 25

Wiertz, Antoine, 5, 31, 47, 57, 59-61, 63-64, 78, 81-82, 138, 140

Woman Eating Oysters, 8n8-9, 145

Woman in Distress, 14, 24-25n45, 145

Woman on a Breakwater, 50-51n60

Zola, Émile, 55n76, 85, 130

zwanze art, 48-50, 52

zwanze humor, 48-50

Library of Congress Cataloging in Publication Data

Lesko, Diane, 1942-
James Ensor, the creative years.

Bibliography: p.
Includes index.
1. Ensor, James, 1860-1949.   2. Artists—Belgium—
Biography.   I. Title.

N6973.E5L47 1985   760'.092'4 [B]   84-26452
ISBN 0-691-04030-3